Wavelength

Intermediate • Coursebook

Kathy
Burke

Ben
Rowdon

Longman

Contents

Units	Grammar	Vocabulary / Pronunciation
① *It takes all sorts* page 6	Present Perfect Simple and Past Simple Present Perfect Simple with *for* and *since* *Used to / would* + infinitive	Describing mood and character Pron: stress and intonation in questions
② *In the city* page 14	Countable and uncountable nouns Present Simple and Present Continuous State verbs Past Simple and Past Continuous	Describing cities British English and American English Pron: strong and weak auxiliary verbs
③ *When Saturday comes* page 22	Defining and non-defining relative clauses First Conditional: *if* and *unless* *Going to* + infinitive	Describing places Strong and base adjectives
Do you remember? **Units 1–3**	1 *Hey! I've done that, too!* 2 *Not like now* 3 *That's a terrible idea!* 4 The beautiful game	
④ *How do you do that?* page 32	Skills and ability Verb + *-ing* Past ability: *could, was able to, managed to, succeeded in*	Talking about skills and ability Talking about work and jobs
⑤ *Culture vultures* page 40	Subject and object questions Modifying adjectives and nouns Present Perfect Continuous	Talking about arts and culture Pron: stressing for emphasis
⑥ *Skin deep* page 48	Superlative adjectives Second Conditional with *would / could / might* *Wish* + Past Simple Infinitive of purpose and *by* + verb + *-ing*	Describing clothes
Do you remember? **Units 4–6**	1 Difficult choices 2 The Arts Café 3 *You don't need to lose weight!*	

Skills	Wavelength pages
Speaking and writing: talking about and describing people Reading and listening: self-help books Listening and writing: television advertisement Listening: conversations	*Writing for work and pleasure 1* **Keep in touch!** Formal and informal language
Listening, speaking and writing: describing a city Listening: interview about living in a city and a description of a disastrous weekend Reading: extracts from modern books about cities Speaking and writing: inventing a short story	*Conversations* **Well, hello!** Greetings and starting conversations Showing interest, asking for clarification and checking Echo questions and statements
Listening, speaking and writing: describing a club / bar Listening and speaking: describing dilemmas and making decisions / offering advice Reading: theme restaurant web pages Writing: designing a theme restaurant	*Day to day English* **How about . . . ?** Making / talking about arrangements Making suggestions and talking about preferences Present Continuous for fixed arrangements *Reading for pleasure 1* **Heat wave** Exercises on *Heat wave* from *Heat wave and other stories*
Reading: *Do great minds think alike?* Listening and speaking: describing jobs and abilities Speaking: job interviews Reading and listening: an actor tells his story Writing: a "rags to riches" success story	*Writing for work and pleasure 2* **I am writing to apply . . .** A CV and a job application letter
Listening: conversations in various venues Listening: conversations about art Speaking: presenting ideas for a community art project Reading: Andy Warhol Writing: describing the achievements of a famous person	*Conversations* **I'm not sure . . .** Language of doubt *Look / look like / look as if* Hesitation phrases Pron: stress and intonation
Listening, speaking and writing: describing clothes and talking about fashions Speaking: talking about the advantages / disadvantages of being rich and famous Listening: imagining a different life Writing: reporting the results of *My fantastic life* questionnaire Reading: *The History of Beauty*	*Day to day English* **If I were you . . .** Suggestions and advice *Reading for pleasure 2* **"Oh, really!"** Exercises on *"Oh, really!"* from *Heat wave and other stories*

Units	Grammar	Vocabulary / Pronunciation
⑦ *Can we talk?* page 58	Past Perfect Simple Reported speech: *say, tell, ask*	Talking about means of communication Phrasal verbs and expressions for telephoning Pron: sentence stress
⑧ *Life, death and the universe* page 66	*Will / going to* + infinitive for predicting Third Conditional	*Otherwise* and *in case* Pron: weak forms and linking in Third Conditional sentences
⑨ *It's a family affair* page 74	*Should / shouldn't have done* *Wish / If only* + Past Perfect Simple Language of criticism Giving reasons and contrasting	Talking about family celebrations
Do you remember? Units 7–9	1 *Tell me more* 2 A sorry tale 3 *It's all your fault!* 4 Max's diary	
⑩ *What's going on?* page 84	The Passive The Passive with *get* and indirect objects Negative questions Modal verbs for laws, rules and social behaviour Verb + *-ing* and verb + infinitive	Talking about news stories and crime Describing behaviour
⑪ *The silver screen* page 92	*All, whole* and *every* Verb tenses for telling stories and jokes Reporting verbs	Talking about films and the cinema Describing film scenes
⑫ *Taking off* page 100	Modal verbs of present and past deduction	Describing travel and holidays Pron: stress in modal verbs of deduction
Do you remember? Units 10–12	1 Disgrace! 2 *You could be telling the truth . . .* 3 A letter to the editor	

Grammar reference	*page 110*	**Information for pair and group work**	*page 130*
Grammar and vocabulary puzzles	*page 120*	**Key to grammar and vocabulary puzzles**	*page 146*
Word lists (unit by unit)	*page 122*		

Skills	Wavelength pages
Reading and speaking: *The funniest thing happened ...* Speaking: victims of a conman role-play Listening and speaking: leaving and taking telephone messages Speaking: narrating stories Reading and speaking: a phone maze role-play	***Writing for work and pleasure 3 Guess what!*** Telling a story
Reading: articles on predicting the future Listening: discussing predictions Speaking: predicting outcomes Reading and writing: a website about regrets	***Conversations Points of view*** Persuading, refusing persuasion, giving opinions, agreeing / disagreeing, interrupting Pronunciation: stress and intonation for emphasis
Speaking and listening: family celebrations Reading: *American Beauty* film script and extract from *Bridget Jones's diary* Speaking: talking about parent / child relationships Listening: cross-cultural wedding Reading: wedding websites Speaking: criticising actions and expressing regret	***Day to day English Isn't it?*** Question tags for checking information and asking for agreement Pron: intonation in question tags ***Reading for pleasure 3 Dear Sue*** Exercises on *Dear Sue* from *Heat wave and other stories*
Reading: newspaper extracts Listening and speaking: news broadcast Reading and listening: *The end of a career?* Speaking: discussing illegal and anti-social behaviour Writing: expressing an opinion on a law or rule	***Writing for work and pleasure 4 On the other hand . . .*** Writing a report
Listening: conversations Reading: memorable film moments Listening and speaking: describing a plot Listening, reading and writing: *The Lost House* film script Writing: a film review	***Conversations Well, actually I . . .*** Asking for permission and making / refusing requests politely Pron: stress and intonation to sound polite
Speaking: describing different types of travel Reading: *The art of travel* Listening and speaking: describing holidays from hell Speaking and listening: making deductions Speaking: holiday advice	***Day to day English Was it worth it?*** Phrases / expressions for giving opinions and recommending, adding emphasis and giving contrasting opinions ***Reading for pleasure 4 Merry Christmas*** Exercises on *Merry Christmas* from *Heat wave and other stories*

Recording scripts	*page 147*	**Guide to pronunciation**	*page 159*
Irregular verb list	*page 159*	***Heat wave and other stories***	*inside back cover*

It takes all sorts

Adjectives / phrases for describing people
Present Perfect Simple and Past Simple
Present Perfect Simple with *for* and *since*
Used to / would + infinitive
Writing for work and pleasure 1: *Keep in touch!*

Is this seat free?

1 a) In groups. Look at the picture. You're going to take a five-hour bus journey. Choose one person to sit next to and say why.

b) In groups. Take it in turns to describe passengers using the adjectives in the Word Box. Begin *He / She looks . . .* The other students guess which person you're describing.

> crazy   friendly   sweet   upset   stupid   intelligent   boring
> miserable   strange   desperate   lonely   chatty   interesting
> weird   shy   unfriendly   talkative   nice   nasty

2 a) 🔊1 In pairs. Look at the two people at the back of the bus. Do you think they know each other? How does the man feel? Why? What do you think the woman is saying to him? Listen and check.

b) 🔊1 Listen again and fill in the gaps in the woman's questions.

Example: <u>Have</u> we <u>met</u> before?

1 .... you .... to India?
2 .... you .... much?
3 Where .... you .... ?
4 When .... you .... there?
5 .... you .... on safari?

Pronunciation: stress and intonation in questions

3 a) In pairs. Underline the stressed words / syllables in the questions in Exercise 2b). Do the questions go up ↗ or down ↘ at the end?

b) 🔊2 Listen, check your answers and repeat the questions. Then read the Language Box.

> #### Questions: stress and intonation
>
> We stress information words in questions, e.g. the question word, nouns, verbs and sometimes adjectives and adverbs. We don't usually stress words like prepositions, articles, pronouns and auxiliary verbs. *Yes / No* questions usually go up at the end. *Wh-* questions usually go down at the end:
> Have you ever eaten octopus? ↗
> When did you eat it? ↘

Present Perfect Simple and Past Simple

4 a) In pairs. Answer questions a) and b) about questions 1–5 in Exercise 2b). Then read the Language Box.

a) Which questions ask about any time before now?
b) Which questions ask about a particular time in the past?

> ### Present Perfect Simple and Past Simple
>
> When we talk about our past experiences:
> * we use the Present Perfect Simple when we only mention the **experience**, not when it happened. It just means *before now*.
> * we use the Past Simple when we mention **when** the experience happened (*yesterday, last month, in 1997*, etc.).
> * we use the Past Simple when we give **details** about a particular past experience (where, how, why it happened, etc.).

b) Look at Recording script 1. Make the answers 1–5 into complete sentences. Use the Present Perfect Simple or the Past Simple.

Example: No, we haven't.
　　　　　No, we haven't met before.

1 No, I haven't.
2 Well, yes, a bit.
3 Well, Europe . . . Africa . . .
4 Two years ago.
5 Yes, I did.

c) The woman at the back of the bus went on talking for the rest of the journey. Underline the correct form of the verbs in brackets.

Oh, yes, I just love travelling. (<u>I've travelled</u> / I travelled) a lot, actually. (I went / I've been)[1] all round Europe. My favourite country is Italy. Oh, I just love the food! (I first visited / I've first visited)[2] Italy, ooh let's see, about seven years ago and (I've been / I went)[3] back many, many times. But you know, in all my life as a traveller (I never went / I've never been)[4] anywhere really wild. I'd love to go somewhere like Alaska. (I wanted / I've wanted)[5] to take a boat to Alaska when I was in Canada last summer but (I haven't had / I didn't have)[6] enough time . . .

d) 🔘3 Listen and check your answers.

I know I know you!

5 a) Have you ever been in the same place at the same time as another student? Go round the class and talk to the other students. Ask questions and try to find at least one place where it is possible you met before, even if you didn't actually meet!

Examples: Have you ever been to . . . ?
　　　　　　When were you there?
　　　　　　Where did you stay?

b) In groups of four. Take it in turns to tell each other what you've found out.

Friends and family

6 a) 4 Listen to Beth having five different phone conversations. Who is she talking about each time? Fill in the boxes with the conversation number.

a) ☐1 an acquaintance
b) ☐ a colleague
c) ☐ her boyfriend
d) ☐ her best friend
e) ☐ a member of her family

b) Read the sentences from Beth's phone conversations. Who is she talking about each time?

1 I know I can always depend on her.
2 She doesn't realise I've got a life of my own.
3 We've got nothing in common.
4 I don't trust her.
5 I've only met him once or twice.
6 She's quite spoilt.
7 We're really close.
8 We don't really get on.
9 He's a friend of a friend.
10 I think I'm in love.

c) 4 Listen again and check. What did Beth mean? In pairs, explain the sentences in Exercise 6b) in your own words.

Present Perfect Simple with *for* and *since*

7 a) 5 Listen to the sentences from conversations 2, 3 and 4. Fill in the gaps.

Conversation 2: She's …………… ……………… ……………… since we were kids.
Conversation 3: We've …………… ……………… ……………… since we were at primary school.
Conversation 4: We've only ……………… ……………… for two months.

b) Answer these questions about the sentences in Exercise 7a). Then read the Language Box and fill in the gaps with *for* or *since*.

Conversation 2: Is she still like this?
Conversation 3: Does Beth still know her?
Conversation 4: Are they still together?

> ### Present Perfect Simple with *for* and *since*
>
> We use the Present Perfect Simple when we talk about a state or situation which began in the past and still continues / is still true in the present.
> We use ……………… with a period of time.
> We use ……………… with a point in time (when the period began).
>
> I know her.
> PAST   NOW
> We were at primary school
> (fifteen years ago)
>
> I've known her **since** we were at primary school.
> I've known her **for** fifteen years.

c) Read the sentences (1–5). These situations are still true. Write the sentences again using the Present Perfect Simple of the verbs in the Word Box and *for* or *since*.

> know ✓   be (x 2)   work   live   have

Example: I met Jeremy five years ago.
 I've known Jeremy for five years.

1 They became Buddhists a year ago.
2 He got a job here when he left university.
3 He bought his car a few months ago.
4 They got married in 1997.
5 He moved to Rome when his wife died.

8 a) Write three true sentences about situations in your life. Use the Present Perfect Simple of the verbs in the Word Box in Exercise 7c) and *for* or *since*.

Example: I've had this ring since I was twelve.

b) In groups. Take it in turns to read your sentences and ask each other questions.

Examples: Was it a present?
Why do you still wear it?

Nice or nasty?

9 a) Here are some more things Beth has said about people recently. Fill in the gaps with adjectives from the Word Box.

> self-confident ✓   insensitive   unsociable
> out-going   generous   impatient
> hard-working   two-faced

1 I'd love to be <u>self-confident</u> like Sue. She seems to feel so good about herself. I'm so insecure.
2 Jay's so .... He won't go out with my friends. He hates parties. He'd rather stay in and watch football. Why can't he be more sociable?
3 She's .... She's always so nice to me but I know she says horrible things about me behind my back. If people can't be sincere, I don't want to know them!
4 I know they're sisters but they're so different. Susan's quite shy but Sally's really ....
5 And then he told me I looked fat in the dress! He's so .... ! He never even tries to think about my feelings! Carl would never do that. He's so sweet, sensitive, handsome.
6 I like my uncle better than my aunt. She's quite mean but he's really .... He always gives us lovely birthday presents.
7 Sheena's really .... She's always getting involved in new projects and staying late at the office. I feel so lazy compared to her.
8 My new boss is really .... She expects things to be done immediately and with no mistakes. I need a patient person who'll take the time to explain things to me.

b) In each of the sentences (1–8) in Exercise 9a) there's the opposite of the missing adjective. Which adjectives are positive? negative? Make a table.

Positive	Negative
1 self-confident	insecure

I know so many people . . .

10 a) In pairs. Student A look at page 142 and Student B at page 136. Then fill in the boxes (1–4).

b) When you finish, take it in turns to look at each other's diagram and ask questions about each box. Learn as much as you can about the information in your partner's diagram.

Example: A: What's that?
B: It's the place where my wife was born.
A: Oh, how long have you been married? What's she like? How did you meet? When / Where did you meet?

c) Choose one of the people you wrote about in Exercise 10a) and write a description. What's he / she like physically? What's his / her character like? Why do you like / dislike this person?

① One-Minute
How to safeguard your heart
Stress
and your sanity —
Management
in sixty seconds a day

Dr DAVID LEWIS

② HOW TO MAKE ANYONE FALL iN LOVE WITH YOU
85 Proven Techniques for Success

LEIL LOWNDES

③ Don't Say 'YES' WhenYou Want To Say 'NO'
Herbert Fensterheim PhD. And Jean Baer

④ MEN ARE FROM MARS, *Women Are from Venus*
A PRACTICAL GUIDE FOR IMPROVING COMMUNICATION AND GETTING WHAT YOU WANT IN YOUR RELATIONSHIPS
JOHN GRAY

You can do it!

11 **a)** In pairs. Look at these book covers. What kind of book are they?

b) Match the covers (1–4) to their blurbs (a–d).

c) Find words in the blurbs which mean:

1 Blurb a): to do the correct thing to solve a problem (phr v)
2 Blurb a): to make something better (v)
3 Blurb b): behaving in a confident way (adj)
4 Blurb c): very, very tired (adj)
5 Blurb c): to rest and relax (phr v)
6 Blurb c): to stay relaxed and not get angry or upset (v + adj)
7 Blurb c): a time when a problem is very bad (n)
8 Blurb d): someone with special skills or knowledge of a subject (n)
9 Blurb d): shown to be true (adj)
10 Blurb d): special skills or ways of doing something (n pl)

d) 🎧 6 Listen to three people. Which book is each person talking about? What does he / she think of it?

e) In groups. Do you agree with any of the people in Exercise 11d)? Do any of the books look useful to you? Why? / Why not? Do you think a book can change your life?

ⓐ Do you ever feel that you and your partner are from different planets? Dr John Gray explains how differences between the sexes can cause problems between men and women in loving relationships. He gives advice on how to deal with differences in communication styles, emotional needs and types of behaviour to improve understanding between partners.

ⓑ **Are you the kind of person who eats a cold bowl of soup because you don't want to complain to the waiter? Do you hate returning something to a shop even if there's something wrong with it?**
This life-changing book will teach you how to be assertive at work, in your marriage, in social situations and in family life. Find out how to say no when you want to, express your anger, be successful and feel good about it. It's easier than you think!

ⓒ Stress is good for you! You just have to learn how to manage it and make it work *for* you – not *against* you. This book can be read in sixty minutes and you can start using the techniques in sixty seconds. It offers fast, effective stress management. You will learn how to:

• **find extra energy when you're exhausted**
• **wind down and sleep well at night**
• **keep calm in a crisis**

ⓓ "I don't understand. I'm attractive, intelligent, sensitive, talented. Why doesn't he or she fall in love with me? Why can't I find love?"
How many times have you asked yourself these questions? Here, finally, are the answers we all need! In this wonderful guide, internationally-acclaimed relationships expert Leil Lowndes shares her scientifically-proven techniques to help you win the heart of anyone you choose.

Another satisfied customer

Used to / would + infinitive

12 a) [OO]7 Read these self-help book titles and listen to the first part of a TV advertisement. The author is interviewing Farrah about his book. Which book (1–5) is the ad about?

1 *Tidy My Room!*
How to make your parents do what you want.
2 *I am You, You are Me, We are Us*
Understanding each other in the twenty-first century.
3 *Get Into the Slow Lane*
Stop killing yourself at work and learn to live.
4 *Queen of the House*
Getting respect from your family.
5 *Get Out of My Life*
Get rid of your boyfriend or girlfriend in three easy stages.

b) [OO]8 Listen to the second part of the ad where Farrah describes her past life. Answer the questions (1–4).

1 Who listens to her now?
2 What did she use to do after work?
3 What did the little voice use to say?
4 How is her life different now?

c) [OO]8 Listen again. Fill in the gaps with *used to, didn't use to, would ('d)* or *wouldn't*.

Example: I used to come home from work, and they would tell me what to cook for supper!

1 I .... wash the dishes and clean the house and I .... finish until midnight or later. I .... feel like a slave!
2 My husband .... come home and eat his dinner in front of the TV and then he .... just go to bed.
3 I .... tell them to help round the house but they .... just ignore me.
4 I .... hear a little voice in my head but I .... listen to it.
5 I .... be depressed but not anymore!
6 They .... fight a lot but they don't any longer.

d) Find two phrases in the sentences in Exercise 12c) which mean *The situation has changed – this isn't true now*. Then read the Language Box.

Used to / would + infinitive

We use *used to* + infinitive to talk about past **states / situations** and **habits / repeated actions** that aren't true anymore.
They **used to** live in Madrid.
I **didn't use to** pay attention to my needs.
We use *would* + infinitive for **habits / repeated actions** to avoid repeating *used to* again and again.
I **used to come** home from work and **they'd (would)** tell me what to cook. Then **I'd** clean the house. I **wouldn't** finish until midnight.
We use *not anymore* or *not any longer* to say that a situation has changed.
I used to be depressed but **not any longer / I'm not any longer**.
They used ignore me but **not anymore / they don't anymore**.

13 a) In pairs. You've written a self-help book. What kinds of problem does your book help people with? What's the title? You can use one from Exercise 12a) or your own idea.

b) Write a TV ad where the author is talking to a satisfied reader. What did the reader's life use to be like? What problems did he / she use to have? How is his / her life different now?

c) In pairs. Act out your ad for the class.

Grammar reference
Present Perfect Simple: page 112
Past Simple: page 111
Used to / would + infinitive: page 111

Writing for work and pleasure

① Keep in touch!

Making the message clear

1 a) Harvey got into serious trouble and decided to leave England as quickly as possible. After he left the country, he wrote a lot of letters and e-mails. Read the e-mail he sent to Pete and answer questions 1–4.

1 Where is Harvey? Why?
2 Who is Pete? Susie?
3 What does Harvey want Pete to do?
4 Is the message formal or informal?

b) Harvey made some punctuation and spelling mistakes when he wrote the e-mail to Pete because he was in a hurry. Underline and then correct the fifteen mistakes.

c) Harvey talks about five different things in his e-mail. Divide the e-mail into five paragraphs.

Dear pete

Just a quick note. I'm really sorry I couldn't make it to your house-warming party I hope it went well and you arent too annoyed with me for not coming. The thing is, Ive had a bit of a problem. A few weeks ago I borrowed a lot of money from the company acount. I was going to return it, but one thing led to another and i lost the money. My boss found out and he threatened too call the police if I didn't give it back imediately. I really panicked and decided to get out of london fast. Susie and I flew to Hong Kong on wednesday and were staying in her brothers flat at the moment. I think we're going to be here for a while. Can I possibly ask you a favour We're getting desperate for money and I need you to sell my computer hi-fi and car for me. I'll write again soon and let you know were to send the money. Thanks for your help.

Harvey

Formal or informal?

2 a) Harvey wrote to five other people. Match the parts of e-mails / letters (1–5) to the people / companies who received them.

Example: 1 = a)

a) a close friend   d) an estate agency
b) a member of the family e) a neighbour
c) an employment agency

① Really sorry but Susie and I can't come to your engagement party after all. We're dying to meet Amanda and really upset we can't make it.

② I am writing in response to your advertisement for an Account Manager in the *Hong Kong Herald* of 2nd March. I would be grateful if you could send me further information.

③ Just a quick note to ask you a favour. Susie and I forgot to arrange for the post office to forward our mail. Would you mind keeping it for us and I'll let you have our new address as soon as we've got one? Also, don't worry if you hear people moving about next door – we've given the keys to the estate agents.

④ Sorry we took off so suddenly and didn't phone you – all a bit last minute, I'm afraid. Don't worry about us – we'll be fine. I'll explain everything one day. Hope Dad is feeling better and taking it easy.

⑤ I am writing to inform you that I would like you to arrange the sale of my flat in London. A set of keys has been left with my lawyer and he will be contacting you in the near future to discuss details.

b) Which messages in Exercise 2a) are formal? informal? Read the Writing Box and find examples of each feature in the e-mails / parts of letters (1–5).

Formal or informal?

Formal
- We don't usually use contractions:
  I have been . . . **NOT** ~~I've been~~ . . .
- We often use the Passive:
  A meeting **has been arranged** . . .
- We use formal language:
  I would like to request . . .

Informal
- We usually use contractions.
- We usually use Active tenses:
  Jenny is arranging a party.
- We use informal language such as phrasal verbs and idiomatic expressions:
  Sorry I couldn't **make it** on Saturday.
- We often use shorter sentences, sometimes without a subject:
  Having a wonderful time.

3 a) Read the e-mail Harvey sent to a friend before he left. Was he telling the truth about why he was cancelling their arrangement?

Dear Amy

Just wanted to let you know that I can't make it to the gallery opening with you tomorrow. I'm afraid my boss has asked me to sort out a few problems urgently so I really can't get away. Thanks anyway – it was nice of you to set it up and I'm sorry about cancelling at such short notice. I'll get in touch soon and fix another time when things are less hectic. Can't wait to catch up. It's been ages!

Love,

Harvey

b) Match the informal expressions (1–11) from Harvey's e-mail in Exercise 3a) with the formal expressions (a–k).

Example: 1 = g)

1 Just wanted to let you know
2 I can't make it
3 asked
4 sort out
5 Thanks
6 set up
7 I'm sorry
8 get in touch
9 fix another time
10 Can't wait
11 Love

a) I apologise
b) requested
c) reschedule
d) I am unable to attend
e) I look forward to
f) contact
g) I am writing to inform you
h) I am grateful
i) resolve
j) Yours sincerely
k) arrange

4 Read the letter Harvey wrote to his bank manager before he left the country. Fill in the gaps with the formal expressions (a–k) from Exercise 3b).

Dear Mr Richards,

g)(1) that ......(2) the meeting with you scheduled for next Tuesday. Unfortunately, I have been ......(3) by my company to ......(4) some problems in one of our overseas offices. ......(5) for cancelling our meeting at such short notice.

......(6) that you have been able to ......(7) a credit limit of £6000 for me until I receive my bonus from work. However, I understand you wish to meet with me to discuss my loan and mortgage repayments. I will ......(8) your secretary on my return to ......(9) our meeting. ......(10) meeting you to discuss these issues.

......(11)

Harvey Collins
Harvey Collins

5 Jack, a close friend, helped Harvey before he left London by lending him some money and organising the flight tickets. Harvey wants to thank him, tell him how he and Susie are feeling, what they're doing, and what their plans are. Write Harvey's letter to Jack a week after arriving in Hong Kong.

Remember!
- Always think about who you're writing to and why you're writing so that you use the correct formal or informal style.
- Organise the information clearly into paragraphs and use correct spelling and punctuation.

In the city

Cities
Countable and uncountable nouns
Present Simple and Present Continuous
State verbs
Past Simple and Past Continuous
Conversations: *Well, hello!*

City scenes

1 a) Look at the photos (1–5) from films. Match a city (a–e) to each photo.

a) Paris   d) London
b) New York   e) Havana
c) Rome

b) In groups. Discuss the questions.

1 Do you know any of these films?
2 Is your city / town (or the capital of your country) in any films?

2 Look at the nouns in the Word Box. In which photos (1–5) can you see these things?

> building   pavement   road sign   postbox
> monument   skyscraper   statue   lamp-post
> traffic lights   cathedral   balcony   phone box
> taxi   corner   railing   steps   rooftop

British English or American English?

3 Match the British English words (1–8) to the American English words (a–h).

Example: 1 = e)

British English	American English
1 pavement	a) downtown
2 taxi	b) elevator
3 shop	c) mailbox
4 car park	d) subway
5 the Underground	e) sidewalk
6 postbox	f) store
7 town centre	g) cab
8 lift	h) parking lot

Countable and uncountable nouns

4 Look at the nouns in the Word Box. Some are countable, some are uncountable. One of the words can be both! Write *C* (countable) or *U* (uncountable) after the words. Then read the Language Box.

> tram C litter U shopping centre fountain
> noise river smog car park pollution
> square nightclub traffic neon sign

Countable and uncountable nouns

Countable nouns can be singular (*a tram*) or plural (*some trams, five trams*).

Uncountable nouns are always singular (*litter, some litter*).

We use *many* with countable nouns in negative sentences and questions:

There aren't **many** car parks in the city centre.

We use *much* with uncountable nouns in negative sentences and questions:

Is there **much** litter on the streets?

We use *a lot of / lots of* with countable and uncountable nouns in positive sentences (and often in questions):

There are **lots of** shops in this area.

Is there **a lot of** traffic on Sundays?

My kind of city

5 **a)** Michael is talking about a city. Fill in the gaps with *there, it, they, much, many* or *a lot of*. Which city from Exercise 1a) is he talking about?

Well, I love the whole city – obviously, but right now my favourite part of the city is near the port. There are two sections, really. My favourite bit is the East Side. During the day ....'s[1] really busy. ....[2] are lots of people working down there – loading and unloading the ships. There's ....[3] noise. Early in the morning ....'s[4] an enormous fish market. ....'s[5] for the locals, really. There isn't ....[6] to see or do so there aren't ....[7] tourists or "outsiders". ....'re[8] usually on the West Side – where the fashionable restaurants are. They can look out at the Statue of Liberty across the water while ....'re[9] eating. But I prefer the East Side. ....'s[10] more real.

b) 🔊9 Listen and check your answers.

6 **a)** In pairs. Have you got a favourite city or part of a city? Is it your city or is it somewhere you've visited? Write a short paragraph describing your city or part of a city.

b) In groups. Take it in turns to read out your descriptions to the group. The group asks questions to try to guess which city or part of a city each student is describing.

Examples: Are there many . . . ?
How many . . . are there?
Is it very . . . ?

In town

7 a) 🔟 In pairs. Listen to Ross and answer the questions.

1 Why doesn't Ross like living in the centre of London?
2 How long has he lived there?

b) 🔟 Listen again. Which adjectives do Ross and the journalist use?

c) 🔟 Fill in the gaps with the Present Simple or Present Continuous form of the verbs in brackets. Then listen again and check your answers.

1 I .... it here. (hate)
2 I .... about moving, in fact. (think)
3 I .... at six every morning. (get up)
4 People .... here and they just .... in the pavement cafés all night. (come, sit)
5 I .... twelve or thirteen hours a day and I swear I .... more than four or five hours' sleep a night! (work, not get)
6 Everybody .... it's so exciting here! (think)
7 What .... they .... to that car? (do)
8 I .... you! (watch)

d) Fill in the gaps in the Language Box with uses 1–4. Then say which use of the Present Simple or Present Continuous each sentence in Exercise 7c) shows.

1 An activity that's happening now – at the moment of speaking.
2 A general habit or routine (something that happens again and again).
3 Temporary activity happening around now (not necessarily at the moment of speaking).
4 Permanent situation (something that's always true or doesn't change).

> ### Present Simple and Present Continuous
>
> We use the Present Simple for .... and ....
> We use the Present Continuous for .... and ....
> **Look!**
> • I'm living in London. (while I'm doing a course = temporary)
> I live in London. (it's my home = permanent)

8 Underline the correct tense in these sentences.

Example: (I'm taking / I take) the train this week because my car's in the garage.

1 (I'm staying / I stay) with friends because our landlord (is painting / paints) our flat.
2 (I'm staying / I stay) with my sister every time I go to New York.
3 (They're building / They build) a supermarket near my house. It's so noisy.
4 Watch out! That man (is driving / drives) on the wrong side of the road!
5 The shops (are closing / close) early on Thursdays.

Pronunciation: auxiliary verbs (strong and weak forms)

9 a) Read the sentences aloud. Are the auxiliaries *do, have, be* strong or weak? Fill in the boxes with *S* (strong) or *W* (weak).

Example: A: Are ☒W you going out?
B: Yes, I am ☒S.

1 I haven't ☐ seen her for weeks. Has ☐ she moved?
2 Lots of tourists have ☐ visited this monument.
3 People say cars aren't ☐ damaging the environment, but they are ☐ .
4 A: Does ☐ everybody here use public transport?
B: No, but most people do ☐ .
5 I think those men are ☐ watching us.

b) 11 Listen and check. Then fill in the gaps in the Language Box with *positive sentences, negative sentences, questions* and *short answers*.

Auxiliary verbs: strong and weak forms

Apart from contractions (*there's, we're,* etc.), auxiliary verbs have two pronunciations: strong and weak.
We use the strong pronunciation in .... and in ....
We use the weak pronunciation in .... and in ....

State verbs

10 Read the Language Box. Then fill in the gaps with the Present Simple or the Present Continuous of the verbs in brackets.

State verbs

There are some verbs (verbs of opinion, having and being, feeling and emotion) that we don't usually use in Continuous tenses, e.g. *agree, be, believe, come from, hate, have, know, like, love, mean, think, understand, want.* These are called state verbs.
We can use some state verbs in both Continuous and Simple tenses – with a change in meaning:
I'm thinking about moving, in fact.
(*think* = mental activity now)
Everybody **thinks** it's wonderful here!
(*think* = opinion)
I'm having a great time in London!
(*have* = experience)
I have a really nice flat.
(*have* = possession)

1 I'm sorry but I .... with you. (not agree)
2 I .... a wonderful time here in Jamaica. I'll write again soon. (have)
3 **A:** What .... about? (you / think)
  B: My boyfriend. I miss him.
4 I'm sorry. I .... you. What .... ? (not understand, you / mean)
5 He's Turkish. He .... Istanbul. (come from)
6 I .... why she .... so badly. She's usually such a good child. (not know, behave)

I am a camera

11 a) In pairs. You're going to make a short (fifteen-minute) film about a city you know well. Do you want to present a positive or a negative image of the city? Choose two different locations that you want in your film. Then think about these questions and prepare your ideas.

1 What kind of film is it? a documentary? a film for the tourist board?
2 Describe your locations. What kind of people go there? Who lives / works there? What happens there? Is it noisy or quiet? When's the best time to go?

b) In groups. Pairs take it in turns to present your film ideas. Tell the group the kind of film you're going to make. Then describe your film locations and say why you've chosen them. The group asks questions to find out more about your film and locations.

THE GLASS CITADEL
Alison Love

ARABIA
Jonathan Raban

BLACK AND BLUE
Ian Rankin

City lights

12 a) Read the book extracts (a–c) quickly and answer the questions.

1 Are they all about European cities?
2 Which one is from a detective novel? a travel book? a love story?

b) Read the extracts again and answer the questions (1–6). Find words in the extracts to support your answers.

1 In which extract is the author leaving?
2 In which extract is the author using public transport?
3 In which extract does the author seem to be happy to be in the city?
4 Which extract mentions the season?
5 Which extract mentions the weather?
6 Which extract mentions the pollution?

c) Find words in the extracts which mean:

1 Extract a): correctly (adv)
2 Extract a): one time (adv)
3 Extract b): to know someone or something because you've seen them before (v)
4 Extract b): thick cloudy air near the ground (n)
5 Extract b): the waste gas that is produced when an engine is working (n pl, two words)
6 Extract b): very small bits of dirt you can see like a powder in the air, on furniture, etc. (n)
7 Extract c): two times (adv)
8 Extract c): waiting in a line of people to do something (v)
9 Extract c): arrived at (v, two words)

ⓐ
It was half past three and the 73 bus was moving slowly along the Euston Road. I was sitting on the top, at the front, where the schoolkids go, looking out across the city. The winter sky was dark blue and apricot: a perfect backdrop for my last view of London.

You only look at a city properly three times: once when you arrive, once when you're leaving. The third time is when you're in love; but let's not talk about that now.

(adapted from *The Glass Citadel* by Alison Love)

ⓑ
As we pushed deeper into the city I really felt as if I was coming home. There was so much to recognise. The brownstone apartment blocks like mountains; the valleys of traffic jams; the blue fog of car exhaust fumes; the thick dust on the office windows; the dead letters falling out of neon signs. Old and slow, Cairo looked and smelled like home. From the taxi window, I saw cafés, bars, bookshops. As soon as the ride was over I could be out there, looking through the shelves, sitting on a bar stool with a glass in my hand, back to the city life again.

(adapted from *Arabia* by Jonathan Raban)

ⓒ
It took Rebus an hour to drive to Raintown, but another forty minutes to find Dumbarton Road. Driving in Glasgow could be a nightmare for the first-timer; one-way streets, badly signposted roads. Rebus had to leave his car twice to call the police station for instructions, both times queuing outside phone boxes in the rain. A wind was blowing in from the west, straight from the Atlantic Ocean. When he got to the police station, he noticed a car in the car park. There were two people inside, smoke was coming from an open window, the radio was playing. "Reporters," thought Rebus.

(adapted from *Black and Blue* by Ian Rankin)

Past Simple and Past Continuous

13 a) Read these parts of the extracts again and answer the questions.

1 Extract a): Read from *It was half past three . . .* to *. . . across the city.* What three things were happening at that time?
2 Extract c): Read from *. . . he noticed a car in the car park . . .* to *. . . "Reporters," thought Rebus.* What two things were happening when Rebus noticed the car?
3 Extract c): In the sentence *When he got to the police station, he noticed a car in the car park,* which action happened first?

b) Underline all the verbs in the Past Continuous in the extracts. Then fill in the Language Box with *Past Simple* and *Past Continuous*.

Past Simple and Past Continuous

We use the .... to talk about finished past actions / states / situations. We also use it to give the (finished) events of a story:
From the taxi window, I **saw** cafés, bars, bookshops.
We use the .... to describe an activity which was already in progress when other events happened, or at an exact moment in the past:
He noticed a car . . . smoke **was coming** from an open window.
We also use it in stories for description – to describe background activity and atmosphere:
A wind **was blowing** in from the west.
When one action closely follows another action, we often use *when* to show which happened first:
When he got to the police station, he noticed a car.

14 a) In pairs. You're going to listen to Ellie describing a weekend in Amsterdam with her boyfriend. Before you listen, look at these words from her story: *delayed, hotel, no answer, public holiday, police cells, drunk.* Try to guess what problems they had.

b) 🔊 12 Now listen to Ellie's story and answer the questions.

1 Why did they decide to go to Amsterdam?
2 What was the weekend like in the end?
3 Were your predictions in Exercise 14a) correct?

c) 🔊 12 Fill in the gaps in Ellie's sentences with the Past Simple or Past Continuous of the verbs in brackets. Then listen again and check your answers.

Example: We <u>were looking forward</u> to getting away. Anyway, the weekend <u>came</u>, we <u>got</u> to the airport, <u>got</u> on the plane – everything <u>was</u> OK. (look forward, come, get, get, be)

1 We .... there, when my boyfriend suddenly .... something. (sit, remember)
2 When we .... there, we .... the bell. (get, ring)
3 I .... really tired and miserable and then it .... to rain. (get, start)
4 We .... down this back street, when we .... a small light. (walk, see)
5 The phone .... all the time and they .... people in all night. (ring, bring)
6 We .... so tired we just .... until the evening. (be, sleep)

It happened one night . . .

15 In groups of four (Pair A and Pair B). Pair A look at page 131 and Pair B at page 137.

Grammar reference
Present Simple: page 110
Present Continuous: 110
Past Simple: page 111
Past Continuous: 112

② Conversations *Well, hello!*

Starting and keeping conversations going

1 In pairs. Look at the words and phrases in the Word Box. Do we use them when we meet someone? when we say goodbye? Make two lists in your notebook. Which words / phrases do you think are formal? informal?

Examples: Meeting someone	Saying goodbye
Hello.	See you later!

> See you later! ✓   Hello. ✓   It was nice to meet you.   Cheerio!
> Goodbye.   Hiya!   How are you?   Bye!   Pleased to meet you.
> See ya.   Bye bye!   Hi!   Nice to meet you.   Cheers!
> How are you doing?   Nice meeting you.

2 🔾🔾 13 Listen to the beginnings of two conversations. What's wrong with each conversation?

3 **a)** In groups. Look at the photo of Antonio and Clara. Antonio wants to begin a conversation with Clara. Look at the list of possible opening lines (1–15). Which are bad ideas?

1 Is there life after death?
2 Are you enjoying the book?
3 Can I sit here?
4 Are you married?
5 I like that author – Stephen King.
6 Have you got a tattoo?
7 Is anyone reading that paper?
8 What sign are you?
9 Oh, no! It's raining again.
10 Have we met before?
11 I'm a vegetarian.
12 Did I see you in here yesterday?
13 My father owns a big company.
14 You're very beautiful.
15 Excuse me, have you got the time?

b) To which three acceptable opening lines in Exercise 3a) could Clara politely and naturally answer *No, I don't think so.*? In pairs, choose three other opening lines from Exercise 3a) and write a polite response to each one. Compare your answers with another pair.

Echo questions and statements

4 **a)** 🔾🔾 14 Antonio and Clara have begun chatting. Listen to their conversation. What's the conversation about? Who speaks more? Who speaks less?

b) 🔾🔾 14 Listen again to the person who speaks less. Tick the words or expressions in the Word Box that he / she uses. Why does he / she use them?

> I see.   Really?   Hmm.
> Yeah.   I know.   Uh-huh.
> Mm-hm.   Sure.   So . . . ?
> Do you mean . . . ?
> Oh yeah?   Absolutely.

c) Write the headings (1–4) in your notebook. Then write the words and expressions from the Word Box in Exercise 4b) under the correct heading.

1 Showing interest
2 Checking
3 Encouraging / Showing you're listening
4 Agreeing

d) Look at Recording script 14. Write in your notebook the words / phrases Antonio uses to:

1 give himself time to think.
2 check that Clara understands.

5 In pairs. Talk to each other about your general impressions of the city you're in. Take it in turns to be the listener using the phrases in Exercise 4c) and the speaker using the phrases in Exercise 4d).

6 a) 🔊 15 Listen to Clara telling Antonio about a problem she had the first time she came to the café. Listen for these words: *bag, purse, waiter, one pound twenty, flatmate*. What happened?

b) Fill in the gaps in Antonio's phrases.

1 **C:** I've been here about eleven times, I think.
   A: .... ? This is my first time here.
2 **C:** Because my school was near here.
   A: .... ? Were you studying English?
3 **C:** I thought I could go from nothing to perfect English in two months!
   A: .... ? .... impossible!
4 **C:** And sure enough, my purse was gone!
   A: .... ? .... go after him?
5 **C:** I tried to explain but he just got angry.
   A: .... ? .... an idiot!

c) 🔊 15 Listen again and check your answers. Then read the Language Box.

> ### Echo questions and statements
>
> We often use echo questions, followed by a further question or statement, to show interest or surprise:
> **A:** He goes everywhere by taxi.
> **B: Does he?** That's unusual.
> We can also repeat the key words as a question:
> **B: By taxi?** Isn't that expensive?

d) Look at Recording script 15 and find the other phrases Antonio uses to react. Fill in the gaps.

1 **A:** I know exactly ....
2 **A:** That's .... Was he a student from your school?
3 **C:** But then I felt so completely alone.
   A: Yeah. I .... !
4 **C:** I couldn't even pay for my lunch.
   A: That's .... What did you do?
5 **A:** No .... ! .... ? How did you feel?

7 In pairs. Take it in turns to read a sentence and reply with an echo question or key words.

Example: A: I'm worried about the environment.
             B: Are you? Me, too – it's terrible.
             OR The environment? Why?

1 My favourite film is probably *Psycho*.
2 Grant doesn't eat red meat.
3 My grandfather was 105 when he died.
4 I've written an English grammar book.
5 Delia wants to buy a Ferrari.

8 In groups of three. Take it in turns to be Student A, Student B and Student C.

STUDENT A: SPEAKER
Choose a subject (1–7) from the list or your own idea and tell Student B about it. Use phrases from Exercise 4d).

1 A terrible accident
2 My favourite building
3 The most important person in my country
4 My favourite kind of music
5 When I started to learn English
6 A journey I took
7 Something in my pocket

STUDENT B: LISTENER
Listen to Student A and react. Use phrases from Exercises 4c), 6b) and 6d). Don't interrupt to tell your own story.

STUDENT C: OBSERVER
Tell Students A and B when to begin and give them exactly three minutes. During this time, take notes on page 133. After three minutes, report to Students A and B, telling them what phrases they used, how natural they sounded, etc.

3 When Saturday comes

Adjectives / phrases for describing places
Defining and non-defining relative clauses
First Conditional: *if* and *unless*
Strong and base adjectives
Day to day English: *How about . . . ?*
Reading for pleasure 1: *Heat wave*
Do you remember? Units 1–3

There's a place . . .

1 a) In pairs. Look at the photos. Where are the people?

b) 🔊 16 Listen to two friends. Which place (a–c) are they talking about? Do they both feel the same about it? Tick the adjectives from the Word Box that you hear.

> modern   cosy   dimly-lit   lively
> bright   packed   cool   simple   crowded
> friendly   comfortable   noisy   colourful
> smoky   quiet   strange-looking   busy
> elegant   fun   dark   spacious   posh
> welcoming   relaxed   traditional
> sweaty   smart   fashionable   casual

c) 🔊 16 In pairs. Did the ticked adjectives describe the place, atmosphere or people? Listen again and check.

d) In your notebook, make a table with three headings: *place, atmosphere, people*. Fill in the table with the adjectives from the Word Box.

2 a) In pairs. Choose one of the places the two friends didn't talk about. Write a short description of the place, the atmosphere and the people. Use at least six adjectives from the Word Box. Add one piece of information which isn't true.

Examples: It's really cosy and . . . but it isn't . . .
It's got . . . and there are . . .

b) In groups. Pairs take it in turns to read your descriptions. Which place is each pair describing? Which information is untrue? Which description is the most detailed? Which description is the most detailed? atmospheric?

Relative clauses

3 Fill in the gaps in these sentences with *which, who, whose* or *where*. Check your answers in Recording script 16. Then read the Language Box.

1 Do you mean the guy .... best friend is a film director?
2 Some of the records .... the DJ put on were a bit too loud.
3 It's the part .... all the media people sit.
4 I saw that guy ....'s in that beer ad.

Defining relative clauses

We use defining relative clauses to identify which person, thing or place we're talking about.
We use *who* (or *that*) for people and *which* (or *that*) for things / places. We often use *that* in conversation.
Do you remember that guy **who / that** we were talking to?
It's the bar **which / that** has got the lizard.
We can also use *where* for places:
That's the club **where** we met.
We use *whose* for possessives:
I met a girl **whose** name was Fran.

4 **a)** Read sentences 1 and 2. Both have the clause *which has enormous windows*. In which sentence does the clause tell you which part of the restaurant? In which sentence does it just add extra description? Now read the Language Box.

1 The upstairs part, which has enormous windows, is really nice.
2 We were sitting in the upstairs part which has enormous windows.

Non-defining relative clauses

Non-defining relative clauses don't tell you **which** person or thing we're talking about – they only give **extra information** about the person or thing. We use commas to separate these clauses from the rest of the sentence:
The restaurant, **which is always full of media types**, is always busy.
Our waiter, **who was an out-of-work actor**, was really funny.
Look!
• We can't use *that* in non-defining relative clauses:
Elmo's bar, **which** (NOT that) I've never been to, stays open all night.

b) In pairs. Read the story. Then put each piece of information (1–5) into the story as a non-defining relative clause.

Example: 4 It was near the station.
We went to a cheap little café, **which was near the station**.

1 She was wearing a fur coat.
2 It had the words "For your eyes only" on it.
3 They looked very expensive.
4 It was near the station. ✓
5 She was wearing a paper hat and a greasy apron.

We went to a cheap little café. We went to the upstairs part and sat down at a corner table. The waitress came and gave us a menu. A woman came in and sat at the next table. Then a man came in and sat down at her table. They were both wearing sunglasses. They were talking very quietly and looking around a lot. She took out a folder and showed him some photos. He wrote things down in a notebook. Then he phoned someone.

c) In pairs. Add two more non-defining relative clauses of your own to the story.

I know a place . . .

5 In groups. Think of a place you often go to that you really like. What's it like? Take it in turns to describe your places and ask questions.

Example: A: There's a café, which is really near my flat, that has nice . . .
B: What's the . . . like?
A: It's really lively. There's this guy who . . .
C: It sounds good. How much is the . . . ?

Decisions . . . decisions . . .

6 a) In groups. Look at the photo. Where are Alison and Stephanie? How often do you go to places like this? Why do you go? Where's the nearest one to you? What's it like?

b) 🔊 17 Listen to Alison and Stephanie's conversation. What two things does Stephanie want Alison to do? Why doesn't Alison want to do them?

c) 🔊 17 In pairs. Fill in the gaps with *I might get, I'll be, I'll spend* or *I won't have*. Then listen again and check.

1 If I stay here, ... all my money.
2 If I spend any more, ... enough for Spain.
3 Unless I leave right now, ... it all.
4 If we go to the pub, ... there all night.
5 If Tom's working on the bar, ... a couple of free drinks.

7 In pairs. Answer questions 1 and 2 about the sentences in Exercise 6c). Then read the Language Box.

1 Do the sentences refer to the past, the present or the future?
2 Which tense follows *if* and *unless* in the sentences?

First Conditional: *if* and *unless*

We use the First Conditional to talk about future possibility.

Possible situation	Possible result
If I spend more money,	I won't have enough for my holiday.
If Tom's working on the bar,	I might get a couple of free drinks.

We use a present tense (usually the Present Simple) in the *if* part of the sentence.
We can use *will / won't* or *might / might not* in the other part of the sentence.

Look!
• We can use *unless* + a positive verb instead of *if* + negative verb:

I'll spend all my money,	**if I don't leave** now.
	unless I leave now.

8 a) In pairs. Match 1–5 with a–e to make First Conditional sentences.

Example: 1 = b)

1 I won't leave a tip
2 She'll be angry
3 If you're scared to ask her to dance,
4 If you buy any more clothes,
5 I'll pay for the taxi

a) I'll ask her for you.
b) if he doesn't serve us soon!
c) if you pay for us to get in.
d) you'll be broke again!
e) if we don't invite her.

b) Match each sentence in Exercise 8a) to each place or situation 1–5.

1 In a café or restaurant
2 Getting ready to go out
3 In a shop
4 Organising a party
5 In a club

c) Read the Language Box. Then find a prediction, an offer, a warning, a threat and a negotiation in Exercise 8a).

Uses of the First Conditional

Making predictions:
If I spend any more, I won't have enough for Spain.
Making an offer:
I'll lend you the money if you need it.
Giving warnings:
You won't have enough for your holiday, unless you stop spending.
Making threats:
I'll call the police if you don't stop bothering me.
Negotiating:
If you go and buy the milk, I'll pay for it.

---

d) In pairs. Write one First Conditional sentence (a prediction, offer, warning, threat or negotiation) for one of the places / situations in Exercise 8b). When you finish, read out your sentence to the class. The class guesses what the place / situation is and decides if the sentence is a prediction, an offer, etc.

Example: PAIR: If you don't take this off the bill, I'll call the manager.
CLASS: You're in a restaurant. You're talking to the waiter. It's a threat.

A bit of a dilemma

9 **a)** [oo] 18 Listen to two conversations. In each one, the speakers are discussing a dilemma. Make notes on who the people are, where they are and what the dilemma is. Do they agree on what to do in the end?

b) [oo] 18 What language do they use when they talk about their plans / intentions? Fill in the gaps. Then listen again, check your answers and read the Language Box.

1 I'm .... her. (phone)
2 I'm just .... that she's fine. (check)
3 So you're .... at home every night. (sit)
4 What are you .... ? (do)
5 Right now, I'm .... this cheesecake. (eat)

Going to + infinitive

We use *going to* + infinitive to talk about our future plans and intentions:
I'm going to write to him. (I've thought about it and I've decided to write to him.)

---

c) In pairs. Pair A look at page 130, Pair B at page 133, Pair C at page 135 and Pair D at page 143.

d) In groups of four (students from an A, B, C and D pair). Take it in turns to say what your dilemmas are and discuss possible solutions. Use the First Conditional and *going to* + infinitive.

Example: Student A has been offered a better job with more money but more work.
A: I've been offered a promotion at work . . .
B: Really? Are you going to accept?
A: Well, I don't know. If I take it, I'll have to work a lot harder. I don't know if I want to . . . I'm not very ambitious really. But the money sounds nice.
C: Yeah, and if you earn a bigger salary you won't have to worry about money all the time.
A: Yes, but . . .

Enjoy your meal!

10 a) Look at these web pages for three different theme restaurants. Read the information quickly. What is the theme of each restaurant?

b) Now read the rest of the information about the restaurants. Match the texts (1–3) to the restaurants (a–c).

①

Don't forget to eat in all the excitement!

An excellent three-course dinner is served by the actors between scenes. A giant Caesar Salad and freshly-baked bread is followed by Chef's choice of the night and finally a mystery dessert. Make sure you arrive before 7:30 – the show begins at 8:00 p.m. There are prizes for those brilliant detectives who correctly identify the murderer! We guarantee an evening of excitement and fun for all! No jeans, please.

②

The menu offers a selection of delicious burgers, enormous juicy steaks, as well as Kickin' Chicken, Macho Man Nachos and Powerhouse Pasta!

Food to satisfy the biggest appetites!

Then try one of our "big boy" speciality drinks, like the Brain Freezer or the Powerbomb Slide! There are regular special guest appearances. Get an autograph and a muscle-crunching handshake from your favourite hero!

③

Begin in our Magic Mushroom Bar, sitting under the biggest mushroom you've ever seen! There are freshly-squeezed fruit and vegetable juices and delicious coffee drinks. Then enjoy fantastic food, from Caribe Chicken to Giant Chocolate Volcano Cake.

Relax and enjoy the sights and sounds of the rain forest – the lush jungle, the star-filled night sky – *it's just like the real thing!*

c) Read about the restaurants again and answer the questions.

1 Where can you watch live shows?
2 Which restaurant has a dress code?
3 Where do you think you can get the biggest portions?
4 Where can you meet famous people?
5 Where do you have to arrive at a specific time? Why?
6 Which do you think young children would enjoy the most?
7 Which restaurant do you think is most educational?

d) In pairs. What do you think of the restaurants? Have you been to a theme restaurant? What was it like?

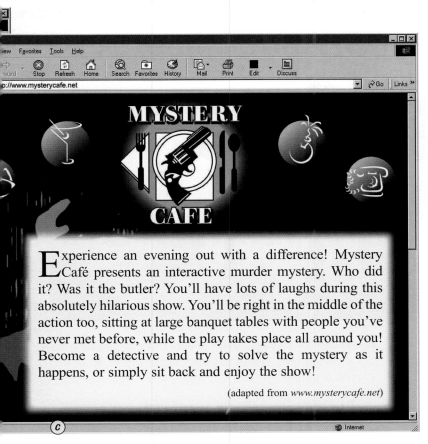

Experience an evening out with a difference! Mystery Café presents an interactive murder mystery. Who did it? Was it the butler? You'll have lots of laughs during this absolutely hilarious show. You'll be right in the middle of the action too, sitting at large banquet tables with people you've never met before, while the play takes place all around you! Become a detective and try to solve the mystery as it happens, or simply sit back and enjoy the show!

(adapted from *www.mysterycafe.net*)

Strong adjectives

11 a) Find adjectives in the texts (a–c and 1–3) with these meanings. Then read the Language Box.

Example: Text 1: extremely intelligent = brilliant

1 Texts a), b) and 1: extremely good (three different adjectives)
2 Texts a) and 2: extremely big (two different adjectives)
3 Text 3: extremely good or tasty
4 Text c): extremely funny

Strong and base adjectives

Strong adjectives have the meaning of *extremely* or *very, very*.

Strong adjective	Base adjective
a **hilarious** show	a very, very **funny** show
a **huge** aquarium	an extremely **big** aquarium

Look!
• We use *absolutely* and *really* with strong adjectives to make them stronger:
It was an absolutely / a really hilarious show.
• We use *very* and *really* with base adjectives to make them stronger:
The burgers are very / really big.

b) Fill in the gaps with the correct strong adjectives from the Word Box.

> freezing ✓   enormous / huge   exhausted
> awful / terrible   boiling   terrified   delicious
> fantastic / wonderful   tiny   furious   starving

Example: A: I was freezing!
B: Really? I didn't think it was that cold.

1 A: I was .... when he arrived late.
  B: I know! You shouldn't get so angry about things!
2 A: I thought it was absolutely .... !
  B: Did you? I didn't think it was that bad.
3 A: I'm ....
  B: Really? I'm not tired at all. I feel like going out.
4 A: It's absolutely .... in here!
  B: Oh! You're always too hot. You should see a doctor.
5 A: I'm .... !
  B: Yeah, I'm quite hungry, too. Let's get a pizza!

c) In pairs. Choose two adjectives that you didn't use from the Word Box in Exercise 11b). Write two similar exchanges and leave gaps for the strong adjectives.

d) Pairs make groups of four. Swap exchanges and fill in the gaps.

Design a theme restaurant

12 a) In groups. Design your own theme restaurant web page. Think about these questions:

1 What is the theme of your restaurant? How are you going to create the right atmosphere?
2 What food are you going to have? Think of adjectives to describe it.
3 What are your waiters / waitresses going to wear?
4 Are the waiters (or the customers!) going to do any special activities?

b) Display your web pages. Then "surf" the classroom and choose a restaurant you'd like to go to (not your own).

Grammar reference
Defining and non-defining relative clauses: page 115
First Conditional: page 116
The Future: plans (*going to* + infinitive): page 114

27

What do you want to do?

1 **a)** 🔊 19 Look at the photo and listen to the extract from *Marty* by Paddy Chayefsky. What are Marty and Angie talking about? What's the problem?

b) Fill in the gaps with the correct form of the verbs in brackets using verb + *-ing*, infinitive with *to* or infinitive without *to*.

ANGIE: What do you feel like .... tonight? (do)

MARTY: I don't know, Angie. What do you feel like .... ? (do)

ANGIE: Well, we have to do something. It's Saturday night! I don't want .... bowling like last Saturday. (go) How about .... up that girl we met at the movies about a month ago? (call) Let's .... her up! (call) What can we lose?

MARTY: I didn't like her, Angie. I don't feel like .... her up. (call)

(adapted from *The Collected Works of Paddy Chayefsky*)

c) 🔊 19 Listen again and check. Then read the Language Box.

Suggestions and preferences

Suggestions
How about **seeing** a film?
Let's **see** a film.
Shall we **see** a film?
Why don't we **see** a film?

Preferences
I feel / don't feel like **seeing** a film.
I'd rather / rather not **see** a film.
I want / don't want **to see** a film.
I'd like **to see** a film.
I'd prefer / prefer not **to see** a film.

2 **a)** 🔊 20 Rae and Brett are also trying to make an arrangement. Listen to their conversation. What's the problem?

b) 🔊 20 Fill in the gaps. Listen and check. Then read the Language Box.

RAE: I .... to Washington at nine! (fly)

BRETT: What .... on Friday from 12:30 until 1:00? (do)

RAE: The boss .... a presentation on plastics. (give)

BRETT: Friday evening. Hey, oh yeah. I .... anything after 6:00 p.m. (not do)

Future arrangements

We use the Present Continuous to talk about definite future arrangements:
I'm meeting Mary at the airport at 6:20.
Where **are you spending** the weekend?

3 In groups of four. You want to go out together some time next week. Go round in circles, making suggestions and giving preferences until you've run out of ideas!

Student A: Suggest an idea.
Student B: You've already made an arrangement. Suggest an alternative arrangement.
Student C: You're against Student B's idea. Suggest an alternative arrangement.
Student D: You're against Student C's idea. Begin again and suggest another idea.

Grammar reference
The Future: arrangements (Present Continuous): page 114

Wavelength page

Reading for pleasure

① Heat wave

Your *Wavelength Intermediate* Coursebook has got a Reader called *Heat wave and other stories* in the back. Do the exercises on this page to help you understand and enjoy the first story, *Heat wave*.

1 *Heat wave* is a film script. The film begins with scenes of people trying to fight the heat. Before you read the film script, imagine what the people are doing. Make a list.

2 **⊙⊙**21 Read and listen to the first part of the film script. Then answer the questions (1–4).

> *Theme music. During the title and credits we see a series of clips showing how city people are trying to fight the heat. When the credits end, we hear the noises of the city. We then see a ten-floor apartment building. It's night. Most of the windows are wide open and lights are on. A long ledge runs below each window. The camera moves slowly from left to right of the top floor.*
>
> *At the first window is a middle-aged man. He is drinking iced mineral water straight from a liter bottle. He is talking to his tomato plant which is growing in a pot outside the window.*
>
> **MAN:** Hey, my sweet tomato? How are you doing? Hot? Thirsty? Do you want some water?
>
> *He pours some water from the bottle into the plastic dish under the pot. Then he leans out of the window and pours some water over his head. Behind him we see the blue light of a TV. The camera moves into the apartment.*
>
> *A middle-aged woman is sitting in front of the TV. She is eating ice cream and fanning herself with a magazine. Over her shoulder we see the newsreader on the TV screen.*

> **NEWSREADER:** So New Yorkers, one and all, get ready for the hottest night in history! Perhaps you haven't noticed but *(he fans himself and laughs)* we're having a heat wave!

1 What kinds of sound effect are asked for?
2 What is the middle-aged man doing to keep cool?
3 What is the woman doing to keep cool?
4 What does the TV newsreader announce?

3 Now read the whole film script. It starts on page 2 of *Heat wave and other stories*. Think about these questions while you read.

1 What kind of relationship have the two middle-aged people got?
2 What's the young man doing?
3 What has he done to keep cool?
4 Who's he talking to before the phone rings?
5 What's the elderly woman doing?
6 What's she doing to keep cool?
7 The young woman makes two phone calls. Who to?
8 What does she do to cool off?
9 Who do you think Tom is?
10 Who do you think the two people in the apartment with no lights on are?
11 What does the elderly woman give the cat?
12 Who steals a piece of chicken?
13 What happens to the tomato plant?
14 What do you think the man who comes out of the shadows is about to do?
15 What happens to the cat in the end?

1 Hey! I've done that, too!

a) Make a list of five to eight things you've done. Think about something unusual, something you're proud of, something you'll always remember, etc. Write a question about each experience.

Example: Have you ever seen a shark?

b) Go round the class and take it in turns to ask and answer questions. If the answer is yes, ask more questions to find out as much as you can and compare your experiences.

Examples: Where were you?
What happened?
What did you do?
How did you feel?

2 Not like now

a) 👀 22 Listen to Mark talking about his parents' life when they were young. What does he describe?

b) 👀 22 What differences does he mention between when his parents were young and now? Listen again and make notes in the table.

	People used to . . .	Now they . . .
Marriage		
Make-up		
Going out		
Public transport		

c) Think about the differences between your generation and your parents' generation: work, leisure, music, social behaviour, clothes, hopes, dreams, etc. Make notes about five things:

1 which your parents used to do when they were your age but your generation doesn't do.
2 which your generation does but your parents didn't use to do.

d) In groups. Discuss the differences. Are you very different from your parents?

3 That's a terrible idea!

a) In pairs. You've decided to change your life. Choose one of the decisions 1–5. Discuss all the advantages so you can defend your life choice.

Example: I'm going to become a private detective. Advantages: It's interesting. It'll be really exciting.

1 I'm going to become a private detective.
2 I'm going to become a professional bank robber.
3 I'm going to sell all my possessions and give the money to a cats' home.
4 I'm going to join the circus.
5 I'm going to go on a six-month trip round Africa with a complete stranger.

b) Make new pairs. Student A, tell Student B about your plans. Student B, you think Student A is making a terrible mistake. Warn Student A about the consequences and try to convince him / her not to do it! Then swap. Student B, tell Student A about your plans.

Example: A: I'm going to become a private detective.
B: What?! You're joking! Have you thought about this carefully?
A: Yeah, and I've decided. I think it'll be really interesting.
B: Yes, but it's really dangerous. What will you do if . . . ?

4 The beautiful game

Read the article. Underline the correct word / words and fill in the
gaps with the adjective forms of the nouns in brackets.

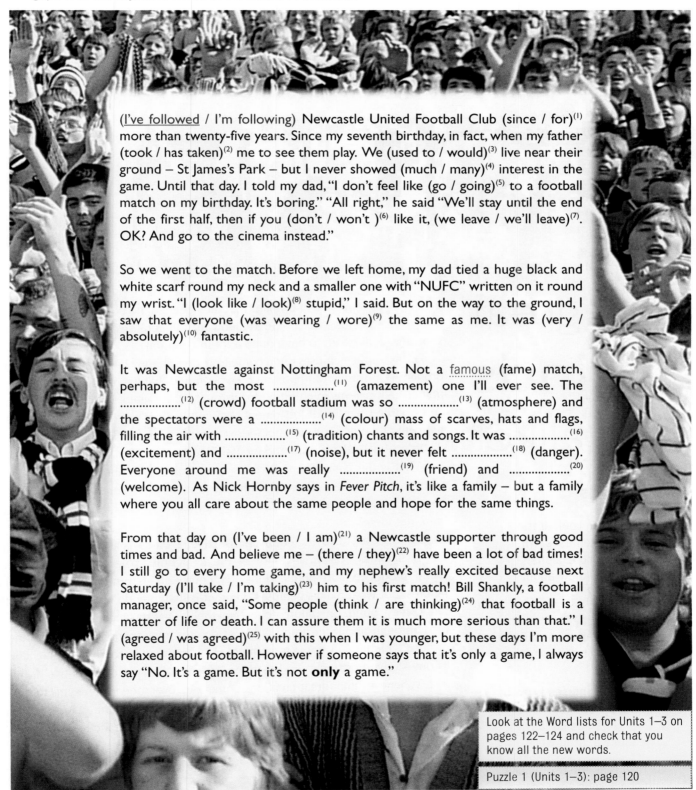

(<u>I've followed</u> / I'm following) Newcastle United Football Club (since / for)[1] more than twenty-five years. Since my seventh birthday, in fact, when my father (took / has taken)[2] me to see them play. We (used to / would)[3] live near their ground – St James's Park – but I never showed (much / many)[4] interest in the game. Until that day. I told my dad, "I don't feel like (go / going)[5] to a football match on my birthday. It's boring." "All right," he said "We'll stay until the end of the first half, then if you (don't / won't)[6] like it, (we leave / we'll leave)[7]. OK? And go to the cinema instead."

So we went to the match. Before we left home, my dad tied a huge black and white scarf round my neck and a smaller one with "NUFC" written on it round my wrist. "I (look like / look)[8] stupid," I said. But on the way to the ground, I saw that everyone (was wearing / wore)[9] the same as me. It was (very / absolutely)[10] fantastic.

It was Newcastle against Nottingham Forest. Not a <u>famous</u> (fame) match, perhaps, but the most ....[11] (amazement) one I'll ever see. The ....[12] (crowd) football stadium was so ....[13] (atmosphere) and the spectators were a ....[14] (colour) mass of scarves, hats and flags, filling the air with ....[15] (tradition) chants and songs. It was ....[16] (excitement) and ....[17] (noise), but it never felt ....[18] (danger). Everyone around me was really ....[19] (friend) and ....[20] (welcome). As Nick Hornby says in *Fever Pitch*, it's like a family – but a family where you all care about the same people and hope for the same things.

From that day on (I've been / I am)[21] a Newcastle supporter through good times and bad. And believe me – (there / they)[22] have been a lot of bad times! I still go to every home game, and my nephew's really excited because next Saturday (I'll take / I'm taking)[23] him to his first match! Bill Shankly, a football manager, once said, "Some people (think / are thinking)[24] that football is a matter of life or death. I can assure them it is much more serious than that." I (agreed / was agreed)[25] with this when I was younger, but these days I'm more relaxed about football. However if someone says that it's only a game, I always say "No. It's a game. But it's not **only** a game."

Look at the Word lists for Units 1–3 on pages 122–124 and check that you know all the new words.

Puzzle 1 (Units 1–3): page 120

4 How do you do that?

> Skills and ability: *I'm good at . . .*
> Work and jobs
> Verb + *-ing*
> Past ability: *could, was able to, managed to, succeeded in*
> Writing for work and pleasure 2: *I am writing to apply . . .*

Mozart (1756–1791)

Edison (1847–1931)

Freud (1856–1939)

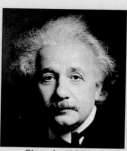

Einstein (1879–1955)

Picasso (1881–1973)

Do great minds think alike?

Great minds

1 **a)** In groups. Look at the pictures of geniuses. What were their professions? What do you know about each person?

b) You're going to read an article about geniuses. Before you read, try to answer these questions.

1 Do most geniuses grow up in happy families?

2 Does a genius usually produce a lot of work?

c) Now read the text quickly and check your answers.

1 What makes a person so brilliant that they change the course of history? Is there a recipe for genius – a list of ingredients that all geniuses share? Perhaps not, but geniuses really seem to have quite a lot in common.

For example, geniuses often come from an unhappy background and many are 5 orphans. One study of important creators found that twenty per cent of them lost one or both parents in childhood. Tolstoy, Michelangelo, Bach, Raphael, Wagner and Charlie Chaplin all lost parents before they were ten years old. Seventy-five per cent of the geniuses in another study came from families affected by poverty, divorce, abuse, alcoholism and mental illness.

10 What is the connection? Perhaps stress made the children escape into their own private worlds – they felt different from other children and so decided to become even more different. Or were they working hard to please parents who were not there?

Geniuses are also incredibly productive. Picasso is responsible for 20,000 15 works. Thomas Edison, inventor of the light bulb, patented 1093 inventions. Freud produced 330 publications. Of course, high productivity will include failures, but what makes geniuses different is that they do not give up when they fail – they build on failure to create their biggest successes. Freud had his breakthrough about the importance of dreams after spending years on another 20 project, which finally came to nothing. He was already over forty – but according to one study, most great work is done between the ages of thirty-five and forty-five. Whenever their great creations come, however, one thing seems to connect all geniuses (even young ones like Mozart) – a "ten-year rule". Geniuses have always worked hard in their chosen areas for at least a decade before they create 25 their first masterpieces.

Finally, could genius also be a question of simple childlike curiosity? Einstein often said that his greatest discoveries came from simply asking the same kinds of questions children ask – but unlike most adults, he never stopped asking them.

(adapted from *The Sunday Times*)

2 a) Read the article again and answer the questions.

1 What have Michelangelo, Wagner and Charlie Chaplin got in common?
2 According to the article, how can the death of a parent influence a child?
3 Did Freud's work on the importance of dreams finally come to nothing?
4 What is the "ten-year rule"?

b) Find words in the article which mean:

1 Lines 1–5: the type of education, family and social experience that someone has (n)
2 Lines 6–10: the time when you are a child (n)
3 Lines 6–10: when people have very little money (n)
4 Lines 6–10: cruel treatment of someone (n)
5 Lines 16–20: the opposite of *successes* (n pl) and *succeed* (v)
6 Lines 16–20: an important discovery or development (n)
7 Lines 20–25: works of art, pieces of writing, etc. of an excellent standard (n pl)
8 Lines 26–28: typical of a child, in a positive way (adj)

c) Read the quotation. What does it mean? Do you agree?

"Genius is one per cent inspiration, ninety-nine per cent perspiration."

(Thomas Edison)

d) In pairs. Were there any facts in the article that surprised you? Can you teach someone to be a genius? Do you think special schools which aim to develop geniuses are a good idea?

3 a) 23 Mr and Mrs Wellorf are having an interview with Professor Blunt. He's the owner of the Blunt School for Geniuses where their daughter, Lucy, is studying. Listen and answer questions 1 and 2.

1 How do Mr and Mrs Wellorf change between the beginning and the end of the interview? Why do they change?
2 How well do you think Lucy is really doing at the school?

b) 23 What did Professor Blunt and Lucy's parents say? Fill in the gaps with phrases from the Word Box. Then listen again and check.

> not very good at ✓ good at not bad at hopeless / useless at
> quite good at very / really good at extremely good at

Example: She's <u>not very good at</u> mathematics.
1 She's .... writing.
2 Picasso himself was .... reading.
3 He was .... artistic work.
4 Do you mean she's .... painting?
5 She's .... drawing.
6 He was .... communicating and dealing with people.

c) Read the Language Box. Then order the phrases in the Word Box in Exercise 3b) from the most positive (1) to the most negative (7).

Talking about skills and ability

We can use *be* + *good / not good at*, etc. + verb + *-ing* / noun to describe what we can or can't do:
He's really good at drawing.
She's useless at mathematics.

Tell me all about yourself

4 In groups of four. You're going to find out about each other's childhoods, schooldays, abilities and skills. Student A look at page 130, Student B at page 132, Student C at page 134 and Student D at page 142.

Frank Dark: stand-up comic

Alan James: advertising executive

Nice work if you can get it

5 **a)** In pairs. Look at the photos and read the job descriptions. What do you think are the good and bad sides of Frank's and Alan's jobs? What do you think these two jobs might have in common?

> Frank Dark is a comedian. He stands up in front of a microphone and tells jokes in clubs. It's not always easy! He also runs a comedy club in London.

> Alan James works for an advertising agency in central London. He's responsible for making sure clients are satisfied with the way their products are advertised.

b) In the same pairs. You're going to listen to Frank and Alan describing their jobs. What do you think they'll say? Read the statements (1–10) and tick (✓) the boxes.

	Frank	Alan
1 You have to be good at dealing with people.	☐	☐
2 It's very stressful.	☐	☐
3 You have to work in a team.	☐	☐
4 You have to take criticism.	☐	☐
5 You have to think quickly.	☐	☐
6 You earn a lot of money.	☐	☐
7 It's hard work, but enjoyable.	☐	☐
8 There's job security.	☐	☐
9 The clothes you wear are important.	☐	☐
10 Nobody tells you what to do.	☐	☐

c) 👓 24 Listen to Frank and then Alan. Check your answers.

6 **a)** Find the words and phrases in the Word Box in Recording script 24. Then copy the table into your notebook and fill it in with the words and phrases.

> a demanding job   deal with people   take criticism
> think on your feet   stressful   a lot of pressure
> job security   for a company / an agency
> in the marketing department   an annual pay rise
> a lot of stress   under pressure   look smart
> well-paid   perks   regular bonuses   long holidays
> long hours   be available   in a team
> deal with problems   make decisions   never boring

It's ...	
There is / are ...	
You get ...	
You have to ...	
You work ...	

b) Use the language in the Word Box to describe your present job or your ideal job.

Verb + -ing

7 Read the Language Box and then underline examples of verb + -ing in sentences 1–6. Which use does each sentence illustrate? Fill in the boxes with a), b) or c).

> ### Verb + -ing
>
> Gerunds (verb + -ing) are the noun forms of verbs. We mainly use them in three ways:
> a) as a subject (like a noun):
> **Running** a club can be very stressful.
> b) after a preposition:
> I'm good at **dealing** with problems.
> c) after some verbs, e.g. *like, hate*, etc.:
> I enjoy **working** on my own.

Example: ☐b I'm responsible for <u>looking</u> after our clients.

1 ☐ I often think about leaving my job.
2 ☐ He hates speaking in public.
3 ☐ Working for a large company can be impersonal.
4 ☐ I don't mind working under pressure.
5 ☐ Sitting in front of a computer screen for long periods is bad for your eyes.
6 ☐ I'm always interested in meeting new people.

Just the job

8 **a)** Read the beginning of the Dynamic Jobs application form. How is this agency different from most normal employment agencies?

b) You've gone to the Dynamic Jobs agency to find a job. Fill in the application form.

c) In pairs. You're going to be interviewers and applicants at the Dynamic Jobs agency. Pair A look at page 135 and Pair B at page 143.

---

dynamic jobs dj

Tired of the same old nine to five? Looking for new challenges?

dynamic jobs will get you out of the office and into the circus!
We'll take you from the concrete jungle to the real jungle!
We'll pull you off the bus and put you into a hot-air balloon!
Just fill in the form below and leave the rest to us!

YOUR SKILLS

Are you very good (✓), quite good (–) or not very good (✗) at:

● organising? ☐
● dealing with people? ☐
● making decisions? ☐
● working under pressure? ☐
● persuading people and selling? ☐
● managing money? ☐
● communicating? ☐

YOUR INTERESTS

Do you really enjoy (✓), quite like (–) or dislike (✗):

● being creative? ☐
● meeting new people? ☐
● working on your own? ☐
● working in a team? ☐
● doing physical work? ☐
● working with nature? ☐
● entertaining people? ☐
● leading others? ☐

YOUR IDEAL JOB

Are these very important (✓) or less important (✗) to you?

● having job security ☐
● working the hours you want ☐
● having independence ☐
● earning a good salary ☐
● having status ☐
● having new challenges ☐
● moving up the career ladder ☐

The sweet smell of success

9 **a)** Look at the cartoons (1–5). Which ones are about success and which ones are about failure? Which ones do you think are funny?

b) In pairs. Choose one of the situations in the cartoons. What do you think they said next? Write four to six lines to continue the conversation.

c) Take it in turns to act out your conversation for the class. The class guesses which cartoon each conversation is based on.

Past ability and linkers

10 **a)** Read Laurence Vague's success story. What's his job? Then fill in the gaps with the correct letters (a–o).

Gaps 1–5
a) I could
b) I studied hard and learnt
c) I had a natural gift for ✓
d) I remember
e) I always knew I wanted to be

Gaps 6–10
f) Sometimes I felt like giving up
g) I tried to
h) However, the problem was
i) I couldn't
j) I went on courses in

Gaps 11–15
k) I managed to
l) I succeeded in
m) Finally
n) After a while
o) I was able

b) 25 Listen and check.

CONGRATULATIONS, PEARSON. A MANAGERIAL POSITION HAS JUST BECOME AVAILABLE.

"I got 6 per cent in maths. Is that good or bad?"

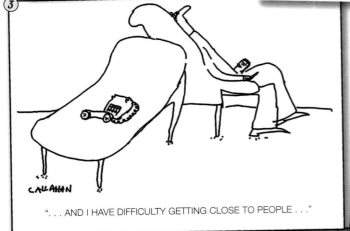

". . . AND I HAVE DIFFICULTY GETTING CLOSE TO PEOPLE . . ."

"Well, we haven't made a very good start have we, Mrs Turnstone?"

MARRIAGE GUIDANCE COUNSELLOR

WE DON'T KNOW WHERE HE GOES ALL DAY BUT HE BRINGS HOME ABOUT 135 THOUSAND DOLLARS A YEAR.

Bizarro by Dan Piraro. Reprinted with permission of Universal Press Syndicate. All rights reserved.

My parents always knew that c) [1] acting. It was something to do with the way I cried as a baby. And ..... [2] an actor, too. It was my destiny! ..... [3] spending all my time as a young boy reading plays and acting them out for my parents and their friends. ..... [4] all the classics. By the time I left school, ... [5] play any part – tragedy, comedy, everything! I was ready for glory. ...... [6] that the rest of the world wasn't ready for me! I was handsome and intelligent, but ..... [7] get any work. ..... [8] contact famous actors and directors, but they weren't interested. It was awful! ..... [9], but I never did! Because I'm strong! Anyway, I had a lot of free time, so ..... [10] stage management and make-up. ..... [11] – two or three months – someone asked me to do the make-up for a production of *Hamlet*. I accepted, but I wanted more! I wanted to be on that stage! ..... [12], my chance came. The actor playing Hamlet fell downstairs on exactly the same night that a famous Hollywood producer was in the audience! Luckily I knew his part and so ..... [13] to take his place. I could see that the producer was impressed with my Hamlet. It was then that I decided to go to Hollywood – and the producer was the first person I contacted. After several phone calls to his secretary (a darling woman!) and trips to his house ..... [14] get a part in the hit film *The Taxman*. And, well, the rest is cinema history. After years of pain and struggling (and of course, my natural talent) ..... [15] becoming what I am today – a Hollywood star, a great actor.

11 Read the Language Box. Then fill in the gaps in sentences 1–5 with *could, couldn't, was able to, managed to* or *succeeded in*.

Past ability

When we talk about general past ability we use *could* + infinitive:
When I was young I **could swim** very well.
To talk about success on one occasion we can use *was able to* + infinitive:
We had plenty of time before the flight so we **were able to have** a meal.
To talk about success on one occasion after difficulty or effort we can use *managed to* + infinitive or *succeeded in* + verb + *-ing*:
The traffic was terrible but I **managed to get** to work on time.
I finally **succeeded in passing** my driving test after three attempts.

Look!
- We usually use *couldn't* in negative sentences:
  I **couldn't** swim very well when I was young.
  The traffic was terrible so I **couldn't** get there on time.

1 John was an incredible child. He .... read and write when he was three.
2 After phoning every day for a week, I finally .... talk to the manager.
3 He tried, but unfortunately he .... persuade her to help him.
4 Stella knew what the problem was so she .... fix the photocopier quickly and easily.
5 She .... finding the formula after many years of research.

Rags to riches

12 In pairs. Choose one of the titles (1–5) or one of your own and write your own success story. Use the language from Exercise 10a). Begin *I always knew . . .*

1 How I became the first man / woman on Venus.
2 How I became an international singing sensation.
3 How I became president.
4 How I became a world-famous film director at twenty-three.
5 How my pet became a Hollywood star.

Grammar reference
Modal verbs (ability): page 118

Writing for work and pleasure

② *I am writing to apply . . .*

Writing a CV

1 a) Ana is a senior duty receptionist in a hotel in São Paulo. What qualifications / skills do you think she needs for her job?

b) Ana is looking for a new job. Read her CV quickly. Were your predictions in Exercise 1a) correct?

2 Fill in the gaps (a–j) in the CV with the headings 1–10.

1 EDUCATION & QUALIFICATIONS
2 Other skills
3 REFEREES
4 Marital status
5 EMPLOYMENT
6 Nationality
7 ADDITIONAL INFORMATION
8 Address
9 Date of birth
10 Interests

3 In groups. Look at the job ads (1–3) from the newspaper *The State of São Paulo* on 26th July. Which one is the most suitable for Ana? Why?

Curriculum vitae

PERSONAL DETAILS

Name
(a) ....
(b) ....
(c) ....
(d) ....

Telephone
E-mail

Ana Helena Ortiz
19th October 1977
Brazilian
Single
Rua Bartolomeu da Silva, 35 – Lapa
05065 – 110 São Paulo SP
11 – 265 – 6192
aho@zipmail.com.br

(e) ....
May 1999–present

Senior duty receptionist at Hotel Excelsior, São Paulo.
Duties include: dealing with bookings and billing and providing tourist information.

June 1998–April 1999

Junior receptionist at Hotel Mendes Plaza, São Paulo.
Duties included: reception work and booking conference facilities.

(f) ....
March 1996–December 1997

University of São Paulo (USP)
Degree course in history (unfinished due to family financial difficulties)

1990–1996

Santa Amelia School, Santos (SP)
School leaving certificate Grade 8.2

1992–1996

Anglo-Brazilian Cultural Centre
Cambridge FCE Examination Grade A

(g) ....
(h) ....

Fluent in English
Computer literate
Swimming and clothes design

(i) ....

(j) ....
Work:

Education:

Mr T Caxias, General Manager, Excelsior Hotel, São Paulo
Professor U Santos, University of São Paulo (USP)

---

① **HOTEL MIDAS**

is looking for a

RESTAURANT MANAGER

The job involves making reservations by fax, telephone, e-mail and in person with the hotel guests. Good standards of English and Portuguese are required. Some knowledge of Japanese would be an advantage. Some evening and weekend work.

② MUSEUM ASSISTANT required by

São Paulo Museum of American Culture

You must be able to speak to our many foreign visitors in English and have an interest in history and art. University degree essential.

③ *NINE STAR AIRLINES*

require a *BOOKING MANAGER* for their new office in Av. Paulista in São Paulo. The manager will coordinate the work of three booking clerks using standardised procedures. You should be computer literate and fluent in Portuguese and English and be used to dealing with members of the public.

Writing a letter of application

4 Read the Writing Box. Then look at the layout of a formal letter of application. Fill in the gaps (a–i) in the layout with the information 1–9.

> ### Letters of application
>
> • A letter of application refers directly to the job being applied for. It doesn't repeat the information in the CV but highlights and expands the information in the CV to say why the person is especially suitable for that job.
> • When we begin a letter without a name, for example *Dear Sir*, we end with *Yours faithfully*. When we begin with a name, for example *Dear Mrs Williams*, we end with *Yours sincerely*.

ⓐ 4

ⓑ

ⓒ

ⓓ

Dear Sir / Madam,

ⓔ

ⓕ

ⓖ

ⓗ

Yours faithfully,

ⓘ

Ana Ortiz

1 their address
2 your signature
3 information about your suitability for the job and why you want the job
4 your address
5 why you're writing
6 additional information
7 the date
8 their name / the name of the company
9 closing

5 **a)** In pairs. Match Ana's thoughts (a–j) to the formal sentences for a job application letter (1–10).

Example: a) = 5

a) I saw your ad in (newspaper) for (job).
b) I've put some other things in with this letter.
c) I can come and see you when you like.
d) I'm getting a bit bored with my job.
e) Can you give me some more information about . . .
f) Write to me.
g) I work in a hotel at the moment.
h) I hope you give me the job.
i) I have to do lots of different things.
j) I love telling the junior receptionists what to do.

1 I am available for interview at your convenience.
2 I would be grateful if you could give me further information concerning . . .
3 Although I am happy in my current position, I would like a post with more responsibility.
4 Thank you for considering my application.
5 I am writing in response to your advertisement for a (job) in the (newspaper) of (date).
6 I look forward to hearing from you.
7 I am responsible for a small team of reception staff and enjoy this aspect of my work.
8 My work involves a variety of duties, including . . .
9 I enclose . . . / Please find enclosed . . .
10 I am currently working as a (job and place of work).

b) In pairs. Which sections (e–h) of the letter in Exercise 4 should sentences 1–10 from Exercise 5a) go in?

Example: 1 = h

c) Write Ana's letter of application for the job of booking manager with Nine Star Airlines.

6 Dynamic Jobs have got vacancies 1–3. In pairs, choose one of the jobs and write a CV and a letter applying for the job. Make sure you include as much relevant information as possible!

1 stand-in for a famous film star
2 bodyguard for a racehorse
3 Hollywood divorce lawyer

> **Remember!**
> • Lay the letter out properly.
> • Organise the information into paragraphs.
> • Impress the employer by highlighting the skills and experience which are appropriate for the job.
> • Use formal language. Don't use contractions.

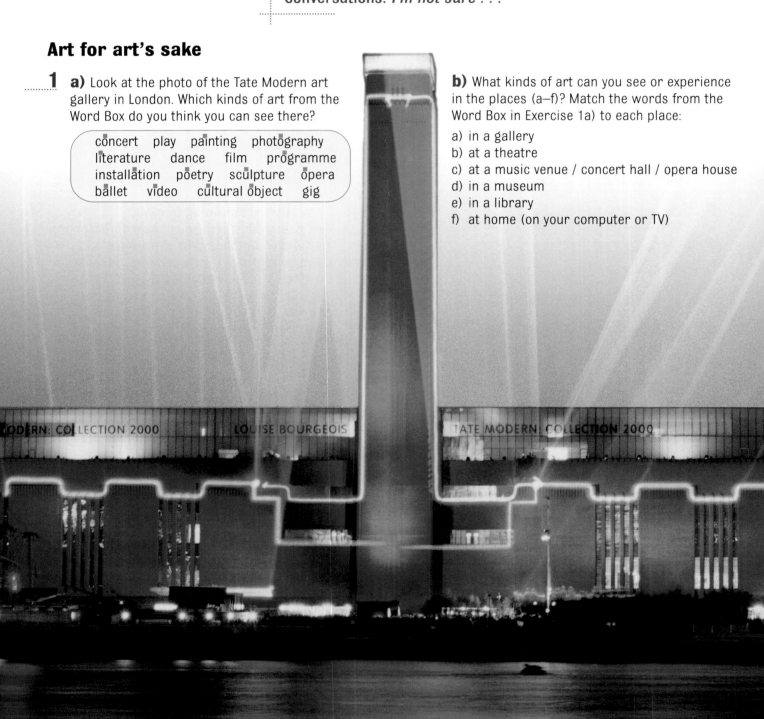

5 Culture vultures

Arts and culture
Subject and object questions
Modifying adjectives and nouns: *It's far less interesting than . . . You're such a snob.*
Present Perfect Continuous
Conversations: *I'm not sure . . .*

Art for art's sake

1 a) Look at the photo of the Tate Modern art gallery in London. Which kinds of art from the Word Box do you think you can see there?

> concert   play   painting   photography
> literature   dance   film   programme
> installation   poetry   sculpture   opera
> ballet   video   cultural object   gig

b) What kinds of art can you see or experience in the places (a–f)? Match the words from the Word Box in Exercise 1a) to each place:

a) in a gallery
b) at a theatre
c) at a music venue / concert hall / opera house
d) in a museum
e) in a library
f) at home (on your computer or TV)

2 a) 🎧26 You're going to hear six short conversations. Where are the people? Match the conversations (1–6) to the places (a–f) in Exercise 1b).

b) 🎧26 Listen again and tick the words from the Word Box that you hear.

> aisle ✓ actor shelf playwright computer
> director composer front row back row
> photographer performance author box office
> presenter stage website audience
> backstage remote (control) exhibit librarian
> visitor exhibition reference book attendant
> interval back issues artist sculptor

c) In pairs. Look at the word map for a gallery, then make similar word maps for places b–f in Exercise 1b). (Some words can go in more than one word map.)

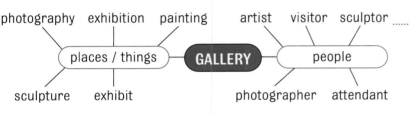

3 In groups. Answer the questions.
1 When did you last go to one of places a–e in Exercise 1b)? What did you see? Who were you with?
2 Which kinds of art do you like / don't you like?

Subject and object questions

4 a) 🎧27 Zara and Mario from conversation 1 in Exercise 2a) are talking in the interval of the play. Listen and answer the questions.

1 What's Mario's problem?
2 In relation to the character John, who is Sarah? Rebecca? Terry?

b) 🎧27 Listen to the conversation again and fill in the gaps in the questions (1–6). Then read the Language Box and fill in the boxes with *S* (Subject question) or *O* (Object question).

Example: ☐O☐ What do you want to know?
☐S☐ Who phoned Sarah that night?

1 ☐ What .... she .... ?
2 ☐ Who .... the letter?
3 ☐ Who .... John?
4 ☐ What .... him do that?
5 ☐ What .... Terry .... that day?
6 ☐ Who .... him?

Subject and object questions

The information *Rebecca phoned Sarah* can create two questions:
1 **Who** did Rebecca phone? (Rebecca phoned **somebody** – who **received** the phone call?)
2 **Who** phoned Sarah? (**Somebody** phoned Sarah – who **made** the phone call?)
Question 1 is an **object question**: we're interested in the **object** of the verb *phone*.
Question 2 is a **subject question**: we're interested in the **subject** of the verb *phone*.
Look!
• We don't use the auxiliary *do* in subject questions.

Arts and culture

5 a) In pairs. How many of these questions can you answer? When you finish, write five more subject questions about arts and culture. Make sure you know the answers to your questions!

1 Who wrote the play *Romeo and Juliet*?
2 Who starred with Hugh Grant in *Notting Hill*?
3 Who designed the tower in the middle of Paris?
4 Who wrote the book *Murder on the Orient Express*?
5 Who created the statue of David in Florence?
6 Who played the drums in the Beatles?
7 Who painted the *Mona Lisa*?
8 Which world-famous opera singer comes from New Zealand?
9 Who composed *The Four Seasons*?
10 Who sang *Love Me Tender*?

b) Make new pairs. Check your answers to questions 1–10 on page 133. Then take it in turns to ask each other your five new questions.

41

Valerie and Mallory

Comparative adjectives

6 Copy the table into your notebook. Fill in the table with the comparative forms of the adjectives in the Word Box.

Adjective + -er	More + adjective + than	Irregular
	more talented than	

> talented ✓ good unusual boring bad
> famous big dark impressive creative
> insecure brave attractive useful far
> enthusiastic lazy smart hard lively
> colourful soft skilful nice
> comfortable cool bright entertaining

7 a) Look at the picture of Valerie and Mallory. Where are they? What do you think they're saying? In what ways are the two paintings similar to each other? In what ways are they different from each other?

b) 🔊 28 Listen. Which painting does Valerie like? Which painting does Mallory like?

c) 🔊 28 Listen again and fill in the gaps. Then read the Language Box.

Example: It's a bit more experimental than his other work – slightly less ordinary.

1 She's .... amazing painter.
2 It's .... black!
3 Her style is .... freer than Frank's.
4 His style is .... exciting.
5 The whole thing is just .... obvious.
6 You're .... snob.
7 I think Frank is .... talented than any artist at this exhibition.
8 It's .... interesting than Mo's work.
9 It isn't .... boring as some of her other stuff.
10 It's .... interesting as some of Frank's early work.

Modifying adjectives and nouns

We make **nouns** stronger with *such a / an*:
He's **such a** talented artist.
She's **such an** interesting person.
We make **adjectives** stronger with *so*:
He's **so** talented.
We use *much, far* and *a lot* with **comparative adjectives** for big differences:
It's **far / much / a lot** less interesting than the other painting.
We use *a bit* and *slightly* with **comparative adjectives** for small differences:
It's **a bit / slightly more** experimental than her other work.
We can also use *nearly as / not quite as* + adjective + *as* for small differences:
It's nearly as / It isn't quite as good **as** the other one.

Pronunciation: sentence stress

8 🔊 29 Listen to sentences 1–5 in Exercise 7c) again and underline the stressed words / syllables. Listen again and repeat, then read the Language Box.

Stressing for emphasis

We stress the words *so, such, far, much, lot, slightly, bit, nearly* and *quite* because they emphasise how much or how little:
You're such a snob.
It's much more interesting.

9 In pairs. Look at the paintings and chairs (1–6). Compare the paintings and then compare the chairs using *far, much, a lot, a bit, slightly, not quite as* and *nearly as*.

Example: This chair is far more comfortable than that one.

10 a) In pairs. Choose two well-known actors / actresses, cities, buildings, TV programmes, singers or films. Make a list of the big and small differences between them.

b) Pairs make groups of four. Discuss and compare the items you've chosen.

Example: A: (name of city) is a lot more exciting than (name of city).
B: Yeah, but it's much more polluted, too!

The people's art

11 In pairs. Your town / city is going to build a huge modern art complex. They're going to put a sculpture in front of the entrance to represent art and culture. You've been asked to decide what you think it should be and to present your ideas at a meeting. Pair A look at page 141, Pair B at page 134, Pair C at page 136 and Pair D at page 138.

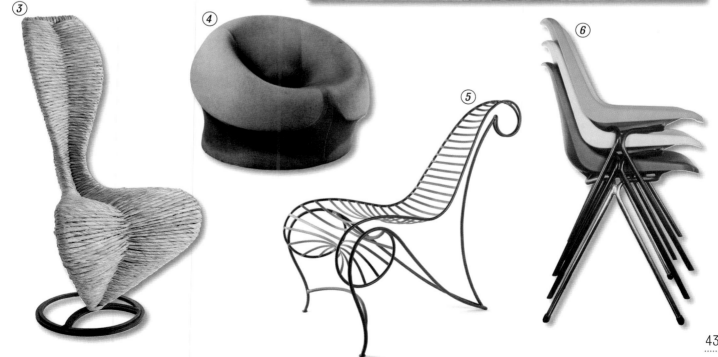

Famous for fifteen minutes

.... **12 a)** Read this article about the artist, Andy Warhol quickly. Which do you think was his most important decade?

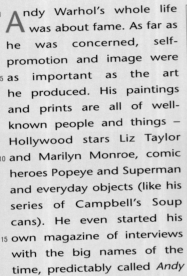

Andy Warhol 1928–1987

¹ Andy Warhol's whole life was about fame. As far as he was concerned, self-promotion and image were ⁵ as important as the art he produced. His paintings and prints are all of well-known people and things – Hollywood stars Liz Taylor ¹⁰ and Marilyn Monroe, comic heroes Popeye and Superman and everyday objects (like his series of Campbell's Soup cans). He even started his ¹⁵ own magazine of interviews with the big names of the time, predictably called *Andy Warhol's Interview*, in the 1960s. Around that time everyone was talking about putting a man on the moon and Ultra Violet, an ²⁰ actress in Andy Warhol's films, asked him whether he thought there was life on other planets. "It's hard enough to be famous here," he replied. In his book of philosophy *From A to B and back again* Andy predicted that "In the future, everyone will be famous for fifteen minutes." This quote became so famous that the MTV programme ²⁵ he presented in the 1980s was called "Andy Warhol's Fifteen Minutes of Fame".

Although Andy was an apparently nervous person in private, he always managed to get his name in the papers. He made sure he was seen at every fashionable nightclub, party or art "happening". ³⁰ "I have a 'social disease'," he said. "I have to go out every night!" Andy's studio, "The Factory", became the centre of avant-garde art in New York and was a never-ending parade of actors, musicians, artists . . . Andy needed to have people around him all the time. Many people think that this constant need to be loved, together ³⁵ with his inability to say no to anyone, led to an unsuccessful attempt on his life. One member of the Warhol crowd, Valerie Solanas, wanted Andy to put on a play she had written. Although Andy wasn't interested, he couldn't tell her to leave him alone and she was "disappointed" that he didn't help her. On June 4th 1968 ⁴⁰ Valerie came to Andy's office and shot him.

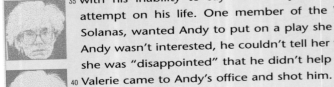

Lou Reed, singer and guitarist in the Velvet Underground whose 1965 album Andy had produced, recognised that Andy wore his "uniform" – the glasses, leather jacket and white hair – to attract attention. However, as Lou pointed out, sometimes you attract ⁴⁵ negative attention as well as positive.

b) Read the text again. Tick the jobs mentioned in the text that Andy Warhol did.

1 pop / rock musician
2 painter
3 sculptor
4 film director
5 record producer
6 architect
7 publisher
8 philosopher
9 television presenter
10 poet
11 writer
12 print maker
13 actor

c) Find an adjective in the text which means:

1 Lines 6–10: famous
2 Lines 11–15: ordinary, usual
3 Lines 21–25: difficult
4 Lines 26–30: shy and not confident
5 Lines 26–30: popular or thought to be good at a particular time
6 Lines 31–35: very modern and different from existing styles
7 Lines 31–35: happening all the time
8 Lines 31–35: not achieving what you wanted to achieve

.... **13 a)** In groups. Make a list of famous people who are famous for more than one thing.

Example: Will Smith: actor, singer, songwriter . . .

b) Choose the person from your list who you know the most about. Write 100–200 words about what he / she has done or did and why he / she is important.

I started this series of portraits six months ago.

Is that all you've done?

Is that all?!

14 a) In pairs. Look at the picture of Nigel and his friend, Duncan. Is Duncan impressed? Why? Answer the questions.

1 How long has Nigel been painting this series of portraits?
2 How many portraits has he painted?

b) Write a complete sentence for each answer in Exercise 14a) beginning *Nigel has . . .*

c) In pairs. Answer the questions (1–4). Then read the Language Box.

1 Which sentence in Exercise 14b) is in the Present Perfect Simple?
2 Which sentence in Exercise 14b) is in the Present Perfect Continuous?
3 Which sentence focuses on the activity?
4 Which sentence focuses on the result?

Present Perfect Continuous

We use the Present Perfect Continuous to talk about an activity which began in the past and **is still continuing**:
He's been working on that portrait for six months. (He's still working on it.)
We also use the Present Perfect Continuous to talk about an activity which began in the past and has produced present results that you can see, hear, etc. (the activity might or might not still be continuing):
A: Why is your face so red?
B: I've been exercising. (I've just finished.)
A: That smells great!
B: Well, it's been cooking since this morning. (It hasn't finished cooking.)

15 🎧30 Nigel wants to be another Andy Warhol. He's telling Duncan about all the things he's been doing. But Duncan wants to know what he has actually done. Which tenses do they use? Listen and fill in the boxes with *S* (Present Perfect Simple) or *C* (Present Perfect Continuous).

Example: C what / do?

1 ☐ create art
2 ☐ make films
3 ☐ not finish / a whole film
4 ☐ write / a novel
5 ☐ how much / write?
6 ☐ explore New York
7 ☐ go to lots of places
8 ☐ go to the Museum of Modern Art?
9 ☐ work on a series of portraits

16 a) In pairs. You're friends who haven't seen each other for a long time. One of you is like Nigel. The other one is the impatient friend. Choose one of the projects from the list and have a conversation similar to the one in Exercise 15.

Example: A: Hi, I haven't seen you around for a while. What have you been doing?
B: I've been trying to organise my life.
A: Really? So what have you done?
B: Well, I've written a list of things to do . . .

1 I've been trying to organise my life.
2 I've been trying to break into the music business / film business / art world.
3 I've been creating a healthier, fitter, more spiritual me.
4 I've been looking for my perfect partner.
5 I've been trying to learn (any subject).
6 I've been saving the planet for our children.

b) When you finish, swap roles, choose a different project and have a new conversation.

Grammar reference
Present Perfect Simple: page 112
Present Perfect Continuous: page 113

5 Conversations *I'm not sure . . .*

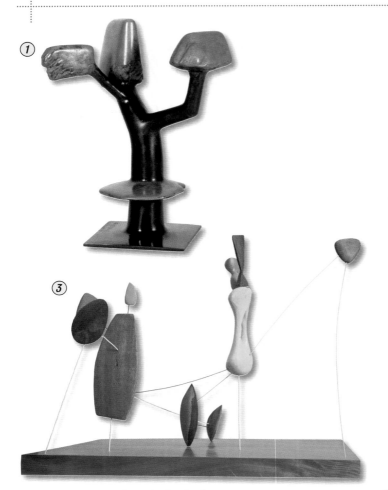

① ② ③ ④

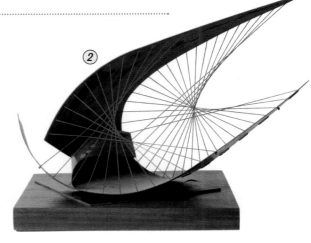

What do you think it is?

1 a) 👀 31 Listen to two friends in the sculpture section of a gallery. They're discussing one of the sculptures (1–4) and trying to work out what it is. Which sculpture do you think they're talking about?

b) 👀 31 Can you remember what they said? Try to fill in the gaps (the first letter of each word is given). Then listen again, check your answers and read the Language Box.

1 It l................ warm.
2 I've got n................ i................ what it is.
3 I s................ it's some s................ o................ animal.
4 It doesn't l................ l................ an animal to me.
5 I t................ it's meant to be two people.
6 It l................ a................ i................ he's whispering.
7 That l................ l................ a giant ear.
8 M................ they're two hands.
9 They m................ b................ holding something.

The language of doubt

When we're not sure about something, we use:
- *Look* + adjective:
  It looks fragile.
- *Look like* + noun (phrase):
  It looks like a bird (in flight).
- *Look as if* + clause:
  It looks as if it's moving.
- *I suppose it's / Maybe it's / I think it's / It might be* + adjective / noun (phrase) or present participle:
  I suppose it's very expensive.
  Maybe it's an animal.
  I think it's / it might be running.

Look!
- We can say:
  It looks as if he's whispering. **OR He** looks as if he's whispering.
- We often use *sort of* when our description of something is not exact:
  It looks **sort of** like a dog.
  Maybe it's a **sort of** plant.
  Perhaps it's some **sort of** animal.

Pronunciation: stress and intonation

2 a) Read exchanges 1–3. How do you think the people sound when they say these things? Underline the stressed words /syllables. Which words / syllables do you think are stressed more? Why?

1 **A:** What do you think it is?
  B: I've got no idea.
2 **A:** Do you know what it is?
  B: I'm not really sure . . . but I think it's some sort of dog. It looks as if it's moving.
3 **A:** Do you think it's alive?
  B: I suppose so. It might be.

b) 🔊 32 Listen, check your answers and repeat.

c) In pairs. Take it in turns to be A and B and practise the exchanges (1–3).

3 In groups. Look at the other sculptures that the friends didn't talk about in Exercise 1a). Use the language from Exercise 1 and talk about them. Do you all agree?

What's the answer?

4 a) In pairs. Look at the picture of Geoff, a contestant on a quiz show. Do you watch quiz shows on TV? How good are you at getting the answers right? Have you ever won money or a prize in a general knowledge quiz or competition?

b) 🔊 33 Listen to Geoff and answer the questions (1–4).

1 How much is the prize?
2 What's the question?
3 How long has he got to answer the question?
4 Does he answer it in time?

c) Do you know the answer to the quiz show question? Check on page 136.

d) 🔊 33 Geoff uses fillers (*um, er, oh,* etc.) to give himself time to think. He also uses phrases, for example, *Hang on.* What other phrases does he use? Listen again and fill in the gaps. Then read the Language Box.

1 Let me ....
2 Don't .... me.
3 It's on the .... of my ....
4 .... a minute.
5 Let me ....
6 .... a second.

Hesitation phrases

When you're not sure about something, don't leave a long silence while you're thinking. Fill in the silence with:
• sounds and words called fillers.
  A: What's your mobile phone number?
  B: Well um, er, hmm, oh, I think it's 0978 1877314.
• short phrases, for example, *Hang on, Hold on,* etc.
  A: When are we having our test?
  B: Oh, **hang on**, er, I think it's on Thursday.
When you can't quite remember a word, a name, etc. you can use the phrase:
It's on the tip of my tongue.

Your time's up!

5 In two teams, Team A and Team B. Team A look at page 135 and Team B at page 144.

6 Skin deep

Clothes and style icons
Superlative adjectives
Second Conditional with *would / could / might*
Wish + Past Simple
Infinitive of purpose and *by* + verb + *-ing*
Day to day English: *If I were you . . .*
Reading for pleasure 2: *"Oh, really!"*
Do you remember? Units 4–6

The way we were

1 a) In pairs. The clothes in the photos (1–6) are from different decades in the twentieth century: the 1940s, 50s, 60s, 70s, 80s and 90s. Which decade do you think each photo is from?

b) In groups. Answer the questions about the fashions in the photos.

1 Which clothes do you like / don't you like?
2 Have you, or has anyone you know, got clothes like these?
3 Which decade's fashions do you think are ugly? stylish? interesting?

2 a) In pairs. Match the Word Boxes (a–f) to the photos (1–6) and find all the items in the photos. Use your *Longman WordWise Dictionary* to help you, if necessary.

b) In pairs. Find the things (1–6) in the photos. Then make a list in your notebook of all the clothes that can have that thing.

Example: sleeve: shirt, jacket, etc.

1 collar
2 button
3 pocket
4 buckle
5 laces
6 shoulder pad

a) polo-neck jumper   jacket   belt

b) tight skirt   high heels   short-sleeved shirt   sleeveless top

c) striped top   flared jeans   scarf   leather jacket

d) T-shirt   baggy jeans   trainers   gloves

e) mini-dress   boots

f) patterned dress   blouse   checked shirt   plain skirt   pin-striped trousers   tie

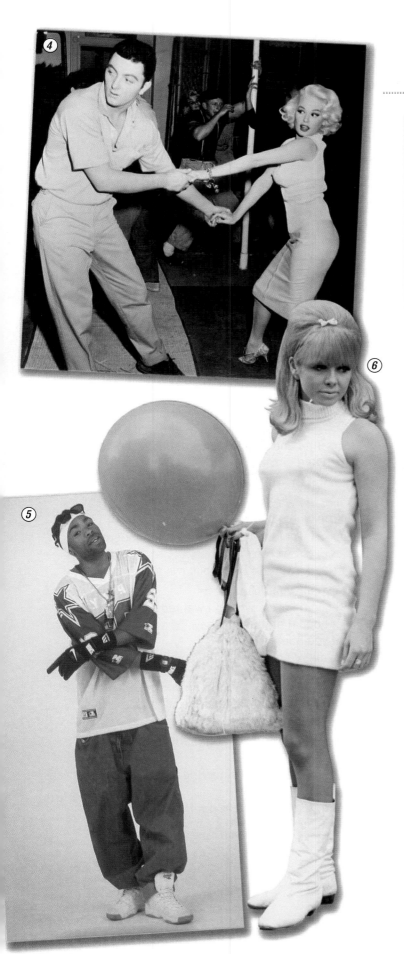

④

⑤

⑥

Fads and fashions

3 **a)** Fill in the gaps in the questionnaire with the superlative of the adjectives in brackets.

1 What is <u>the weirdest</u> thing you've ever done in the name of beauty? (weird)

2 What is .... item of clothing you've ever bought? (expensive)

3 What is .... item of clothing you've got? When and where did you buy it? (new)

4 What is .... item of clothing you've ever bought? (good)

5 What is .... fashion mistake you've ever made? (bad)

6 What is .... , ... or .... hairstyle you've ever had? (strange, stupid, wild)

7 Who is .... or .... person on the planet at the moment, in your opinion? (cool, stylish)

8 What is .... fashion these days, in your opinion? (unattractive)

b) 🔊 34 Listen to Amy and Tim answering two questions from the questionnaire in Exercise 3a). Which questions are they answering?

c) 🔊 34 Listen again. Then read the sentences (1–8). Which express what Amy said? Which express what Tim said? Fill in the boxes with A (Amy) or T (Tim).

Example: ☐A I met a student who asked me to be a model for him.

1 ☐ I wanted something that looked cool and didn't look brand-new.
2 ☐ The style was completely different from my usual style.
3 ☐ People recommended a place where I could get the kind of thing I wanted.
4 ☐ There was a huge selection.
5 ☐ It was just the kind of thing I wanted.
6 ☐ This was my only chance to look like this.
7 ☐ It was something I could wear with anything.
8 ☐ I looked crazy.

d) In pairs. Take it in turns to ask and answer the questions in the questionnaire in Exercise 3a).

Rich and famous

4 a) Look at the photos of style icons. Do you know who they are? Do you think they influence / influenced style or fashion? Can you think of any other style icons, past or present?

b) In pairs. What do you think are the advantages and disadvantages of being rich and famous? Discuss the ideas in the Word Box.

> plastic surgery   clothes   lifestyle   taxes
> therapy   friends   marriage   privacy
> the press   drugs and alcohol   the public

Second Conditional

5 a) 🔊 35 Tina and Ryan are talking about the advantages and disadvantages of being rich and famous. Listen and answer the questions.

1 Who sees the advantages, Tina or Ryan?
2 Which of the ideas in Exercise 4b) does Tina mention? does Ryan mention?

b) 🔊 35 Match 1–5 with a–e to make sentences from Tina and Ryan's conversation. Then listen again and check.

Example: 1 = b)

1 TINA: If I were famous,
2 RYAN: Would you really be happy
3 TINA: I wouldn't care what people thought
4 TINA: If it weren't fun,
5 RYAN: If I were in the public eye all the time,

a) people wouldn't want it.
b) I could have anything I wanted.
c) if I had that much money.
d) if you had everything?
e) it might get depressing sometimes.

c) Answer the questions (1–4) about the sentences in Exercise 5b). Then read the Language Box.

1 Are Tina and Ryan rich and famous?
2 Are they talking about situations that are real or unreal?
3 Are the sentences referring to the past or the present / future?
4 What tense is used in the *if* part of each sentence?

Second Conditional

We use the Second Conditional to talk about situations in the present / future that are unreal or very unlikely (will probably never happen):
If I had loads of money, I'd (would) have plastic surgery.
We use the Past Simple in the *if* part of the sentence to show unreality. We use *would / wouldn't, could / couldn't, might / might not* + infinitive in the other part of the sentence:
If I were rich, I could have anything I wanted.

6 Write Second Conditional sentences.

Examples: Living on a tropical island is my dream but only rich people can do that.
I'd live <u>on a tropical island if I were rich.</u>
He wants to leave his job, but he needs the money.
If he didn't <u>need the money, he'd leave his job.</u>

1 She isn't tall so she can't get modelling jobs.
If she were . . .
2 They want to spend more time together but they're too busy.
If they weren't . . .
3 I don't earn much money so I can't afford a car.
I could . . .
4 The press bother me all the time because my wife is famous.
If my wife weren't . . .
5 Joe wants to be a singer in a rock band but he can't sing.
If Joe could . . .

My fantastic life

7 a) In pairs. You're going to interview other students about how their lives would be different if they were rich and famous. Write at least two more questions for each category.

1 Home: How many homes would you have?
2 Appearance: Would you dress differently?
3 Leisure: Who would you spend time with?
4 Lifestyle: What could you do that you can't do now?

b) In new pairs, take it in turns to interview each other. Then write a paragraph about your partner.

Wish + Past Simple

8 a) 🎧 36 Listen again to Ryan's first sentence from the conversation in Exercise 5a). Fill in the gaps.

I .... I .... live on an island like that.

b) In pairs. Answer questions 1 and 2. Then read the Language Box.

1 Can Ryan live on an island? Why / Why not?
2 Would he like his situation to be different?

Wish + Past Simple

We use *wish* + Past Simple when we would like a present situation or reality to be different, but this is improbable / impossible:
I wish **I didn't have to** work.
(**I have to** work but I don't want to.)

c) What do the people in Exercise 6 wish? Write wishes for sentences 1–5.

Examples: I wish I could live on a tropical island. I wish I were rich.
He wishes he didn't need the money. He wishes he could leave his job.

I wish . . . I wish . . .

9 a) If a genie offered you three wishes, what would you wish for?

Example: I wish I lived in a villa on the Amalfi coast.

b) Go round the class. Take it in turns to ask and tell each other about your wishes.

10 In groups. You're going to read an article about the things people have done through history in the name of beauty. Before you read, discuss what different things people do / have done to their bodies to improve / change their appearance.

11 a) Sentences 1–5 are the first sentences from paragraphs a–e in the article. Read the sentences. Then read the article quickly and match the sentences to the paragraphs. Fill in the boxes with the sentence number (1–5).

1 At the beginning of the last millennium, baths were not considered healthy, because of the cold and often dirty water.
2 There was a revolution when we realised we could use underwear to change the shape of the body.
3 In Tudor days, black rotting teeth were a big problem.
4 Suntans first became popular in the twentieth century.
5 Hairstyles have had their ups and downs through the ages.

b) In pairs. Answer the questions.

1 Which historical periods are mentioned?
2 Paragraph a): Which two dangerous ingredients were used in make-up?
3 Paragraph b): Find the word that means *protective tooth covering*. What happened to this protective covering when people cleaned their teeth with pumice stone?
4 Paragraph b): Find a noun connected to unhealthy teeth.
5 Paragraph c): Why are mice mentioned twice?
6 Paragraph d): Apart from water, what liquids were used for washing?
7 Paragraph e): Find words that mean *paying no attention to* (v) and a *bad effect* (n).
8 Paragraph e): What do you think were the bad effects of the platform shoes? corsets?

12 In pairs. Which of the methods in the article do you find the strangest? the funniest? the most disgusting? What do you think of the law that was passed in 1770?

The History

What would you do to have "Marilyn Monroe" looks? Just how far would you go? Well, you'd be amazed at some of the weird (not to mention deadly!) things people have done throughout history in the name of beauty.

ⓐ [ ] Until then, only peasants who worked the land had tanned skins – not the kind of image aristocrats wanted! In the sixteenth century the idea was to look as pale as possible. Women – including Elizabeth I (1533–1603), covered their faces in chalky powders to make them look very pale – almost white. Unfortunately, these powders often contained lead and if it got into your mouth you would be pale . . . and dead. In eighteenth-century Italy more than 600 men died from getting too close to wives wearing arsenic make-up.

ⓑ [ ] Toothbrushes didn't exist until the seventeenth century so a piece of cloth was used with a bit of pumice stone. It eventually removed the tooth enamel completely! It was customary (if you could afford it) to rinse your mouth with wine to make the breath smell sweeter, but that only made the decay worse.

ⓒ [ ] However, nothing has ever compared to the two-metre high wigs of the 1770s that were held up with a wire frame and smoothed in place with pig fat. This attracted mice, which the servants had to deal with on a weekly basis. In Britain in those days, women didn't shave their legs – but they did shave their eyebrows. They then stuck on new ones cut from the skins of mice.

of **Beauty**

d In the sixteenth century Elizabeth I only took four baths a year! Mary Queen of Scots chose to bathe in wine. Milk was recommended for a pale skin. In the next century water was still considered unhealthy and the wife of Samuel Pepys (1633–1703) preferred to wash her face in puppy's urine.

e It was the Georgians who developed the corset to make the waist smaller, push out the chest and straighten the back – completely ignoring the damage to their health. And how did women stop their dresses dragging in the mud of medieval Britain when they weren't even allowed to show their ankles? By wearing platform shoes, of course. They were uncomfortable and completely impractical, as any modern wearer of platform shoes knows. However, given the terrible conditions of the roads they were also very dangerous.

In 1770, the British government passed a law that said that a woman who tricked her husband with make-up was as bad as a witch. If he married her and found that she was ugly underneath all the powder and paint, then he could be "unmarried" any time he wanted.

Only time will tell what future generations will think of our techniques for achieving physical perfection and keeping our youthful looks. In the meantime, keep taking those vitamins and stay young and beautiful!

(adapted from *The Sunday Mirror*)

Verb forms for *Why?* and *How?*

13 a) Look again at paragraphs a) and e). Answer questions 1 and 2. Then read the Language Box.

1 Why did women in the sixteenth century cover their faces in chalky powders?
2 How did women in medieval Britain stop their dresses dragging in the mud?

Verb forms for *Why?* and *How?*

- We use the infinitive of purpose (*to* + infinitive) to talk about **why** we do things (the purpose):
  Women wore corsets **to make** their waists look smaller.
- We use *by* + verb + *-ing* to talk about **how** we do things (the method):
  Women made their waists look smaller **by wearing** corsets.

b) Fill in the gaps with the correct form of the verbs in brackets using *by* + verb + *-ing* or *to* + infinitive.

Example: He dresses like that <u>to attract</u> attention
    – and he attracts a lot of attention
    <u>by dressing</u> like that! (attract, dress)

1 She makes her hair shiny .... it in beer. (wash)
2 She washes her hair in beer .... it shiny. (make)
3 I lost weight .... between meals. (not eat)
4 He made his fortune .... a face cream that makes you look twenty years younger. (develop)
5 She went to a clinic .... drugs. (get off)

Grammar reference

Second Conditional and *wish* + Past Simple: page 116

Day to day English *If I were you . . .*

Suggestions and advice

1 🔊 37 Listen to Tony, an actor, talking about an audition he had. Answer the questions (1–4).

1 What was the audition for?
2 Why was Tony worried?
3 What advice did his friend give him?
4 What problem did Tony have at the audition?

2 a) In pairs. Match each picture (A–F) to a suggestion / piece of advice.

Example: A = 4b)

1 a) Have you tried drinking tomato juice with a raw egg in it?
  b) Put a cold cloth on your head.
2 a) If I were you, I'd put a plaster on that.
  b) You'd better see a doctor. You might need stitches.
3 a) Put your head between your knees.
  b) You'd better lie down.
4 a) You should run cold water on it.
  b) You could put some ointment on to cool it.
5 a) Why don't you tilt your head back?
  b) You should pinch your nose.
6 a) Try breathing into a paper bag.
  b) How about holding your breath?

b) In pairs. Match the problems (a–f) to the suggestions / advice (1–6) in Exercise 2a).

Example: a) = 6a) and b)

a) He's got hiccups.
b) He's got a hangover.
c) He's going to faint.
d) He's cut himself.
e) He's burnt himself.
f) He's got a nosebleed.

3 In groups. Which of the ideas in Exercise 2a) are new to you? Have you got any other suggestions?

4 a) 🔊 38 Colin's got a cough. His friend's giving advice. Which suggestion / piece of advice is the strongest? Listen and fill in the boxes with 1–5 to show how the suggestions / advice get stronger.

a) ☐ You really ought to see a doctor.
b) ☐ Why don't you try some of this cough medicine?
c) ☐ Here – have some water.
d) ☐ Look! You have to do something about that cough!
e) ☐ Maybe you should see a doctor about that cough.

b) Look at the suggestions / advice in Exercise 2a). Then fill in the gaps in the Language Box.

Suggestions and advice

Suggestions
You could drink some hot lemon juice.
Why .... drink some hot lemon juice?
.... drinking some hot lemon juice.
How .... drinking some hot lemon juice?

Advice
You should / ought to see a doctor.

Stronger advice
If ...., I'd see a doctor.
You'd better see a doctor.

Orders
You must / have to do something about this.

5 a) In pairs. Think of suggestions / advice for each problem (1–6).

1 She's got a cold.
2 She's got a sore throat.
3 She's got sunburn.
4 She's got a headache.
5 She's got a stomachache.
6 She's got a toothache.

b) In groups. Take it in turns to read out your suggestions / advice and guess the problem.

Reading for pleasure

② "Oh, really!"

1 This story takes place in a twenty-four-hour supermarket. Who do you think the people are who shop for food outside normal opening times? Can you add to the list?

1 People who don't have time during the day.
2 People who have trouble sleeping.
3 People who find they have run out of something they urgently need.

2 **⊙⊙ 39** Read and listen to the first part of the story. Then answer the questions (1–3).

Ambrose parked his Maserati right outside the entrance of the supermarket. It was, after all, 2 a.m. Honest people were all asleep in their respectable beds. Only the dishonest – people who might steal Ambrose's magnificent car – were out and about at this time of night!

The supermarket was the only place that was open in the neighbourhood. Its name lit up the dark and empty street. "SUPERSAVE SUPERMARKET", it said in coloured neon lights. "OPEN 24 HOURS".

Supermarkets were Ambrose's passion, especially those that stayed open all night. He loved the rows and rows of shelves full of tins, packets, bottles, jars; the bright displays of fruit and vegetables; the freezers full of frozen delights. He was fascinated by the sleepy atmosphere, the strange people who chose to do their shopping while the rest of the city slept.

1 Why do you think Ambrose parked his car right outside the entrance to the supermarket?
2 What made it easy to identify the supermarket?
3 Why did Ambrose particularly like all-night supermarkets?

3 Now read the whole story. It starts on page 10 of *Heat wave and other stories*. Think about these questions while you read.

1 How did Ambrose avoid paying the full price for the mangoes?
2 What did he get at the bread counter?
3 Where did he go next?
4 Who did he see on his way there?
5 Where did he put the goat's cheese, the Parma ham and the jar of caviar?
6 Why did Ambrose put six tins of tuna fish in his trolley?
7 Why did the young woman knock over the tins of tuna fish?
8 Why was she uncertain about what to buy?
9 What did Ambrose offer to do?
10 Ambrose put some expensive items in Julia's trolley. Why was she worried?
11 What did Ambrose put inside the pizza box?
12 What did Ambrose do so that Julia didn't have to pay for expensive soap?
13 What made Julia think that Ambrose wasn't poor?
14 What explanation did Ambrose give for his behaviour?
15 What did Ambrose realise when he went through the checkout?

Wavelength page

1 Difficult choices

a) 📀 40 Listen to two people answering the same question. What do you think the question was? In pairs, try to fill in the gaps to make the complete question.

If you had to .... a .... , what .... and where?

b) 📀 40 Listen again. What were the people's answers?

c) In pairs. Answer the questions.

1 If you could choose only one of your senses (sight, hearing, smell, taste, touch) to be perfect and the rest not very good, which one would you choose? Why?
2 If there was a pill that made you immortal, would you take it? Why / Why not?
3 If you had to live in another country, where would you live? Why?
4 Do you think your life would be better if you were a member of the opposite sex? Why / Why not?
5 If you had to give away all of your possessions except one, what would you keep?

d) In pairs. Write one more question like the ones in Exercise 1c).

e) In groups. Take it in turns to ask and answer your questions.

2 The Arts Café

a) 📀 41 Look at the picture. Valerie and Mallory have decided to open an arts café. A journalist is interviewing them about it. Listen and tick the kinds of artist and performer in the Word Box that Valerie and Mallory are looking for.

| actor | musician | photographer | painter | dancer |
| video artist | sculptor | writer | singer | poet |

b) 📀 41 In the interview, Valerie and Mallory talk about the kinds of art and entertainment they're going to have and not going to have. Listen again and write in your notebook:

1 two kinds of live music
2 one kind of dance
3 four kinds of visual art
4 one thing connected with literature
5 one kind of performer they definitely don't want
6 one thing they don't want their customers to do

c) In pairs: Pair A (Valerie and Mallory) and Pair B (artists and performers). Valerie and Mallory are interviewing artists and performers for their café. Pair A look at page 135 and Pair B at page 132.

d) In groups of four. Valerie and Mallory and two different artists from different pairs.

VALERIE AND MALLORY
Interview both artists. Find out about their past experience.

ARTISTS
You're competing for one spot. Do your best!

e) In pairs. Artists: tell each other how you changed your experience for the interview. Valerie and Mallory: decide on one of the artists for your café. Then tell the artists who you chose and why.

3 *You don't need to lose weight!*

Underline the correct word / words.

SERENA: I think (<u>I'll try</u> / I'm trying) this revolutionary diet in the paper. It says if I follow it for two weeks (I'll lose / I'd lose)⁽¹⁾ ten kilos.

TANYA: But you're already on a diet!

SERENA: I know – but it's (such / so)⁽²⁾ boring and slow! (I've been following / I'm following)⁽³⁾ the diet for two weeks and I've only (been losing / lost)⁽⁴⁾ one kilo! I want something which is (much / very)⁽⁵⁾ more effective. With this diet, I can eat everything but I (don't have to / can't)⁽⁶⁾ mix some foods. And I (have to / can)⁽⁷⁾ eat a whole grapefruit before every meal because it makes you feel full so then you don't eat so much. That's the worst part. I hate grapefruit! But that's the rule and . . .

TANYA: That's enough! I'm so tired of (hearing / hear)⁽⁸⁾ about diets and plastic surgery . . . (Who does say / Who says)⁽⁹⁾ we have to be thin to be beautiful? There's nothing bad about (having / to have)⁽¹⁰⁾ a woman's body! The important thing is your personality!

SERENA: I wish (that's / that were)⁽¹¹⁾ true. But when people meet you, the first thing they see is your body.

TANYA: Oh, come on! (You are / You're being)⁽¹²⁾ ridiculous! I'm sure people (don't think / aren't thinking)⁽¹³⁾ you're fat.

SERENA: Hang on! I didn't say I was fat. I'm only doing it (to lose / for lose)⁽¹⁴⁾ a bit of weight. If I manage (to lose / in losing)⁽¹⁵⁾ five kilos, I'll be happy. And this diet guarantees five kilos in two weeks!

TANYA: It can't be true. If it (were / is)⁽¹⁶⁾ that easy to lose weight, everybody (will / would)⁽¹⁷⁾ do it. You can only lose weight by (eat / eating)⁽¹⁸⁾ less and (do / doing)⁽¹⁹⁾ exercise.

SERENA: I hate (jog / jogging)⁽²⁰⁾. I've always been really bad (in / at)⁽²¹⁾ sports. I suppose that's why I've never succeeded (to lose / in losing)⁽²²⁾ much weight. And why I've always been (such / so)⁽²³⁾ miserable.

TANYA: (Going / To go)⁽²⁴⁾ on a lot of diets is not the answer. You've got to accept yourself as you are!

SERENA: I know. But I wish I (can / could)⁽²⁵⁾ be as thin as you.

TANYA: What! You're joking! I'm not thin. I'm . . .

Look at the Word lists for Units 4–6 on pages 124–126 and check that you know all the new words.

Puzzle 2 (Units 4–6): page 120

Wavelength page

Can we talk?

Means of communication
Past Perfect Simple
Reported speech: *say, tell, ask*
Telephone phrasal verbs and expressions
Writing for work and pleasure 3: *Guess what!*

Communication

1 In pairs. Look at the cartoon and discuss the questions.

1 Do you think it's sad? old-fashioned? true?
2 Have you got a mobile phone? If yes, how was your life different before you got it?
3 What are the advantages and disadvantages of mobile phones?

2 **a)** In pairs. What are the people talking about? Fill in the gaps (1–5) with *notes, computers, e-mails, mobile phones* or *television.*

1 .... **I use it all the time.**
It went off in the cinema!
Turn it off during the class!

2 .... I watch it most days.
Could you turn it down, please?
It's always on in the background.

3 .... **I couldn't read her writing.**
It said, "Meet at cinema – at 7 p.m.".
She wrote it on the back of an envelope.

4 .... *I'm on it for hours.*
It crashed this morning.
Mine doesn't have enough memory.

5 .... *I'm not going to reply to it.*
I deleted it by accident.
I forgot to attach the document.

b) Which sentences in each group (1–5) could be about other means of communication in Exercise 2a)?

Example: 4 I'm on it for hours: mobile phones.

c) In pairs. Think of another means of communication. Write sentences from Exercise 2a) about it. Add three more sentences of your own.

d) In groups. Take it in turns to read your sentences and guess each other's means of communication.

Telling stories

3 **a)** Felix is a terrible storyteller because he often misses out important details. You're going to listen to him telling a story to a friend. Before you listen, read the main events of the story.

1 Tony forgot to bring his wallet.
2 Tony got to the restaurant at nine.
3 Tony got a taxi home again.
4 The manager gave their table to some other people.
5 Tony finally got back to the restaurant at about ten.
6 Tony started screaming at the manager.

b) 📼 42 Now listen to Felix's story. Which two events from 1–6 in Exercise 3a) did he miss out?

And then I . . .

c) 📼 42 Listen again to Felix's story and underline the tense you hear in each sentence. In each pair of sentences, which event happened first, a) or b)? Read the Language Box.

1 a) He (took / had taken) a taxi home.
  b) He (forgot / had forgotten) his wallet.
2 a) He (started / had started) screaming at the manager.
  b) The manager (gave / had given) our table to someone else.

Past Perfect Simple

We form the Past Perfect Simple with *had / hadn't* + past participle:
We knew he wasn't coming because **he'd (had) telephoned.**
We use the Past Perfect Simple to show that something happened **before** another event in the past. This makes the order of events in a story clear and gives important background information:
He didn't have any money because **he'd forgotten** his wallet.
(He didn't have any money **at that time** because he forgot his wallet **before that time**.)

---

4 **a)** In pairs. Look at stories A and B. If you keep the events in this order, which two sentences in each story need the Past Perfect Simple tense? Practise telling the stories using the Past Simple and Past Perfect Simple. Then write them in your notebooks.

Examples: Alfie opened the door. He **saw** that the room was empty. Someone **had stolen** everything! . . .

Story A
Alfie opened the door . . .
1 He (see) that the room was empty.
2 Someone (steal) everything!
3 He (decide) to phone the police . . .
4 . . . but the thief (take) the telephone!
5 He (go) to the next-door flat.

Story B
Jilly arrived at the office late . . .
1 She (miss) her train.
2 She (run) upstairs to the meeting room.
3 She (saw) a notice on the door: "Today's meeting cancelled".
4 Her secretary (not tell) her.
5 Jilly (be) furious.

b) In pairs. Make new sentences in Story A and Story B by joining two events using *because* or *so*. How many sentences can you make?

Examples: He saw that the room was empty **because** someone had stolen everything!
Jilly arrived at the office late **so** she ran upstairs to the meeting room.

The funniest thing happened . . .

5 In groups of four (Pair A and Pair B). Pair A look at page 139 and Pair B at page 140.

Ten days ago
1 It won't cost more than £150.
2 It's only a small job.
3 You haven't done any serious damage.
4 It only needs one or two new parts.
5 I can fix it in a day.

Ten days ago
6 You don't have to worry about anything.
7 Nothing can go wrong.
8 The other side hasn't got a case.
9 The jury will find you innocent.
10 I've fixed everything.

Well, of course I'm angry about a bill for £900.
a) You told me it wouldn't cost more than £150!
b) You said it was only a small job!
c) You told me . . .
d) You said . . .
e) You told me . . .

f) You told me I didn't have to worry about anything.
g) You said nothing could go wrong.
h) You told me . . .
i) And you said . . .
j) Then you told me . . .
You should be in here with me!

What did they say?

6 a) Look at the pictures of Mandy and Sam. Who are they speaking / writing to? Why are they angry?

b) In pairs. Compare Mandy's sentences (a and b) with what the mechanic said ten days ago (1 and 2). Then compare Sam's thoughts (f and g) with what the lawyer said ten days ago (6 and 7). What happens to the verb when a sentence is reported? Read the Language Box and check your answers.

c) 📼 43 Finish the sentences (c–e and h–j). Then listen and check.

Reported speech: sentences

When we report sentences we usually move the main verb back one tense:

Direct speech	Reported speech
"I'm leaving Jack."	She told me she **was leaving** Jack.
"He **shouted** at me."	She said he'**d (had) shouted** at her.
"I **haven't told** him yet."	She said she **hadn't told** him yet.

We change *can* → *could*, *will* → *would* and *must* → *had to*:
"I'**ll do** my best."   He told them he'**d (would) do** his best.
Could, should and *might* **don't** change:
"You **might be** right."   She said I **might be** right.
Pronouns, possessive adjectives, time and place references change:
"**You** can leave **yours here** until **tomorrow**." He told her **she** could leave **hers there** until **the next day**.

Look!
• We use an indirect object (*them, the doctor*, etc.) after *tell*, but **not** after *say*:
He told **me** he was leaving the next day.
He said ~~me~~ he was leaving the next day.

7 a) Who do you think asked the questions (1–8)? Fill in the boxes with *M* (Mandy) or *S* (Sam).

1 [M] When will it be ready?
2 [S] Do you feel confident?
3 [ ] Will we win?
4 [ ] What's the problem with it?
5 [ ] Are you going to look at the brakes?
6 [ ] Have you spoken to the newspapers?
7 [ ] Can you check the tyres?
8 [ ] Why's the jury looking at me like that?

b) In pairs. Compare reported questions 1 and 2 with questions 1 and 2 in Exercise 7a). What happens to a question when it's reported? Read the Language Box and check your answers.

1 Mandy asked (the mechanic) when it would be ready.
2 Sam asked (the lawyer) if she felt confident.

Reported Speech: questions

When we report a question:
• the word order is like a sentence, not a question
• we don't use the auxiliaries *do, does, did*
• there's no question mark
We can include the object but we don't have to.

Direct speech	Reported speech
"Where **do you live**?"	She asked (me) where **I lived**.

We use *if* or *whether* with *Yes / No* questions:
She asked (me) if / whether I lived near the station.

c) Write reported questions for direct questions 3–8 in Exercise 7a).

He lied to me!

8 a) Look at the picture and read the newspaper article. Who's Dickie Garret? What's his crime?

Con-artist charged

b) In pairs. Imagine you're a couple / two friends who are among Dickie Garret's many victims. How did he get the money from you? Look at the questions and decide what happened.

1 How and where did you meet him?
2 What did he say his name was?
3 How much money did you give him?
4 Why did he say he needed money? a cure for disease? to build a hospital? a charity? to start a fantastic new business?
5 What lies did he tell you? *I'm going to . . . I have to . . . My mother / hospital / castle / community needs . . . It's an amazing idea! It can't fail!*

c) In groups of four (Pair A and Pair B). You're sitting in a café together and you see the newspaper article about Dickie Garret. You recognise him instantly. Tell each other your stories.

Example: PAIR A: I don't believe it! Look! That's . . .
PAIR B: Who? He told **us** his name was . . . ! **We** met him in . . . **He** said he needed . . . because he was . . .
PAIR A: He told **us** he was starting a . . . **He** said it was an amazing idea!

9 You're very angry because someone told you something which you then discovered wasn't true. Write a letter to a friend telling him / her what happened and how you feel. Think about these questions.

1 Who was it? What did he / she say? Use reported speech: *She said the hotel was near the beach. He didn't tell me he had a wife! She said she didn't care about my money. He told me he was in the media.*
2 What happened as a result?
3 How did you find out the truth?

After a seven-year career conning innocent victims out of thousands of pounds throughout the British Isles, Dickie Garret, also known as Doctor Thomas Kramer, Lord Soames, the Reverend Martin Banks and many others, was finally sentenced yesterday in London. Since his arrest there have been reports from all over the country of people losing their life savings, sometimes as much as twenty thousand pounds, because of Garret's amazing stories of business ventures, charities, personal misfortunes, family needs

I'm on the phone!

10 a) In pairs. Look at the phone maze on page 63. Take it in turns to be the secretary (purple boxes) and the caller, Mr Trink (green boxes). Read the conversation four times, taking different routes, until you reach *Success! Connection!* or *Failure! No connection!* each time. The secretary begins each conversation with *Scoop Limited*.

b) Which of the more formal expressions and sentences from the phone maze mean the same as the informal expressions and sentences (1–10)?

Example: Is Rocco there?
= Could I speak to Mr Rocco, please?

1 Sorry. He's out.
2 Who's that?
3 Sure, it's Trevor.
4 Just say Trevor rang.
5 No idea – sorry.
6 Do you want to leave a message?
7 What's your number?
8 Hang on. / Just a minute.
9 Sure.
10 OK. Cheers.

c) In pairs. Read the sentences in A, B and C. What do the phrasal verbs in green mean? Use your *Longman WordWise Dictionary* to help you if necessary. Put the sentences in each group in a logical order.

A
a) I looked up his number in the phone book.
b) As soon as I mentioned my name to him, he hung up.
c) I rang him up at home.

B
a) Then she put me through to Edward.
b) His secretary answered and she took down my name.
c) Edward said he was busy and asked me to call him back later.

C
a) He finally got back to me half an hour later.
b) Unfortunately, after two minutes, we were cut off.
c) I got through to Mr Vinton at 6:15.

11 a) 🔊 44 Listen to five people leaving phone messages. Are the phone calls formal or informal? Fill in the boxes with *F* or *I*.

1 [F]   2 ☐   3 ☐   4 ☐   5 ☐

b) 🔊 44 Listen to conversation 1 again and read the secretary's notes. What information did she include in her notes and what did she ignore?

Date *17/4*   Time *9:30*

Mr Jack Pearson   called.

To speak to *Mr Gibson (Marketing)*

Message *change meeting from Monday 11:30 to Friday 11:30 – room 706 (not 704). If problem, phone his secretary.*

c) 🔊 44 Listen again to messages 2–5. Make notes on the important information.

Pronunciation: sentence stress

12 a) 🔊 45 Listen again to this sentence from conversation 1 in Exercise 11a). Underline the stressed words / syllables. Then practise saying the sentence.

SECRETARY: So that's Mr Pearson, on Friday, at eleven thirty, room seven oh six.

b) In pairs. Look at the notes you made in Exercise 11c). Take it in turns to confirm the important information from conversations 2–5. Remember to stress the important words / syllables.

13 In pairs. You're going to make and receive formal and informal phone calls. Student A look at page 138 and Student B at page 140.

The phone maze

7

Scoop Limited.

Hello. Could I speak to Mr Rocco, please?

Oh, dear. When will he be back?

I'm afraid Mr Rocco is out at the moment.

Could I ask who's calling, please?

I'm afraid I can't say, sir. Can I take a message?

I see. Um . . . could I leave a message?

Certainly. This is Trevor Trink.

It's Trevor Trink.

Certainly, sir. Go ahead.

How do you spell that?

Oh, Mr Trink! I'm sorry! I didn't recognise your voice. Mr Rocco is expecting your call. Hold the line a moment.

No, thank you. I'll ring back later.

Could you tell him that Trevor Trink called?

T – R – I – N – K.

Of course, sir.

Could you hold a moment, Mr Trink? I think Mr Rocco has just come in.

Could I have your phone number, please?

SUCCESS! CONNECTION!
Rocco here. Hey, Trinky! How are things?

All right. Thank you very much.

Certainly.

Certainly. It's 01222 854702.

Thank you very much. Putting you through!

Thank you for calling. Goodbye.

I'm sorry, sir. It wasn't Mr Rocco. But I will tell him you called.

A *very bad recording* of "My Way".

"My Way" another eleven times.

FAILURE! NO CONNECTION!

Oh, I give up! *(hangs up)*

Grammar reference
Past Perfect Simple: page 113
Reported speech: page 115

Writing for work and pleasure

③ Guess what!

Telling a story

1 a) Heather wrote a letter to her friend, Andy. Andy has moved to Edinburgh and Heather wanted to tell him about something that happened in their home town. Read the letter and fill in the gaps (1–7) with the linkers (a–g) and the gaps (8–14) with (h–n).

Gaps 1–7
a) as soon as
b) a couple of days after
c) because of
d) at first
e) as you know ✓
f) unfortunately
g) however

Gaps 8–14
h) while
i) by the time
j) when
k) luckily
l) in the end
m) later
n) then

b) In pairs. Read the story in the letter again. Put the events (a–j) in the order in which they happened.

a) The men drove off in a car.
b) People painted their houses.
c) Bill phoned the police.
d) Tom and Jo walked round town wearing their trendiest clothes.
e) The town found out that the film crew were coming.
f) Three masked men put jewellery into bags.
g) The young man started to film.
h) Bill realised that the men were robbers.
i) The film crew arrived.
j) The young man asked to film a robbery in the shop.

Dear Andy

How are things? Sorry I haven't written for ages but I haven't had much news. _e_,(1) nothing ever really happens here. ......(2) last week was quite eventful, for a change.

You know that law series on TV that your brother's always talking about? Well, everyone round here got really excited ......(3) the arrival of a TV crew to film a couple of episodes. We'd known for about two months that they were coming, so lots of people had painted their houses and tidied their gardens. I just wanted to see the actors but Tom and Jo really wanted to be in the programme! ......(4) the crew arrived, Tom and Jo started walking round town in their trendiest clothes. ......,(5) this didn't work. No-one asked them to appear as extras!

Anyway, ...(6) the crew arrived, a young man went into Bill Mortimer's jewellery shop and asked if he could film a robbery. ......(7) Bill wasn't sure but ......(8) he agreed and a couple of hours ......,(9) the man came back with a video camera and three other men. They were wearing masks and one was carrying a gun. The young man started filming and the man with the gun pointed it at Bill ......(10) the other two men filled their bags with jewellery.

Bill was really starting to enjoy himself ......(11) the men suddenly ran out of the shop, got into a car and drove off! It was only ......(12) that Bill realised that perhaps they hadn't been actors after all. He called the police but ......(13) they arrived, the men had completely disappeared.

...............(14) all Bill's jewellery was insured so he didn't lose his business. Anyway, enough of small-town dramas.

c) In pairs. Answer questions 1–6 about the story. Then read the Writing Box.

1 What had lots of people done before the film crew arrived?
2 How long had the film crew been in town when the young man visited Bill Mortimer?
3 What were three of the men wearing when they robbed the shop?
4 What was one of the masked men carrying?
5 What was the young man doing while the men were stealing from the shop?
6 What did Bill do when he realised the men weren't actors?

Writing or telling stories

When we tell stories we use:
- linkers and other expressions to show the order of events and to join the story together so that it flows smoothly.
  We left **when** the fighting started.
  As you know, I can't stand action movies.
- different tenses to show the order of events.
  We use the Past Simple to talk about single finished events:
  He **walked** into the shop.
  We use the Past Continuous to describe activity which was already in progress when other events happened.
  They **were driving** away when the police arrived.
  We use the Past Perfect Simple to show that something happened before another event in the story and to give background information.
  Everyone **had worked** really hard to prepare for the arrival of the film crew.

d) Look again at your answers to questions 1–6 in Exercise 1c). Which tense did you use in each answer?

2 In pairs. Choose one of the basic plots (1–3). Write a short story to put in a letter to a friend. Use different past tenses to show the order of events and at least six linkers from Exercise 1a).

1 Two friends went to New York. They had a problem. They met someone. He helped them.
2 A woman was babysitting. Ten police officers came to the door. They arrested her.
3 A man discovered his wallet was missing. He attacked a man. He went home.

Making a story more interesting

3 a) In pairs. Add adverbs, adjectives and strong adjectives to sentences 1 and 2 to make the stories more interesting and dramatic.

Example: One **beautiful, sunny** morning, a **glamorous, middle-aged** woman walked **calmly** into the **tiny** bank in Little Trumpton, looked **straight** at the **shy, young** cashier and said **coldly** "Give me the money or you're dead."

1 Tim woke up one night, heard a noise downstairs, picked up an object and walked down the stairs.
2 A man drove into a town, parked his car outside a pub, went inside, sat down at a table and started talking to a woman.

b) In groups of four. Compare your stories. Which story is the most interesting? dramatic?

4 In the same pairs as in Exercise 2. Swap the story you wrote in Exercise 2 with another pair. Add adjectives and adverbs to make the other pair's story more interesting.

5 Choose a first line of a story (1–5) and a last line (a–e). Write a letter to a friend (120–180 words) telling the story.

First lines
1 I had the most incredible luck recently.
2 Pat had the party of the decade last Saturday.
3 Chris changed jobs just before Christmas.
4 Leslie decided to go on the trip of a lifetime.
5 I think Jody has gone completely mad.

Last lines
a) So it's hard to say when I'll see him / her again.
b) So he / she is in hospital for at least six weeks.
c) And suddenly I've got five children to look after!
d) I hope I never have to do that again.
e) Do you think anything else can go wrong?

Remember!
- Use linkers, other expressions and different past tenses to show the order of events in the story and to make the story flow smoothly.
- Make your story interesting by using a variety of adverbs and adjectives.

8 Life, death and the universe

Will and *going to* + infinitive for predicting
Third Conditional
Otherwise and *in case*
Conversations: Points of view

Visions of the future

1 a) In groups. Read these quotations. What have they all got in common?

① "Well-informed people know it is impossible to transmit the voice over wires and (if it were possible) the thing would be of no practical value."

(*The Boston Post*, 1865)

② "Heavier-than-air flying machines are impossible."

(Lord Kelvin, pioneer in thermodynamics and electricity, 1895)

③ "Man will never reach the moon, regardless of all future scientific advances."

(Lee Deforest, inventor of the vacuum tube, 1957)

④ "Nuclear-powered vacuum cleaners will probably be a reality within ten years."

(Alex Lewyt, manufacturer of vacuum cleaners, 1955)

⑤ "The one prediction coming out of futurology that is undoubtedly correct is that in the future, today's futurologists will look silly."

(Steven Pinker, 1997)

(adapted from *How The Mind Works* by Steven Pinker)

b) Which quotation focuses on what makes a machine work? is about planes? is about phones?

c) How many years passed between Lee Deforest's prediction and man walking on the moon? Check your answer on page 141.

d) Do you agree with Steven Pinker's comment (5)?

2 Read the text quickly. Which title (1–3) best summarises the ideas in the text?

1 Transport in the twenty-first century.
2 We're no good at predicting the future.
3 The future looks bright!

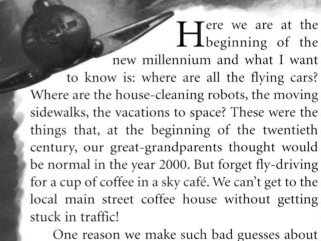

Here we are at the beginning of the new millennium and what I want to know is: where are all the flying cars? Where are the house-cleaning robots, the moving sidewalks, the vacations to space? These were the things that, at the beginning of the twentieth century, our great-grandparents thought would be normal in the year 2000. But forget fly-driving for a cup of coffee in a sky café. We can't get to the local main street coffee house without getting stuck in traffic!

One reason we make such bad guesses about the future is that we imagine our future lives filled with the same things that we already have, only better, but in fact the things that really change our world are entirely unexpected. The Victorians never predicted TV, because they couldn't

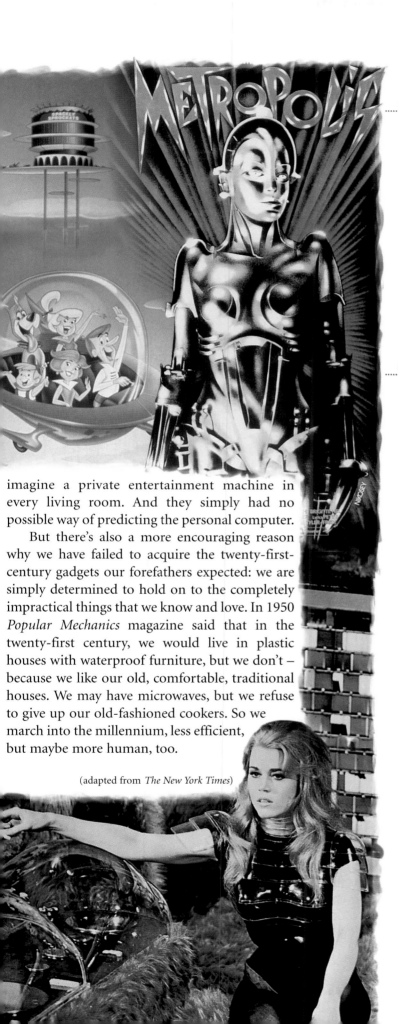

imagine a private entertainment machine in every living room. And they simply had no possible way of predicting the personal computer.

But there's also a more encouraging reason why we have failed to acquire the twenty-first-century gadgets our forefathers expected: we are simply determined to hold on to the completely impractical things that we know and love. In 1950 *Popular Mechanics* magazine said that in the twenty-first century, we would live in plastic houses with waterproof furniture, but we don't – because we like our old, comfortable, traditional houses. We may have microwaves, but we refuse to give up our old-fashioned cookers. So we march into the millennium, less efficient, but maybe more human, too.

(adapted from *The New York Times*)

3 a) Read the text again and answer the questions.

1 In the first paragraph, does the writer feel worried? disappointed? bored?

2 The writer gives two reasons why we haven't got the things we predicted. Tick (✓) the two reasons.

a) We can only imagine variations of our present lives.
b) We always try to predict things we cannot imagine.
c) We don't use technology to help us.
d) Plastic houses, microwaves, etc. are impractical.
e) The things we predicted are potentially dangerous.
f) We don't want to give up the things we already have.

b) Read the first six lines of the text again. Do you think we're closer to any of these things than the writer believes?

4 a) Read the Language Box. Then look back at the quotations in Exercise 1a). Which word is used with *will* to show that the prediction isn't quite certain?

> ### Predicting the future: will + infinitive
>
> We use *will* + infinitive to give our opinions, predictions, guesses about the future based on what we know about a situation, person, etc.:
> Man will walk on Mars.
> (Space technology is advancing all the time. So, in my opinion, man will one day walk on Mars.)
> He'll have a heart attack before he's forty.
> (He works too hard, drinks too much, smokes, etc. This is my opinion / prediction based on my knowledge of his lifestyle.)

b) Order the sentences (a–j) from the least likely to happen (1) to the most likely to happen (7).

Example: 1 = b) and e)

a) It might not / may not happen.
b) I'm sure it won't happen.
c) It probably won't happen.
d) It'll definitely happen.
e) It definitely won't happen.
f) It may well happen.
g) It might / may happen.
h) I doubt if it'll happen.
i) I'm sure it'll happen.
j) It'll probably happen.

c) How does the word order change in positive and negative sentences with *probably* and *definitely*?

The shape of things to come

5 **a)** In pairs. It's New Year's Eve, 1799. Max Ranting and Professor Karl are discussing the future on Earth. Look at the predictions Max is making. Tick (✓) the predictions which have already come true or are happening now.

1 We will control the weather.
2 People will fly.
3 We will find a cure for all diseases.
4 People will walk on other planets.
5 Money will no longer exist.
6 We will discover the secret of life itself.
7 Everybody will speak the same language.
8 People will live for over two hundred years.
9 Animals will no longer exist.
10 People will travel under the sea.

b) In groups. Discuss the predictions which aren't true now / yet. Do you think they'll definitely happen? they might happen? they probably won't happen?

c) Read the Language Box. Then fill in the gaps in sentences 1–4 with *in case* or *otherwise*.

Otherwise and *in case*

We use *otherwise* to talk about a possible bad result if something happens, or doesn't happen, now:
Listen carefully, **otherwise** (= because if you don't) you won't understand.
Don't eat any more cake, **otherwise** (= because if you do) you might be sick.
We use *in case* when we talk about something we do now to protect ourselves from a possible problem later:
I'll take a torch **in case** there are no lights. (I've decided to take a torch now because there might not be any lights when I get there in the future.)

Look!
We don't use future tenses after *in case*.

1 We have to reduce pollution, ... we'll continue to damage the ozone layer.
2 They've developed strict laws about cloning .... people abuse it.
3 They're testing the new anti-aging drug carefully before putting it on the market .... there are side effects.
4 Whale hunting will have to stop, ... whales will become extinct.

68

6 a) 🔘 46 Listen to Max and Professor Karl. Which prediction from Exercise 5a) are they discussing? What is Max working on? What happens in the end?

b) 🔘 46 Professor Karl makes two predictions. Listen again and fill in the gaps. What evidence does the professor have to support his predictions? Read the Language Box.

1 There .... be a terrible storm tonight!
2 That .... explode!

Predicting the future: *going to* + infinitive

We use *going to* + infinitive when we make a prediction based on present evidence / information (things that we read, see, hear, etc. now).

Present evidence / information	**Prediction**
The brakes aren't working! We've lost control of the car!	We**'re going to** crash.

Look!
- *Will* + infinitive:
  He'll be sick if you give him that. (I know him. He's got a sensitive stomach and spicy food makes him sick.)
- *Going to* + infinitive:
  He's going to be sick! (I'm looking at him now. His face is green and he's got his hands over his mouth.)

---

7 Match the predictions (1–6) to the present evidence / situations (a–f).

1 He'll win the race – no problem.
2 He's going to win the race!
3 He'll be late.
4 He's going to be late.
5 He'll fall.
6 He's going to fall!

a) He's overtaking the front runner!
b) He's really clumsy.
c) He's never on time for anything.
d) He's a very fast runner and he hasn't lost a competition all year.
e) He's on the edge of the wall and he's losing his balance.
f) He's just phoned from Brighton. That's an hour's drive from here and the wedding begins in forty-five minutes.

8 a) In pairs. Look at the pictures (1–3). What do you think is / isn't going to happen? Write predictions for each picture.

Example: 1 The woman's going to . . . They aren't going to . . .

b) Pairs make groups of four. Take it in turns to read your predictions. Did you predict the same things? What evidence did you use for your predictions?

Looking back

9 **a)** 🔊47 Listen to what actually happened after each scene shown in the pictures on page 69. Which person is speaking each time? Fill in three of the boxes (a–d) with *1, 2* or *3*. Were your predictions correct?

ⓐ

ⓑ

ⓒ

ⓓ

b) 🔊47 Listen again and fill in the gaps.

1 If I hadn't .... to read this poster, it .... hit me!

2 If I'd .... her some flowers or something, she .... done this.

3 If I hadn't .... to buy her a present, this .... happened!

10 **a)** Answer the questions and then read the Language Box.

1 a) Did the piano hit him? Why? / Why not?
   b) How does he feel?
2 a) Did she leave him? Why? / Why not?
   b) How does he feel?
3 a) Did she get a ticket? Why? / Why not?
   b) How does she feel?

Third Conditional

We use the Third Conditional when we imagine different possible past situations and their results. We often use it to express relief, regret or blame.

We use *if* + Past Perfect Simple for the imagined past situation and *would / wouldn't* or *might / might not* + *have* + past participle for the imagined result.

Imagined past situation	Imagined past result
If I **hadn't run** away,	he **would have hit** me!
(Reality: I **ran** away.)	He **didn't hit** me. = relief)
If I'**d worked** hard,	I **might not have lost** my job.
(Reality: I **didn't work** hard.	I **lost** my job. = regret)
If we **hadn't waited** for you,	we **wouldn't have been** late.
(Reality: We **waited** for you.	We **were** late. = blame)

b) Write Third Conditional sentences.

Examples: He stopped to look at the poster so the piano didn't hit him.
The piano <u>would have hit him if he hadn't stopped to look at the poster</u>.
He forgot their anniversary so she left him.
If <u>he hadn't forgotten their anniversary, she might not have left him</u>.

1 The poster had a really interesting design so he stopped to look at it.
   He . . .
2 The piano fell to the ground because the rope broke.
   If . . .
3 He was really stressed so he didn't remember their anniversary.
   If he . . .
4 He was really tired because he worked all weekend on a report.
   He . . .
5 She was in a hurry so she parked in a "No parking" zone.
   She . . .

Pronunciation: weak forms and linking

11 **a)** 🔊48 Underline the stressed words / syllables in the Third conditional example sentences in Exercise 10b). Listen and check your answers. How is the auxiliary verb *have* pronounced? Read the Language Box.

Third Conditional: weak forms and linking

The auxiliary verb *have* is weakened and the beginning *h* sound disappears when it links onto the final consonant sound of the word which comes before:
If I'd seen him I **would have** /wʊdəv/ said hello.

If I hadn't shouted, I might **not have** /nɒtəv/ lost my job.

If I'd treated her better, she **wouldn't have** /wʊdəntəv/ left.

b) In pairs. Practise saying the sentences you wrote in Exercise 10b).

12 a) American writer Barry Cadish has got an Internet website for his book *Damn! Reflections of Life's Biggest Regrets*. Read the messages people sent him. Find the mistake or bad decision they made in the past and the result that it had. Write a Third Conditional sentence for each situation (1–5).

Example: 1 If he'd / he hadn't . . . he would / wouldn't have . . .

b) In pairs. Compare your answers.

13 a) Think of a story to send to the website. Write the story in a paragraph (50–80 words). End the paragraph with a Third Conditional sentence which summarises the regret.

b) In groups. Take it in turns to read only your Third Conditional sentence. The other students build up the complete story by asking you questions.

Sample regrets

When I was creating this website, people told me I needed to include a few real regrets as examples. So I asked these people if I could use theirs. To my surprise, they all said yes. And here they are:

1 Name withheld, 52, private investigator
I was born clever. According to tests I am a genius. Back in the 1970s, my younger sister got involved in the growing computer industry and she asked me if I wanted to learn about them, because I was thinking about a career change. I thought about it and decided that the uses for computers would be very limited.

A few years later she suggested that I invest money in Microsoft, but my instinct told me it wouldn't last long, so I said no. Of course, my sister and her husband became very rich. I didn't. Sometimes I regret being so intelligent.

2 Name withheld, 30, technical support
I can't go into details, but I regret not thinking more about my family and friends. I regret being nasty for no reason. One good friend just stopped talking to me forever because I was so unkind. Why did I do that? I don't know.

3 Stephanie, 18, sales associate
I once got off with my boyfriend's brother. Not a good decision. Bye-bye boyfriend.

4 Isobel, 15, at school
I regret that my dad got a new job and so we had to move to this stupid place.

5 Mark, 8, at school
I regret getting angry with my little brother and hitting him because my mum sent me to my room and I couldn't watch TV.

(adapted from *www.regretsonly.com*)

Grammar reference
The Future: page 114
Third Conditional: page 116

That's easy for you to say!

1 In groups. When was the last time you tried to persuade someone to do / not to do something? When was the last time someone persuaded you to do / not to do something?

2 a) 🔊49 Look at the photo and listen to Kath and Alan. Where are they? What does Kath want Alan to do? Does Alan want to do it?

b) Who says these things? Fill in the boxes with *K* (Kath) or *A* (Alan).

1 ☒K☒ Be a sport.
2 ☐ You can't be serious!
3 ☐ That's easy for you to say!
4 ☐ No way!
5 ☐ Don't be such a wimp.
6 ☐ What have you got to lose?
7 ☐ Just have a go.

c) 🔊49 Listen again and check. Then fill in the Language Box with sentences 1–7 from Exercise 2b).

> ### Persuading and refusing
>
> **Persuading**
> Imperatives / set phrases:
> Go on. / Come on.
> You only live once.
> _____
> _____
> _____
>
> Putting yourself in their position:
> If I could sing, I'd be on stage now.
>
> **Refusing persuasion**
> Set phrases:
> You must be joking!
> Are you joking?
> _____
> _____
>
> Stressing that it's you, not the other person, who has to do it:
> It's all right for you.
> _____

Pronunciation: stress and intonation

3 a) Read the Language Box. Then underline the words which are "stretched" in sentences 1–5.

> ### Stress and intonation: emphasis
>
> When we really want to emphasise a word we "stretch" it out. We often do this in conversation when we're trying to persuade someone:
> Oh, p–l–e–a–s–e. I'll pay for the meal.

1 Oh, go on. Just once.
2 I really want you to do it.
3 It'll be a laugh.
4 Just have a go.
5 What have you got to lose?

b) 🔊50 Listen and check. Then in pairs, practise saying the sentences.

Oh, come on!

4 In pairs. Choose two of the situations (1–4). Take it in turns to be the persuader and the person who doesn't want to do something.

1 Your friend wants to buy a second-hand car. Persuade him / her to buy a new one.
2 You know your friend fancies a certain person. Persuade your friend to ask him / her out.
3 Persuade your friend to take a day off work with you when neither of you is ill.
4 You go to collect your friend from work. Persuade him / her to let you make an international telephone call from one of the office phones.

I disagree!

5 a) 51 Listen. What are George and Bernard arguing about? In groups. Who do you think is right, George or Bernard?

b) 51 Listen to the conversation again. Tick the words / phrases from the Word Box that George and Bernard use.

> I see your point.   That's true.
> You can't seriously believe . . .   Hold on.
> I think . . .   Yes, but what about . . . ?
> I don't think so.   If you ask me, . . .
> Absolutely!   I see what you mean.
> As far as I'm concerned, . . .   Come on.
> The thing is, . . .   You're joking!
> But really, . . .   As I said, . . .
> I suppose so.   I disagree.   I agree.

c) Copy the table into your notebook and fill it in with the words / phrases from the Word Box.

1 Giving an opinion	
2 Interrupting (to make a point)	
3 Insisting / repeating an opinion	
4 Agreeing	
5 Accepting an argument	
6 Disagreeing	

6 In pairs. Discuss the situations (1–6). Have opposite opinions for each situation.

Example: A: Well, of course he should do it. I think . . .
         B: You're joking! That's a terrible idea. I think he should . . .

1 A friend is going to Las Vegas to gamble. But she has told her husband that she's going to Denver on business. One of you thinks it's a great idea.
2 Your friend always cheats on his tax forms. He saves a lot of money every year. One of you is shocked.
3 A friend of yours is beginning a campaign to make alcohol illegal. One of you thinks this is an excellent idea.
4 A couple you know are both having secret affairs. One of you thinks they should both be completely honest.
5 A man at work was fired for losing some computer files. But you both know that it was your friend who wiped them accidentally. One of you thinks he should keep quiet – what's done is done.
6 You have found out that a colleague at work is using his company credit card to pay for expensive dinners with his girlfriend. One of you thinks you should tell the boss.

Wavelength page

9 It's a family affair

Family celebrations
Should / shouldn't have done
Wish / If only + Past Perfect Simple
Giving reasons, contrasting and criticising
Day to day English: *Isn't it?*
Reading for pleasure 3: *Dear Sue*
Do you remember? Units 7–9

Say "cheese"!

1 In pairs. Discuss these questions.

1 Do you carry any photos with you? Who / What are they of? Does anyone carry a photo of you?
2 Have you got any photos on the walls / on shelves at home? in photo albums?
3 Do you like looking at other people's photos?

2 a) Look at photos A–E. Which family occasions do they show? Match the nouns in the Word Box to the photos. Which words in the Word Box aren't in the photos?

> ceremony   gift / present   cake   guest
> newborn baby   host   birthday   balloon
> wedding   relative / relation   celebration
> anniversary   candle   party   decorations   bride
> couple   turkey   champagne   bridegroom

b) Choose one of the photos (A–E) and write a description of what's happening. Make your description as detailed as possible. Include one piece of incorrect information.

Example: The mother is smiling and holding the baby. The father is holding a bottle of milk. He looks . . .

c) In groups. Take it in turns to read your descriptions and point out each other's mistakes.

3 In groups. Describe the last special occasion in your family. What were you celebrating? Why was it memorable? How did you celebrate? Did you enjoy it?

You shouldn't have done that!

4 **a)** 🎧 52 Listen to four conversations about family events which have gone wrong. What's the occasion in each conversation? What's the problem in each situation?

b) 🎧 52 Which conversation do these sentences come from? Who says them? Fill in the boxes with *1, 2, 3* or *4* and the gaps with *wife, husband, bride, bridegroom* or *mother*. Then listen again and check.

Example: ☐4 BRIDE I should never have listened to you.

a) ☐ .... You shouldn't have asked the children to organise it.
b) ☐ .... I should have left him at home.
c) ☐ .... They shouldn't have been so close to the house.
d) ☐ .... If only I'd married Nigel.
e) ☐ .... You should have been here.
f) ☐ .... I wish I hadn't asked them.

5 Look at the sentences in Exercise 4b). Are the people talking about a mistake in the past, present or future? Which three things are the speakers expressing: criticism, admiration, regret, blame or satisfaction? Fill in the gaps in the Language Box with the three things.

> ### Wish / If only + Past Perfect Simple and should have
>
> We can express ...., ... and .... about events in the past in different ways.
> *Wish / If only* + Past Perfect Simple (*had / hadn't* + past participle):
> I wish / If only I'd been here. (I wasn't here, and I'm sorry about that.)
> *Should / shouldn't have* + past participle:
> You shouldn't have eaten so much cake. (You ate too much cake and now you feel sick.)
> **Look!**
> • We often use *never* to make negative ideas stronger:
>   I should never have listened to you!   I wish I'd never married you!

6 Complete the second sentence so that it means the same as the first.

Example: I didn't make enough food!
   I should <u>have made more food.</u>

1 It was wrong of me to drink so much.
   I shouldn't . . .
2 She thinks it was a mistake to come to the party.
   She wishes . . .
3 I feel terrible that I didn't buy him a present!
   I should . . .
4 It was a really bad idea to invite Gary!
   If only we . . .
5 We didn't hire a DJ and the music was a disaster.
   I wish . . .

7 In groups of eight. Pair A look at page 130, Pair B at page 134, Pair C at page 141 and Pair D at page 138.

Let's get married

8 In groups. Read about a traditional British wedding reception. Who are the people (a–e) in the picture? Answer the questions.

And finally the speeches started. The bride's father stood up and made a speech about his daughter. Then the bridegroom thanked everyone and proposed a toast to the bridesmaids. After that the best man made a really funny speech about the groom. Well, we thought it was funny, but the bride's father

1 Is this different from a traditional wedding in your country? Is the style of weddings changing?
2 Have you ever been to / seen a wedding in Britain? What was it like?

9 **a)** ⓞⓞ 53 Listen to Martin talking about a cultural difference he discovered when he got married. Answer the questions.

1 Where's Martin from? Where's his wife from?
2 What was the cultural difference connected with?

b) ⓞⓞ 53 Listen again and answer the questions.

1 What did Ana's aunts and cousin give them?
2 What did Martin's brother give them?
3 Did Martin think his brother's present was bad?

c) What does *get* mean in sentences 1–4 from Recording script 53? Fill in the gaps with *receive, obtain, become* or *arrive*.

1 We got (= ....) home after the honeymoon.
2 We still had to get (= ....) a lot of things for the house.
3 What did we get (= ....) from your brother?
4 I got (= ....) a bit embarrassed.

10 Read the Language Box. Then fill in the gaps in sentences 1–6.

Giving reasons and contrasting

Reasons
For, to, in order to, so that
We use *for* + noun; *to* or *in order to* + infinitive; *so that* + subject + verb:
He married her **for** her fortune.
He married her **to** / **in order to** be rich.
He married her **so that** he could be rich.
Because, because of
We use *because* + subject + verb; *because of* + noun:
She was attracted to him **because** he was powerful / **because of** his power.

Contrast
Although, even though, despite, in spite of
We use *despite* / *in spite of* + a noun, a gerund or *the fact that* + clause:
In spite of / **Despite** the bad weather / having bad weather / the fact that they had bad weather, they had a lovely honeymoon.
We use *although* / *even though* + subject + verb.
Even though gives more emphasis:
Although the weather was bad and **even though** their hotel was flooded, they had a lovely time.

Example: Her parents liked him <u>even though</u> he was a musician.

1 He married her .... she was pretty.
2 They stayed together .... they were unhappy.
3 It was a great day .... the bad weather.
4 She married him .... make her parents angry.
5 She divorced him .... his affairs.
6 He married her .... her money.

Las Vegas Weddings
wedding packages

Traditional Church Weddings
Chapel Weddings
Weddings Anywhere
Theme Weddings

- Fairy Tale Wedding
- Elvis Weddings
- Nature Weddings
- MORE Theme Weddings
- Theme Hotel Rooms
- Helicopter Tours
- Limo Photo Special

Make your wedding a legend with "The King" of Rock and Roll!

Get married in the "Elvis shrine"
Elvis fanatics will love this shrine decorated in honour of "The King" with Elvis stained glass windows, guitar candelabra and "The King's" framed gold records. Elvis himself will perform the ceremony and sing his most memorable tunes.

Let "The King" be your personal guide on the Las Vegas Strip
"The King" will arrive in your choice of a Super Stretch Limo or Pink Cadillac and will be your guide for one hour.
A must for any fan of "The King"!

(adapted from www.lasvegasweddings.com)

---

b TOURISM — EMPIRE STATE BUILDING ◆

VALENTINE'S WEDDINGS

Thinking about getting married at the Empire State Building?

Valentine's Day couples get married on the eightieth floor of the building and automatically become members of the Empire State Building Wedding Club. This entitles them to free admission to our observatories on their anniversary.

The feeling and spirit of New York City is embodied in the Empire State Building. People who fell in love here, return with their children and grandchildren. Everyone recognises the building as the unequalled symbol of American ingenuity and Art Deco architecture – an awe-inspiring landmark which offers one of the most spectacular views on Earth and creates magical romantic moments.

(adapted from www.esbnyc.com)

RELATED LINKS

▼
Upcoming Events
Events at the Empire State Building, lobby / window exhibits, and other activities.

Visitor Information
Directions, hours, and ticket information.

Lighting Schedule
Information regarding the Tower Lights during holidays and special occasions.

Observatory
Information regarding the 86th Floor Observatory and 102nd Floor Tower.

Wedding Dreams of Las Vegas
Looking for something different or daring?
Skydiving style
Take the Plunge $1,350

This package includes private use of a passenger jet liner, jump masters, minister, skydiving for the bride, groom, maid of honour and best man. A beautiful spring bouquet (delivered to your hotel), twenty-four pictures and negatives, video of the ceremony and of the jump.

- Tandem jumps are available for the bride and groom at no charge.

(adapted from www.weddingdreams.com/Extreme.htm)

---

11 a) Read the Internet ads for weddings quickly. In which country do these weddings take place?

b) In pairs. Read the ads (a–c) again and answer the questions (1–8).

1 In which weddings are the views important?
2 Which weddings include transport?
3 Which wedding includes music?
4 Which wedding includes flowers?
5 Which wedding mentions a time limit?
6 Which wedding offers a future benefit or extra?
7 Which wedding involves a famous person?
8 Which wedding offers danger and excitement?

c) In pairs. Which wedding would you prefer? What details would you change?

d) In pairs. Look at the other theme weddings (1–4). What do you think they're like?

1 *Titanic* wedding
2 Haunted house wedding
3 Hawaiian paradise wedding
4 Wild West wedding

12 In groups of four (Pair A and Pair B). Pair A look at page 140 and Pair B at page 142.

Parents and kids

13 a) Extracts A and B are about family relationships. Read them quickly. Where are the people in each extract?

b) Read the extracts again and answer the questions.

1 Which family relationships are represented in each extract?
2 Which family issues (a–i) are illustrated in each extract? How do the different characters feel? Use information from the extracts to explain your answers.

   a) money
   b) communication
   c) boyfriends / girlfriends
   d) sharing jobs round the house
   e) respect / politeness / manners
   f) sharing the living space, TV, etc.
   g) freedom / independence
   h) parental control
   i) education

A

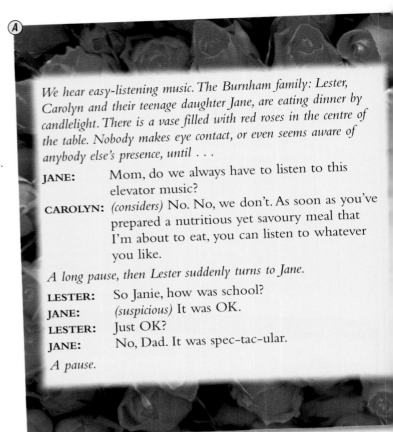

We hear easy-listening music. The Burnham family: Lester, Carolyn and their teenage daughter Jane, are eating dinner by candlelight. There is a vase filled with red roses in the centre of the table. Nobody makes eye contact, or even seems aware of anybody else's presence, until . . .

JANE: Mom, do we always have to listen to this elevator music?

CAROLYN: *(considers)* No. No, we don't. As soon as you've prepared a nutritious yet savoury meal that I'm about to eat, you can listen to whatever you like.

A long pause, then Lester suddenly turns to Jane.

LESTER: So Janie, how was school?
JANE: *(suspicious)* It was OK.
LESTER: Just OK?
JANE: No, Dad. It was spec-tac-ular.

A pause.

B

Monday 17 April 8st 13, alcohol units 6 (drowning sorrows), cigarettes 19 (fumigating sorrows), calories 3983 (suffocating sorrows with fat-duvet), positive thoughts 1 (vg)

11.59 pm

'Helen Fielding is one of the funniest writers in Britain and Bridget Jones is a creation of comic genius'
Nick Hornby

Bridget Jones's diary
Helen Fielding

11.30 a.m. Why oh why did I give my mother a key to my flat? I was just – for the first time in five weeks – starting a weekend without wanting to stare at the wall and burst into tears. I'd got through a week at work. I was starting to think maybe it was all going to be OK, maybe I wasn't *necessarily* going to be eaten by an Alsatian, when she burst in carrying a sewing machine.

'What on earth are you doing, silly?' she trilled. I was weighing out 100 grams of cereal for my breakfast using a bar of chocolate (the weights for the scales are in ounces which is no good because the calorie chart is in grams).

'Guess what darling?' she said, beginning to open and shut all the cupboard doors.

'What?' I said, standing in my socks and nightie trying to wipe the mascara from under my eyes.

'Malcolm and Elaine are having the ruby wedding in London now, on the twenty-third, so you will be able to come and keep Mark company.'

'I don't want to keep Mark company,' I said through clenched teeth.

'Oh, but he's very clever. Been to Cambridge. Apparently he made a fortune in America . . .'

'I'm not going.'

'Now, come along, darling, let's not start,' she said, as if I were thirteen.

(from *Bridget Jones's diary* by Helen Fielding)

LESTER: Well, you want to know how things went at my job today?

Now she looks at him as if he's lost his mind.

LESTER: You couldn't possibly care less, could you?

Carolyn is watching this closely.

JANE: *(uncomfortable)* Well, what do you expect? You can't all of a sudden be my best friend, just because you had a bad day.

She gets up and heads towards the kitchen.

JANE: I mean, hello. You've barely even spoken to me for months.

She's gone. Lester notices Carolyn looking at him critically.

LESTER: Oh, what, you're mother-of-the-year? You treat her like an employee.

CAROLYN: *(taken aback)* What?!

(adapted from *American Beauty* by Alan Ball)

14 Find words / phrases in the extracts which mean:
1 (Extract A) good for your health but having a pleasant taste (three words)
2 (Extract A) You don't care at all, do you? (seven words)
3 (Extract A) very surprised or shocked (two words)
4 (Extract B) entered suddenly and with a lot of energy (two words, phrasal verb)
5 (Extract B) be with someone so they don't feel lonely (three words)

15 a) 🔊 54 Read the questionnaire. Then listen to three people answering questions from it. Which question is each person answering? What do they say?

a) When should your parents stop being your parents?
b) What's the perfect number of children to have?
c) Do you think teenagers should rebel against their parents?
d) At what age should children leave home?
e) Why don't people get on with their parents-in-law?
f) What can you learn from your grandparents?

b) In groups. Discuss the questions in the questionnaire.

I'm fed up with him!

16 a) 🔊 55 Listen. Who are the family members? What's the problem?

b) 🔊 55 Listen again and fill in the gaps. Then read the Language Box.
1 You're .... his side.
2 You're .... him.
3 I'm so tired .... this argument.
4 I'm sick .... answering the phone for you.
5 She's .... to cause trouble.
6 I'm fed up .... it.

Language of criticism

We use the Present Continuous and *always* about a habit which happens a lot and irritates us:
He**'s always** complaining.
She**'s always** using my things.
We also use *tired of*, *sick of* and *fed up* **with** + gerund / noun / pronoun to express anger or irritation:
I'm getting tired of **your attitude**. (noun)
She's fed up with **him**. (pronoun)
I'm sick of **telling** you what to do! (gerund)

Look!
• The opposite of *always* + Present Continuous is *never* + Present Simple:
You never help round the house! **NOT**
~~You're never helping~~ round the house!

17 a) In pairs. You live together but you're very irritated with each other so you have an argument. Who are you? What's the argument about? Look at issues (a–i) in Exercise 13b) and each think of at least two complaints. Plan your argument and practise it.

b) Act out your argument. The class decides who you are and which issue you're arguing about.

18 Choose a character from one of the extracts in Exercise 13a). Write a diary extract (60–80 words) where your character writes about how he / she feels about the other member / members of their family and the family situation.

Grammar reference
Wish / If only + Past Perfect Simple: page 117
should / shouldn't have done: page 119
Present Continuous with *always*: page 110

Day to day English *Isn't it?*

A family reunion

1 a) The Forsythes are having a family reunion. Match the exchanges (1–5) to the couples talking (A–E) in the picture. Then match the question tags (a–e) to the exchanges.

1 ☐A A: Your name's Barry, ...c)....
   B: Er, no. It's Harry, actually.
2 ☐ A: There isn't much food, ...
   B: No, there isn't.
3 ☐ A: You remember Gail, ...
   B: No, actually, I don't think we've met.
4 ☐ A: She's put on weight, ...
   B: Er, yes, she has.
5 ☐ A: You can't see my glasses anywhere, ...
   B: They're on your head.

a) can you?   c) isn't it?   e) don't you?
b) hasn't she?   d) is there?

b) 🔊56 Listen and check your answers. Then read the Language Box.

Question tags

We often add question tags to the end of sentences to check information or to ask for agreement.
- If the sentence contains an auxiliary verb or a modal verb, we use it in the question tag:
  You **can't** find my handbag for me, **can** you?
  He's grown, **hasn't** he?
- If there is no auxiliary verb, we use *do* in the question tag (except with the verb *be*, which we repeat):
  You know Gordon, **don't** you?
  You**'re** Wendy's daughter, **aren't** you?
- Positive sentences have negative question tags. Negative sentences have positive question tags.

Look!
- We can use *actually* to correct information:
  No, it's Harry, **actually**.

Pronunciation: intonation in question tags

2 🔊57 Listen to questions 1 and 2 from Exercise 1a). Which question tag rises at the end? Which falls at the end? Who is only expecting agreement? Who is checking information he / she isn't sure about? Read the Language Box.

Intonation in question tags

- We use **rising** intonation when we're checking information that we're not sure about:

  You can't see my glasses anywhere, can you?

- We use **falling** intonation when we're confirming what we think is true or asking for agreement:

  She's put on weight, hasn't she?

3 a) What do you know about the other students (their opinions, lifestyle, etc.)? Write six sentences with question tags to check information (*You're twenty, aren't you?*), confirm information (*You drive a Golf, don't you?*), or ask for agreement (*This classroom's quite small, isn't it?*).

b) Go round the class. How much can you confirm or find out?

Example: A: You're twenty, aren't you?
   B: Yes, I am. / Yes, that's right.
   OR No, I'm twenty-four, actually.

Wavelength page

Reading for pleasure

③ Dear Sue

1 In this story, a young woman receives a number of mysterious messages without knowing who they're from. How many of these ways of sending this kind of message do you think might be used? Can you add to the list? Remember that the message must be untraceable!

1 An unsigned letter.
2 An e-mail sent through a free server.
3 A message left on an answering machine.

2 🎧58 Read and listen to the first part of the story. Then answer the questions.

Sue sat watching the rain on the windscreen of her car. The traffic wasn't moving so she'd turned the engine off. The raindrops looked like tears. "Tears!" she said aloud. "I'm sick of tears!" It was Monday morning of week two AD – after Dave. After Dave had said to her: "I really like being with you, Sue. But I don't feel ready for a serious relationship." In other words, he just didn't love her. They'd had six wonderful, exciting months together and Sue had never been happier. And now it was over. Sue wasn't the kind of person who cried much, but she had wept in private, off and on, for days and days. Now she was beginning to get tired of feeling so unhappy. She turned on the radio to cheer herself up.

". . . all you lucky Londoners on your way to work! And now I have a special request for Miss Sue Saunders from a mysterious Mr Sunshine with a message that says, 'Dear Sue, don't be blue!' And the song he's chosen for her is 'You light up my life'!"

Sue sat staring at the radio as the song started. Had she heard right? A message for her on Radio Five? Impossible! But if it hadn't been for her, who could it have been for? Surely there couldn't be another Sue Saunders in London who was blue! Just then the cars behind her started hooting. The traffic was at last beginning to move.

1 Where was Sue?
2 What was the weather like?
3 Why has she been so unhappy?
4 Who was the radio message from?

3 Now read the whole story. It starts on page 17 of *Heat wave and other stories*. Think about these questions while you read.

1 Why had there been a party on Saturday night?
2 Why hadn't Sue gone to the party?
3 How did she think her boss knew about Dave?
4 Who had sent the last e-mail that Sue read before going to her meeting?
5 Who did Chris suggest should produce Sue's programme?
6 What kind of relationship did Sue have with this person?
7 What stopped Roy telling Sue about his weekend?
8 What was the message on Sue's voice mail?
9 Who did Sue have lunch with on Tuesday?
10 What item of gossip did Sue learn about Roy?
11 Who did Sue think all the messages might be from?
12 What did Sue do on Tuesday and Wednesday evenings?
13 Who did she find waiting for her on Thursday after work?
14 Who did she find waiting for her at the entrance to her block of flats?

Do you remember? Units 7–9

1 Tell me more

a) 👀 59 Listen to the beginnings of four conversations. Match the conversations (1–4) with the means of communication (a–d).

a) e-mail   c) letter
b) television   d) telephone

b) 👀 59 Listen again. What do you think was in the e-mail, TV episode, letter? What do you think Tanya said in the phone call?

c) In groups of four. Student A look at page 141, Student B at page 145, Student C at page 136 and Student D at page 139.

d) In groups of four (Students A, B, C and D). Take it in turns to report your information and make notes on each other's information.

e) Check your notes against the original letter (page 141), e-mail (page 145), TV script (page 136) and phone call (page 139). Did the students who reported the information forget anything?

Example: You said that . . . but you didn't say
that . . .

2 A sorry tale

a) In groups of four. You're each going to read one paragraph of a story. Student A look at page 134, Student B at page 139, Student C at page 130 and Student D at page 144.

b) In your same groups. Take it in turns to tell each other your paragraph. Then put the paragraphs in the correct order and tell the story.

c) In your same groups. What was Jed and Jemima's situation at the end? Discuss the different things that happened and who was responsible each time. Who do you think was the most / least responsible?

Example: It's his fault because if he hadn't . . . ,
he wouldn't have . . .

3 It's all your fault!

a) In groups. You're scriptwriters for the TV soap opera *Enemies*, about a powerful but very dysfunctional family. You're going to write the script for the dramatic final scene of this week's episode. All the characters are at a family occasion. But something unexpected happens – with disastrous results! Before you write, answer the questions.

1 Who are the characters?
2 What's the occasion?
3 What's the atmosphere like at first? What's each person doing and saying?
4 What disaster happens? What does everyone do and say?
5 Do they sort out the problem by the end of the scene?

b) Write the script for the scene. Use *should / shouldn't have done, wish / if only* + Past Perfect Simple and the language of anger and irritation.

Examples: A: It's all your fault! I wish we'd never invested that money! I should never have believed you.
B: You're always criticising me. I've never been good enough for you!

c) Practise your scene. Then act it out for the class.

4 Max's diary

Read this extract from Max Ranting's diary. He wrote it the day after his conversation with Professor Karl and the explosion. Underline the correct word / words and fill in the gaps with the correct tense of the verb in brackets.

and I returned home at about one in the morning. And so I sat there alone in my laboratory by the fire. (Although / But) the explosion a few hours earlier had not been (not be) serious, it .... (1) (take) me more than an hour to clean up the broken glass and chemicals. I was drinking brandy (for / to) (2) calm my nerves and studying my notes in detail, in (order / try) (3) to discover exactly what .... (4) (go) wrong with the experiment. It was essential to find out why. (even though / despite) (5) I had been very careful, the mixture had exploded. Just imagine! If Professor Karl .... (6) (not be) between me and the explosion, I'm sure I .... (7) (die)! Perhaps I shouldn't .... (8) (put) in so much sulphuric acid? Perhaps I should .... (9) (use) different equipment? Questions, questions. Soon. (because of / because) (10) the fire's heat and the brandy, I started to fall asleep.

Suddenly, there, in front of me, I saw the ghost of Professor Karl! I could hardly speak! But (despite / in spite) (11) my terror, I managed to ask him what he .... (12) (do) there. There was no answer. "But you aren't a ghost!" I said.

"The doctor (said / told) (13) me that you only .... (14) (have) some cuts and bruises. He said that he'd (probably / might) (15) send you home the next day." Still he did not speak, he only looked round the room. Again I asked him why he .... (16) (come). "Have you returned in order (for / to) (17) show me that science does not have all the answers? Please answer me, spirit! I know I should .... (18) (listen) to your wise words more when you were alive! Oh, if only I .... (19) (not think) that I had all the answers!" "Oh, be quiet, Max!" the Professor said. "I'm not a ghost. I'm just trying to remember where I left my glasses. Now please be silent (for / so that) (20) I can concentrate. You're (always / often) (21) getting so excited about nothing, Max. That's (because / why) (22) you make so many mistakes. You really must learn to stay calm, (in case / otherwise) (23) you will never be a great scientist." I was so relieved! I had another large brandy (for / so that) (24) my nerves and gave one to the professor. "Good advice, Professor," I said. "(Despite / In spite) (25) of our differences, we make an excellent team. Happy New Century!"

Look at the Word lists for Units 7–9 on pages 126–128 and check that you know all the new words.

Puzzle 3 (Units 7–9): page 121

Wavelength page

10

What's going on?

> News stories and crime
> The Passive
> Negative questions: *Didn't you suspect . . .?*
> Modal verbs for laws, rules and social behaviour
> Verb + *-ing* and verb + infinitive
> Writing for work and pleasure 4: *On the other hand . . .*

Have you heard the news?

1 In pairs. Answer these questions.

1 Where do you get your news? a newspaper? the television? the Internet? the radio?
2 Which part of a newspaper do you read first? Which part do you never read? Do you always believe what you read in the newspapers?

2 a) Read the newspaper articles (1–3) quickly. Which one is international news? national news? a human interest story?

b) Read the articles again and answer the questions.

1 Which two groups were involved in the riot?
2 Why did Jennifer change the hamster's name from Hammy to Houdini?
3 How did the virus work? Why was it so effective?

c) Find these words in the articles (1–3).

1 a) robbed during a riot (v)
  b) thrown using a lot of strength (v)
  c) entered using force (phr v)
  d) completely destroyed (v)
2 a) the box in which a dead person or animal is buried (n)
  b) sleeping all the time during winter, a natural process for some animals (v)
  c) bit something repeatedly without eating it (v)
3 Underline the words connected with computers.

The Passive

3 a) Which articles (1–3) do these events come from?

a) The schoolchildren and teachers said prayers.
b) As soon as people opened this e-mail, their personal computers received over a thousand more messages.
c) The police brought in hundreds of officers in riot gear.

① **Protests erupt in violence**

A protest against capitalism in central London involving 4,000 people descended into ugly scenes of violence yesterday when shops were looted and bricks and bottles were hurled at police. Hundreds of officers in riot gear were brought in to break up the demonstrators after a McDonald's restaurant and a bureau de change on Whitehall were broken into and wrecked shortly after 2 p.m.

(adapted from *The Guardian*, 2nd May 2000)

② **Houdini the hamster comes back from the grave**

There were floods of tears the day Jennifer Wildes' pet hamster died. Prayers were said at school and her father held a funeral service when the animal was buried in a tiny cardboard coffin. The trouble was, he wasn't dead – he was simply hibernating. And the next day he chewed his way out of his box and dug back into the world from his grave. Jennifer, eight, of Droylsden, Manchester, said: "I'm so happy. I was sure my hamster was dead. I used to call him Hammy, but in future he'll be called Houdini."

(adapted from *The Daily Express*, 22nd October 1999)

b) Look again at the articles and answer the questions. Then read the Language Box.

1 How are sentences a–c in Exercise 3a) different from the original sentences in the articles?
2 Which information from sentences a–c is missing from the sentences in the articles?

The Passive

- We form the Passive with the correct tense of the verb *be* + past participle:
  He'**ll be called** Houdini.
- The Passive is more common in formal written texts:
  Ten people **were arrested** after the incident.
- We use the Passive when:
  - the action is the important idea, not who did it:
    As soon as this e-mail **was opened**, . . .
  - the person who did the action is obvious:
    Shops **were looted**. (Obviously by the rioters.)
  - when we don't know who did the action:
    The virus was sent as an e-mail.
- We use *by* to say who or what did the action:
  We've been hit **by** six or seven viruses this year.

③

Cash bug strikes

A computer virus promising unexpected cash cost worldwide businesses millions of pounds yesterday. The virus was sent as an e-mail with the title "Annual Bonus". As soon as this e-mail was opened, personal computers received over a thousand more messages, causing the systems to crash. Nearly twenty per cent of companies in the USA and a total of thirty million European workers were affected. The boss of one company paralysed by the bug said: "We've been hit by six or seven viruses this year, but this one is easily the worst. Normal business is made impossible by something like this because customers can't be contacted by e-mail. It's like having a power cut."

4 a) Write the sentences in the Passive using the correct form of the verb *be*.

Example: People **buy** millions of papers every day. (Present Simple)
Millions of papers **are bought** every day.
Somebody must **stop** him! (infinitive without *to*)
He must **be stopped**!

1 The police are interviewing the suspects.
2 They found the money.
3 They have arrested a lot of people.
4 They'll kill him if he goes there!
5 Someone needs to send supplies to the area.
6 I like people interviewing me.

b) In pairs. Underline all the Passive sentences in the articles in Exercise 2a).

5 a) 🔊 60 Listen to part of a news broadcast and answer the questions.

1 Which of the articles (1–3) is this story similar to?
2 What do these numbers refer to?
   a) 2000   c) 12   e) hundreds   g) 4:30
   b) 10 or 11,000 d) 20   f) 30

b) 🔊 60 Listen again and fill in the gaps. Then read the Language Box.

1 A police officer in riot uniform .... hit by a bottle.
2 Cheryl .... knocked down by a police horse.
3 Shops .... wrecked.
4 A lot of people .... hurt for no reason.
5 The people who started the trouble .... arrested.

The Passive with *get*

We can use *get* with the Passive in informal spoken and written English especially to show that something happened quickly, unexpectedly or by accident:
His glasses **got broken** in the fight.

Broadcast news

6 In groups of four or four pairs. You're journalists preparing for a meeting about that afternoon's news broadcast. Student / Pair A look at page 133, Student / Pair B at page 136, Student / Pair C at page 141 and Student / Pair D at page 145.

Scandal

7 **a)** Read the article about politician Andrew Chalmers quickly. Is the article for or against him?

 **DAILY WORLD**
HOME NEWS

Charmless Chalmers

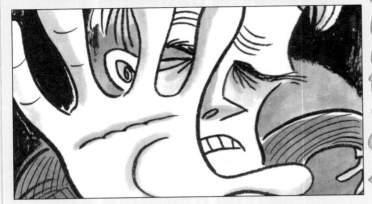

Who does Andrew Chalmers think he is? He thinks he can come out of prison and go straight back into government! Well, here at *The Daily World* we think you – the voters – have got a right to the full story! So here's our list of his "mistakes"!

1 Drink-driving

While in Paris for a European summit meeting about road safety, Chalmers was stopped for speeding. He was then arrested when he was also found to be drunk. He said to the arresting officer, "You're overreacting! I do this all the time in England!"

2 Fiddling expenses

While he was an MP, Chalmers' expenses for business trips often totalled thousands of pounds. He had to be more careful when an accountant noticed that he had charged for lunch in three different luxury hotels on the same day – in three different European cities!

3 Shoplifting

Chalmers was stopped by store detectives at a top department store in West London as he attempted to leave the shop with three bottles of champagne under his coat. Chalmers claimed that he had forgotten they were there. He was released with a warning.

4 Burglary

A week later the police were called by a witness who had seen a man climbing out of a window of the Houses of Parliament. Andrew Chalmers was arrested at the scene of the crime carrying two bottles of champagne which he had taken from the fridge in the MPs' dining room. "All the shops are closed," he told the police.

5 Forgery

In order to show how popular his ideas were, Chalmers sometimes forged his colleagues' signatures on various documents and letters of support. "I knew they would

support me. I didn't want to bother them with details like signing papers," he argued.

6 Fraud

Chalmers' worst "mistake" was his business venture with known fraudster Seymour Cripes-Tottingly. Chalmers used his position and name to get rich and famous people to invest in their new company, "Grow Richer", which made farm equipment for the Third World. But all the money went into overseas bank accounts under the names of Chalmers and Cripes-Tottingly and no-one actually started any company! Chalmers was found guilty of fraud at his trial, where his excuses failed to impress the jury. He was sentenced to nine months in prison.

After his release from prison on 9th January, Chalmers went on a six-month cruise. Maybe he was hoping that everyone would forget. Sorry, Andy – *The Daily World* never forgets!

b) In pairs, explain the crimes / offences (1–6) in the article in your own words.

c) Find these words connected with the law in the article.

1 Paragraph 1: driving faster than you're legally allowed to (n)
2 Paragraph 3: allowed to go free (v)
3 Paragraph 4: the place where an illegal activity happened (5 words)
4 Paragraph 6: a legal process where a court of law decides whether someone is innocent or guilty of a crime (n)
5 Paragraph 6: twelve ordinary people who listen to the evidence in a trial and decide whether someone is innocent or guilty (n)
6 Paragraph 6: given a legal punishment because you're guilty of a crime (v)

d) In groups. Do you think Andrew Chalmers is unusually dishonest for a politician?

8 a) 📼61 *The Daily World* decided to interview Andrew Chalmers after his release from prison about the "Grow Richer" scandal. Listen to the first part of the interview and answer the questions.

1 Does Andrew Chalmers admit he was guilty?
2 Does he say he behaved in an honest way?
3 Why, according to Chalmers, didn't he know how the investors' money was spent?

b) 📼61 Listen again and fill in the gaps. Then read the Language Box.

1 The jury .... false information.
2 They .... the whole story.
3 I .... never .... about how the money was spent.

c) Rewrite these sentences in the Passive.

Example: They told him to phone his lawyer.
 He was told to phone his lawyer.

1 Somebody told me to come here.
2 They didn't give me any choice.
3 Somebody will inform the Prime Minister.
4 They told Jane to wait in reception.
5 Someone asked me a couple of questions.

9 a) 📼62 Listen to the second part of the interview and answer the questions.

1 Who is Chalmers talking about when he says, "We all do crazy things when we're young."? Why is this a bad excuse?
2 Why has he cut off all business connections with Cripes-Tottingly?

b) 📼62 Listen again and fill in the gaps. Then read the Language Box.

1 .... you the financial director?
2 .... you know, Mr Chalmers, right from the beginning, that Seymour Cripes-Tottingly was a known criminal?
3 .... you see that he was simply putting the money into foreign bank accounts?
4 .... you and your wife just returned from a holiday with Mr Cripes-Tottingly and his wife?

But haven't you ever . . . ?!

10 In groups of four. Student A look at page 135, Student B at page 133, Student C at page 136 and Student D at page 144.

It shouldn't be allowed!

11 **a)** Look at pictures 1–3. Where are the people and what's happening? Use the adjectives in the Word Box and talk about each picture.

> irritating   polite   fun
> annoying   dangerous   cool
> illegal   unusual   charming
> selfish   impressive   stupid
> necessary   rude   anti-social

① BEEP BEEP BEEEEP

②

③ SILENCE

b) 🔊 63 Listen to three people talking about the pictures (1–3). Which adjectives in the Word Box in Exercise 11a) do they use?

c) 🔊 63 Which expressions do speakers 1–3 in Exercise 11b) use? Listen again and fill in the boxes with *1, 2* or *3*.

a) [1, 2] It's / It's not against the law (to)
b) [   ] It's / It's not rude (to)
c) [   ] It's / It's not against the rules (to)
d) [   ] It's / It's not illegal (to)
e) [   ] It's / It's not good / bad manners (to)
f) [   ] You're / You're not allowed to
g) [   ] You're / You're not supposed to
h) [   ] You can / can't
i) [   ] You should / shouldn't
j) [   ] You have to / don't have to

d) In pairs. Which expressions in Exercise 11c) are about the law, which are about rules, which are just about good or bad behaviour? Read the Language Box and check your answers.

> ### Modal verbs: Laws, rules and social behaviour
>
> **Laws**
> It's / It's not illegal (**to carry** a weapon).
> It's / It's not against the law (**to drink** alcohol in public).
> You have to / don't have to (**carry** ID).
> You can / can't (**smoke** on public transport).
>
> **Rules and regulations**
> You're / You're not supposed **to** (**do that**).
> It's / It's not against the rules (**to take** drinks outside).
> You're / You're not allowed **to** (**talk** in here).
> You can / can't (**smoke** in here).
> You have to / don't have **to** (**do that**)
>
> **Behaviour**
> You should (**wait** your turn in queues).
> You shouldn't (**talk** in the library).
> It's / It's not rude / anti-social / bad manners (**to eat** in public).

Verb + *ing* and verb + infinitive

12 **a)** In pairs. Look at sentences 1 and 2. What happens to the verb *drive* and the word order in sentence 2? Is there a difference in meaning between sentences 1 and 2?

1 It's illegal to drive without a licence.
2 Driving without a licence is illegal.

b) Write the alternative for each sentence (1–5) using verb + infinitive or verb + *-ing*.

Example: It's rude to stare at people.
~~Staring at people is rude.~~

1 Carrying a gun is illegal.
2 It's not against the rules to smoke in here.
3 Criticising the government isn't against the law.
4 It's anti-social to use a mobile phone in the cinema.
5 Parking on the pavement is selfish.

Who do they think they are?

13 a) In groups. Match an item / items from the Word Box to each picture (a–j).

> queue-jumping   fiddling taxes   dropping litter   sexism
> stealing from work   breaking the speed limit / speeding
> cheating   hitting / smacking   fare-dodging   jaywalking

b) 🔊 64 Listen to two people talking about two different situations from pictures a–j and answer the questions.

1 Which situation is each person talking about?

2 Which countries are they talking about?

3 What happened in listening 2?

c) In groups. Discuss questions 1–4 about pictures a–j.

1 In your country which of these things are illegal / against the rules or anti-social / bad manners?

2 Has anyone you know ever done any of these things? What happened as a result?

3 Have you ever been a witness to any of these things? What did you do?

4 Which things in the pictures are always wrong? Or does it always depend on the situation?

14 Use the language in this unit and write 60–100 words about one of the questions (1–3). Use your own experience, the experiences of people you know or stories from the news to support your views.

1 Is there a law or rule which you think is frustrating or unnecessary?

2 Is there something which isn't against the law, but which you think should be illegal?

3 People say "Rules are made to be broken." Do you agree?

Grammar reference

The Passive: page 117
Modal verbs: page 118

Writing for work and pleasure

Writing a report

1 a) A journalist from the magazine *Modern Living* is conducting a survey on how family size affects children. What do you think are the advantages and disadvantages of being an only child? being a child in a large family? In pairs. Copy the word map into your notebook and add your own ideas.

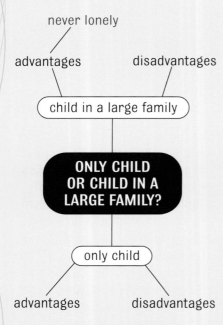

never lonely

advantages   disadvantages

child in a large family

ONLY CHILD OR CHILD IN A LARGE FAMILY?

only child

advantages   disadvantages

b) The journalist interviewed 500 people and wrote a report for the editor of the magazine. Read the report. Which of your ideas are mentioned?

c) The journalist used a word map to organise the information from the interviews and write her report. Look at the word map in Exercise 1a) and write headings for paragraphs 1–4 in the gaps in the report.

How does family size affect children?

This report outlines the findings of my recent survey which compared the advantages and disadvantages of being either an only child or part of a larger family. The information was gathered from 500 interviews with parents and their children aged 4–16.

1 ....

Many parents felt that there were advantages to a child having brothers and sisters, despite the possible increased financial burden on the family. Firstly, they stressed that there was less chance of a child feeling lonely or isolated if he / she were part of a larger family. Secondly, parents believed that siblings have a positive effect on the social skills of the growing child, teaching tolerance of others and promoting co-operation through the sharing of household duties. In addition, it was considered an advantage that children with siblings would not have sole responsibility for their ageing parents in later life.

2 ....

The children interviewed, on the other hand, complained that they did not have enough of their parents' attention and that they often had to do things they did not want to do, for example, looking after younger siblings. Moreover, they felt that they were often compared unfavourably with their siblings.

3 ....

In contrast, the parents of only children generally had more time and money to spend on them. For example, if the child showed an interest or ability in something, such as, music, this could be supported. Many of the parents interviewed also felt that only children tended to develop better social skills because they were more often in adult company and also had to make greater efforts to find friends outside the family.

4 ....

The downside for the only children was that they often felt under pressure to live up to their parents' expectations. As well as this, many people felt that only children tended to be spoilt and were therefore not adequately prepared for adulthood.

On the whole, there seem to be advantages and disadvantages to both situations, although, interestingly, there were fewer disadvantages for only children than might have been expected. The advantages for children in large families were mostly seen through the eyes of the parents, as many of the children interviewed had stories to tell about frequent arguments between siblings. In conclusion, if we decide to write an article on this subject, I recommend that we write it from the viewpoint of the children themselves.

d) Look at the first and last paragraphs of the report. What information do these two paragraphs contain? Then read the Writing Box.

Writing Reports

A report is a factual piece of writing based on research or information which the writer has collected.

A report needs to be written so that it is easy for the reader to follow. This means that:
- there is an introductory paragraph saying what the report is about and how the information was gathered.
- there is a final summarising paragraph with an opinion and recommendation where appropriate.
- the information in the report is organised into sections.

In reports we use formal language and often use the Passive: Several families **were interviewed** . . .

2 a) Copy the table into your notebook. Fill in the table with the linkers and phrases in green from the report which:

1 list examples in order	Firstly, Secondly
2 add more details to support an idea	
3 contrast with a previous idea	
4 summarise or conclude the main ideas	
5 make recommendations	

b) Look at the linkers and phrases in the Word Box and add them to the table in Exercise 2a).

> To summarise   however   I propose that   thirdly   furthermore

3 a) In pairs. Choose a topic (1–5). Discuss the advantages and disadvantages.

1 Being self-employed or working for a company.
2 Having children when you're young or waiting until you're older.
3 Going straight to university or college after school or having a gap year to travel or do voluntary work.
4 Learning a language in a class or with an individual tutor.
5 Having one long holiday every year or several short breaks.

b) In the same pairs. Make a word map for your topic. Write the topic in the middle. Then fill in the word map with your main ideas, supporting ideas and examples.

c) Write a report on your topic (150–200 words) for the editor of *Modern Living*. Use the linkers and phrases from Exercises 2a) and 2b).

Remember!
- Always think about the purpose of your report. Who is going to read your report and why?
- Write a word map, plan or clear notes before you begin.
- Refer to your word map / plan / notes as you write. Make sure your report keeps to the most important points.

11

The silver screen

Films and cinema
All, whole and *every*
Speaking skills: telling stories, describing films
Reporting verbs
Conversations: *Well, actually I . . .*

When the lights go down

1 In groups. Discuss the questions.

1 Where do you like to sit in the cinema? Why?
2 When was the last time you laughed out loud during a film? cried during a film?
3 Have you ever walked out of a film?

2 a) In groups. Can you think of one famous film for each kind in the Word Box?

> war romantic comedy science fiction
> animated crime comedy action
> fantasy thriller western musical
> drama adventure romance horror

b) Which kinds of film in the Word Box need the word *film* after them?

Example: action film

c) ⏺⏺ 65 Listen to two people talking about films. Which kinds do they like? don't they like?

d) In groups. Do you agree with the people in Exercise 2c)? What kinds of film do you like? What kinds don't you like? Why?

3 In pairs. Look at the photo. Fill in the spaces (1–8) with the words and phrases connected with films in the Word Box. (Some can go in more than one space).

> It's based on . . . popcorn back row
> front row audience screen
> It was directed by . . . star special effects
> stunt review actor / actress soundtrack
> seat ad / advert It was dubbed into . . .
> extra low budget ice cream script aisle
> screenplay film critic subtitles car chase
> producer credits blockbuster It's about . . .
> independent foyer usher trailer scene
> merchandise director It's set in . . . plot

3 Kinds of studios / film

1 Talking about films

2 Things you buy

4 People

4 **a)** 🔲66 Listen to three conversations and tick the words / phrases in the Word Box in Exercise 3 that you hear.

b) 🔲66 Listen again. Which conversation (1–3) is between an actress and a director? two people in the cinema during a film? two people after a film?

5 **a)** In pairs. Write a short conversation between two people at the cinema. Use five words or phrases from the Word Box in Exercise 3, but put gaps in the conversation where they should be.

b) Swap your gapped conversation with another pair and fill in the missing words / phrases. Then check each other's answers.

5 Before the film

6 In the film

7 Things in the cinema

8 Things you read

All, whole, every

6 **a)** 🔲67 Listen to Jake. Which question from Exercise 1 is he answering?

b) 🔲67 Listen again and fill in the gaps with *all, whole* or *every*. Which word / words is / are used with singular nouns? plural nouns? uncountable nouns? Then read the Language Box.

1 I've stayed to the end of .... film I've ever been to.
2 It just seems silly to spend .... that money.
3 I always sit through the .... film.
4 .... films have some good points.

All, whole *and* every

All, whole
We usually use *all* with uncountable nouns and plural countable nouns. We use *his, my, the,* etc. after *all*.
We usually use *whole* with singular nouns. We use *his, my, the,* etc. before *whole*:
We spent **all our money** on posters and T-shirts.
All the people / **The whole audience** cheered in the fight scene.

All, every
All and *every* have similar meanings but *every* is always singular:
All the children **were** / **Every child was** under twelve.

Look!
• **Every** *time* means on every separate occasion.
• **All** *the time* means always or very often.
• We can say **the whole** *day / month,* etc. or **all** *day / month,* etc. to mean the entire time.
• We can say **his whole** *life* or **all his** *life*.

c) Underline the correct word / phrase.

Example: The (all / <u>whole</u>) family love going to the cinema.

1 He ate (all / whole) my popcorn.
2 He ate the (all / whole) bag of sweets.
3 He ate (all / whole) the chocolates.
4 (All / Every) seat was booked.
5 (All / Every) the seats were booked.
6 (All the time / Every time) I go to that cinema I have to queue!
7 They both love films. They go to the cinema (all the time / every time).
8 We got to the cinema at 11 a.m. and stayed there (all / every / whole) day.

Scene by scene

7 a) These texts are from a list of the one hundred most memorable film moments of the twentieth century. Match each text (1–5) to a film poster (A–E). What kind of film do you think each one is?

b) Match the summary titles (a–e) to the texts.

a) We don't take no for an answer
b) A new world over the rainbow
c) A man alone
d) Emotion on the ocean
e) They're behind you

c) In groups. Which adjectives from the Word Box would you use to describe each scene (1–5)? Use your *Longman WordWise Dictionary* to help you if necessary.

> gripping   exciting   shocking
> romantic   sexy   predictable
> depressing   dramatic   moving   sad
> tense   gory   funny   frightening

The plot thickens

8 Underline the verbs in these sentences from the texts in (1–5). Which tenses are used? Read the Language Box.

1 Dorothy watches as her house rises high into the air.
2 Sheriff Kane will have to stand alone.
3 Melanie is sitting with her back to the school playground.
4 Woltz gradually wakes up.
5 Rose has told Jack that she cannot go on seeing him.

> **Verb tenses for stories and jokes**
>
> To increase the drama when we describe the plot of a book or film, or tell jokes, we often use present and future tenses: Michael **has spent** the whole day searching for Annie. He **comes** out of the lift and she**'s standing** there. As soon as they **see** each other they **know** they**'ll** always **be** together.

① Hiding in her bedroom, Dorothy watches, terrified, as her house rises high into the air. Things fly past her window and the scene becomes more and more surreal. Old Elvira Gulch from the village appears on her bicycle and turns into a terrifying witch. There's a crash and Dorothy's black-and-white world turns into a world of spectacular colour. "Toto," she says to her little dog, "I've a feeling we're not in Kansas anymore."

② With no help from the townspeople, it's clear that Sheriff Kane will have to stand alone. When the clock strikes twelve, he gets up and walks out into the street. But even then he's no fighting machine: he's an anxious, middle-aged man, looking nervously around. That's what makes him so heroic.

③ Melanie is sitting with her back to the school playground, waiting for the children and smoking – unaware of the crows gathering on the climbing frame behind her. The camera stays on Melanie for a long time, as we hear the children singing in the classroom. The suspense is maintained with the camera cutting back and forth from Melanie to the climbing frame as the crows gather. Finally she turns, sees the climbing frame covered in birds and rushes to the classroom. The crows attack.

④

Hagen is in Hollywood to convince producer Mr Woltz to put Sinatra-esque singer Johnny Fontaine into a movie. Woltz entertains Hagen in style, showing off his $600,000 stud horse, but refuses to give Johnny a part. Hagen tells him that Don Vito "never asks for a second favour". The next day, in the early morning light, the camera moves slowly towards Woltz's huge California mansion. In his bedroom, Woltz gradually wakes up, looking confused. He sees blood on his sheets. He pulls them back – and there is the head of his $600,000 horse.

⑤

Rose has told Jack that she cannot go on seeing him because she's engaged, but she cannot stop herself from secretly meeting him once more. At the ship's bow under the reddening evening sky, Jack persuades her to step up onto the railings, stretch out her arms and lose herself in the ocean air. "Jack, I'm flying!" she exclaims. To the music of worldwide chartbuster "My Heart Will Go On", Jack moves in for a long, slow kiss.

(adapted from *The Observer*)

9 a) 🎧 68 Listen to Jake beginning to talk about one of the scenes described in texts 1–5. Which scene is he going to talk about?

b) 🎧 68 Listen again and fill in the gaps. Then read the Language Box.

It's such a great film. I mean, it's not horror, exactly, but it's so frightening. It's about this woman, Melanie Daniels. She goes to this little island for ....(1) reason, um, I think she wants to visit someone, or does Mitch Brenner invite her? Er, I can't really remember. But ....(2), she's on this island with Mitch and she's got ....(3) kind of relationship with him, you know, or she wants to start a relationship with him. ....(4), they're together and everything's going well, but then all the birds on the island start attacking people. You know, just for no reason, um, I think one person has ....(5) theory about it, but ....(6), the birds are attacking – killing people and, well, everyone's terrified. Nobody knows what to do – there's a feeling of confusion. So Melanie decides to collect Mitch's sister from the school.

Telling stories: speaking skills

- We can use *some* instead of *a* and *an* when we're not quite sure about "what" or "who":
  For **some** reason, she shoots him.
- We use *anyway* when we want to come back to the main subject:
  John's in the car park. I think he's waiting for Jane – or maybe he's looking for Steve. **Anyway**, he's in the car park and suddenly . . .
- We use the linkers, *and* (addition), *but* (contrast) and *so* (consequence) a lot when telling a story to keep the story moving.

10 a) Think of a film scene that you remember well. Why do you remember it? Is it a classic film moment? Is it funny? moving? terrifying? Prepare to describe it (and the basic plot of the film).

b) In groups. Check that the others know your film. If they don't, describe the basic plot. Then take it in turns to describe and discuss your film moments.

Examples: A: Have you seen X? (No, I haven't.) Well, it's about (plot), and there's this bit / scene where . . .
B: Have you seen Y? (Yes, I have.) Well do you remember that bit / scene where . . . ?

11 Write a review of a film you've seen.

Paragraph 1: Give the title, kind of film, director, actors, etc.
Paragraph 2: Describe the basic plot and the atmosphere. Use *It's set in . . .* , *It's based on . . .* , *It's about . . .* , *It's very (moving, frightening, etc.).*
Paragraph 3: Give your opinion of the film and why you did or didn't like it. Would you recommend it?

The Lost House

12 **a)** What kind of film are the photos from? Do you like films like this? In each photo, what do you think is happening? has just happened? is going to happen?

b) [oo] 69 You're going to hear the beginning of an old film, *The Lost House*. Listen and answer the questions.

1 What's the relationship between the man and the woman?

2 Where are they? Why are they there?

3 What do you think is going to happen?

c) [oo] 70 Listen to and read the rest of the scene. Then answer questions 1–4 in pairs.

1 How can Bud and Betsy see round the house?

2 Why does Betsy scream twice?

3 Where are their suitcases?

4 What do you think is in the cellar?

BUD:	Hey, come on in, honey. Come out of the rain.
BETSY:	No! I will not take one more step, Bud! There's no light. I won't go in!
BUD:	Oh, honey. We'll **find** a light. Just come in out of the rain, will you?
BETSY:	No. Let's go back.
BUD:	Honey? *(Bud holds out his hands to Betsy.)* Please?
BETSY:	Oh . . . but . . . *(She goes in.)* OK . . . I'm in. Happy?
BUD:	Great. Now where can we find a candle or something? *(He holds up his lighter and looks round.)* Wow, this place is big! And there's a candle right there. I'll just . . . *(The door slams. Betsy screams.)*
BUD:	Er . . . I guess it was the wind . . . I'll just light this candle. *(He lights the candle.)* That's better. Er . . . hello? Anybody? Is anyone at home?
BETSY:	Bud, I'm frightened.
BUD:	Gee, Betsy, I know . . . I'm sorry I brought you here. I'm sorry I got lost. I . . . *(He sees a door.)* Hey! That's the cellar, I bet. Let's go down into the dark cellar and see if we can fix the electricity. You hold the candle, and I'll . . .

(Suddenly Glutz, the servant, appears out of the shadows and puts his hand on the cellar door.)

GLUTZ:	**Don't** . . . go into the cellar, sir.

(Betsy screams.)

BUD:	Say, who are you? We thought the house was empty.
GLUTZ:	I am Glutz, the family servant. You must not go into the cellar, sir. It's . . . strange . . . down there.
BUD:	OK, I won't, really.
GLUTZ:	Never, sir. Not the cellar.
BUD:	OK, OK, if it's that important to you.
GLUTZ:	It's important to **you**, sir. But there is a room for you . . . **up**stairs. Shall I get your luggage from the car?
BUD:	I . . . don't know . . . a room . . . but . . . ?
GLUTZ:	Or would you like a glass of warm milk? You must be . . . **dead** tired.

(We hear laughter from somewhere.)

BETSY:	That . . . that came from the cellar, didn't it?
GLUTZ:	Go . . . **up**stairs, madam . . . sir . . . go upstairs **now**! And **don't** come back down!

Reporting verbs

13 a) 🔊71 Listen to Betsy talking to a police officer the next day. Why is she at the police station? What do you think has happened?

b) 🔊71 Listen again and fill in the gaps.

Example: He asked me <u>to come</u> out of the rain.

1 I refused .... one more step.
2 Finally I agreed .... in.
3 He apologised .... lost.
4 He wanted .... the candle.
5 He warned .... into the cellar.
6 He promised .... down there.
7 He offered .... our bags from the car.
8 He offered .... a glass of milk!
9 He told .... upstairs.
10 He told .... back down.

c) Match Betsy's reported sentences to the correct sentences in the film script on page 96. Then read the Language Box.

Reporting verbs

- **Ask, tell, warn, want**

Subject	Verb	Object	to + infinitive
She	told	him	to go home.

- **Agree, promise, offer, refuse**

Subject	Verb	to + infinitive
They	agreed	to stay.

- **Promise** and **offer** + nouns

Subject	Verb	Object	Noun
He	promised	me	money.

- **Apologise**

Subject	Verb	for	verb + -ing
He	apologised	for	getting lost.

14 The scene between the scenes in Exercises 12c) and 13a) was never made. All that's left of the script is seven lines. Which lines do you think are Bud's? Betsy's? Glutz's? someone else's? Report sentences 1–7 using a verb from the Language Box.

Example: 1 **Bud** promised to find a telephone first thing in the morning.

1 Don't worry, Betsy. I'll find a telephone first thing in the morning!
2 Shall I go and see what that noise is, honey?
3 No, Bud! Don't leave the room!
4 Just open the door, my dear. I'll tell you where your husband is.
5 Don't let the mad old woman in, madam!
6 I let her out of the cellar, madam. I'm very sorry.
7 Oh Glutz! Where's Bud? Please tell me!

15 a) In groups of four. Read sentences 1–7 in Exercise 14 again. What do you think happened? Think about questions 1–5 and write the missing scene using sentences 1–7 in your script.

1 What was the noise?
2 Where did Bud go when he left the room? What happened to him?
3 What did Betsy do?
4 Who was the old woman? What did she do?
5 What happened next?

b) Now act out your scene for the class.

> **Grammar reference**
> Tenses in narrative: page 113

The right thing to say

1 In pairs. Student A look at page 144 and Student B at page 132.

2 a) 🔊72 Listen to five conversations. Where do you think the people are? What's the relationship between them? What's happening?

b) 🔊72 Listen again and fill in the gaps. Which questions are more polite? Which are less formal?

1 .... taking our picture?
2 .... I leave a bit early on Friday?
3 .... I use your phone?
4 .... borrow it?
5 .... answer the phone?

c) 🔊73 Listen again. Write the answers the five people give to questions 1–5 in Exercise 2b). Then read the Language Box.

Permission, requests

Permission and "yes" answers
A: Can / Could I use your phone? **OR** Is it all right if I borrow this book?
B: Yes / Yeah, sure / go ahead / no problem.
A: **Do you mind if I leave** a bit early? **OR Would you mind if I left** a bit early? (more polite)
B: **No**, not at all / that's fine / of course not.

Requests and "yes" answers
A: Can / Could you help me?
B: Yeah / Yes, sure / go ahead / no problem.
A: **Would you mind opening** the door?
B: **No**, not at all / that's fine / of course not.

Pronunciation: stress and intonation

3 a) 🔊73 Listen to questions 1–5 from Exercise 2b). Underline the stressed words / syllables.

b) 🔊73 Listen again and check your answers. Then read the Language Box and practise saying the sentences.

Intonation to sound polite

Is it OK if I use your phone?
Remember that if your intonation is flat you won't sound polite.

---

4 a) 🔊74 Listen to a conversation between two neighbours. What does the man want? What does the woman want? What's strange about the conversation?

b) Now read this conversation between two strangers in a café. What's strange about it?

MAN: Is anybody sitting in this chair?
WOMAN: No.
MAN: I want to sit here.
WOMAN: Then sit here. I can't stop you.
MAN: I'm going to smoke.
WOMAN: OK.
MAN: Is this your newspaper?
WOMAN: Yeah. So what?
MAN: Have you finished with it?
WOMAN: Yeah.
MAN: Give it to me.
WOMAN: OK.
MAN: I've got to post a letter. I'll be gone for a few minutes. Watch my bag.
WOMAN: I suppose I'll have to.

c) In pairs. Change the language to make the conversation in Exercise 4b) more polite, friendly and natural. Then take it in turns to be the man and the woman and practise the conversation.

Example: Excuse me. Do you mind if I . . . ?

①

Freddy on the Riviera

5 **a)** Look at picture 1. What do you think Freddy's doing? What do you think he's saying? What do you think he wants?

b) 🔊 75 Listen and check your suggestions.

c) In pairs. How does the woman feel? Does she want to give Freddy what he wants or does she want to refuse? Can you remember what she says? Try to fill in the gaps.

1 Well, ... I was just about to drink it.
2 I'm .... I don't eat meat.
3 .... , they're my husband's.

d) 🔊 75 Listen again and check your answers. Then read the Language Box.

> ### Refusing requests politely
>
> If we refuse someone's request we usually give a reason:
>
> | Well, | actually, | I was just about to drink it. |
> |---|---|---|
> | | I'm afraid | |
> | Sorry, | | |

Pronunciation: stress and intonation

6 **a)** 🔊 76 Listen to the sentences from Exercise 5c). Underline the stressed words / syllables.

b) 🔊 76 Listen again and check your answers. Then practise saying the sentences.

Sorry, I was just about to . . .

7 **a)** In groups of four. (Pair A and Pair B). Each pair choose one of the other pictures (2 or 3) and write a conversation where Freddy makes different requests and the other person refuses politely each time.

b) In your groups. Pairs take it in turns to act out your conversations. (Say who you are before you begin.) The others listen and tick the phrases in the Language Boxes in Exercises 2c) and 5d) that you use.

③

②

Taking off

Holidays and travel
Modal verbs of present and past deduction
Day to day English: *Was it worth it?*
Reading for pleasure 4: *Merry Christmas*
Do you remember? Units 10–12

Come fly with me

1 **a)** Look at the photos (1–5) of people on holiday. Which words / phrases in the Word Box can you match to the photos? (Some words / phrases can go with more than one photo.)

> breathtaking scenery   a holiday romance
> backpacking   exploring   off the beaten track
> all the comforts of home   seeing the sights
> getting away from it all   first-class travel
> souvenirs   on a budget   chilling out
> package holiday   it's for tourists   taking it easy
> travelling light   doing Europe

b) In pairs. Which photos show the kinds of holiday that you like? Why do you like them? Which kinds of holiday do you hate? Why? Which photos remind you of holidays or trips you've had?

12

THE ART OF TRAVEL

1 Why do so many backpackers travel alone? Is it because finding the right travelling companion is nearly impossible? In normal life people don't spend as much time together or have to make as many decisions (often based on **very** little information) as they do when they travel together. This
5 can cause real stress between people.

There would probably be fewer divorces if people travelled together for a few months before tying the knot because they would really get to know each other first! Just because someone is a good friend doesn't mean he or she will automatically make a good travelling companion. If you haven't
10 fully discussed goals, money and even personal habits before you go, then you might destroy your relationship on a backpacking trip from hell! As someone wrote: "Finding you're hopelessly, completely, absolutely incompatible in a tent at 8,000 feet when it's freezing outside is not a good situation."

15 *The three basic categories of travel problems are:*
1 One has an hourly itinerary, the other doesn't own a watch.
2 One prefers first class, the other prefers the back of a bus.
3 One's make-up case is heavier than the other's backpack.

Don't underestimate these differences!

20 If you find that problems are beginning between you, take it in turns to be the decision-maker. For example, first one of you chooses the itinerary, then the other – me chief today, you chief tomorrow. Give each other time to explore alone, perhaps meeting for dinner – or next week in Paris. But always have a fallback plan for meeting (for example, the same place but the next day) so
25 that if your original plan doesn't work you don't lose each other forever!

Both travellers must understand that a good travel relationship needs compromise from both sides. Constant whining is usually the result of one partner feeling he or she isn't being treated fairly. Listening is the most important and most abused skill between people and travelling is all
30 about people.

(adapted from *www.artoftravel.com*)

2 **a)** Read this extract from an Internet website quickly. What is it about? Choose the best answer (1–3).

1 Travelling alone compared with travelling with another person.
2 Advice about travelling alone.
3 Advice about travelling with another person.

b) Match the pictures (a–d) to the correct line / lines of the extract.

c) Find words / phrases in the extract for the definitions (1–7).

1 used as a starting point to develop a plan or idea (v, two words)
2 getting married (three words)
3 too different to be able to live together (adj)
4 think something is less important than it is (v)
5 alternative arrangement (two words)
6 agreement after negotiation (n)
7 complaining in an irritating voice (n)

Travel troubles

3 **a)** In groups. Look at the picture. Are the family having a good time? What possible problems can parents or children have on a family holiday?

b) 🔵🔵 77 Listen to two people talking about family holidays. What problems do they mention about parents? children? Which of your ideas do they mention?

c) In pairs. How can you avoid the family holiday from hell? Make two lists of dos and don'ts: one for parents and one for children.

Examples: PARENTS: Let your children help with the planning. Don't ask your son / daughter lots of questions every time he / she wants to go off somewhere.

CHILDREN: In the car, don't ask "Are we there yet?" more than twice. Suggest alternatives if there's something you don't like.

d) In groups of four. Use your lists to write an article for an Internet website called "The art of family travel". Use headings 1–4.

1 Introduction: typical problems on family holidays
2 Advice for parents
3 Advice for children
4 Conclusion

That can't be right!

4 **a)** 🔵🔵 78 Look at the photo of Sarah Carmichael. Where is she? Who's she talking to? Now listen to the conversation. What's the problem?

b) 🔵🔵 78 Listen again and fill in the gaps with *must, can't, could, might* or *may*. Who said what? Fill in the boxes with *R* (receptionist) or *S* (Sarah).

1 ☐ The room .... be occupied!
2 ☐ You .... be in another room.
3 ☐ I .... be on the list!
4 ☐ You .... be looking at the wrong day.
5 ☐ You .... be thinking of the Queen's Hotel.
6 ☐ The booking .... be under your husband's name.

c) Match sentences 1–6 in Exercise 4b) to sentence a), b) or c).

a) I think this is possible. = sentences 2, ... and ..... .
b) I'm sure this is true. = sentences ..... and ..... .
c) This is impossible. = sentence ..... .

d) Read the Language Box. Then fill in the gaps with *must, can't, could, might* and *may*.

Logical deduction: the present

We use *must, can't, might, could* and *may* + infinitive to make guesses (logical deductions) about the present.
- When we're sure that something is true, we use .... + infinitive:
  Steve failed the exam. He .... feel awful.
- When we think something is possibly true, we use .... , ... or .... + infinitive:
  I don't know where they are. They .... be upstairs.
- When we're sure that something is impossible or not true, we use .... + infinitive:
  You .... be hungry! You've just had lunch!
- To talk about continuous actions, we use *must, might, may, could, can't* + *be* + verb + *-ing*:
  He must **be** work**ing** late again. His light's still on.

Look!
- To say that something perhaps **isn't** true we use *might / may not* **NOT** ~~couldn't~~.
- We don't usually contract *might / may not* and we don't use *It can be . . .* or *It mustn't be . . .* to express logical deduction.
- *May* is more formal than *might* or *could*.

Pronunciation: stress in modal verbs of deduction

5 a) 🔊79 Listen to sentences 1–6 in Exercise 4b) again. Underline the stressed words / syllables.

b) 🔊79 Listen again and check your answers. Then read the Language Box and practise saying the sentences.

Logical deduction: stress

We stress
- the modal verb of deduction *must, can't, could, might, may*
- the important new information:
  A: She might be Italian.
  B: Yeah, she can't be Spanish because . . .
We don't normally stress repeated information:
  A: Is that Sarah?
  B: No, it can't be Sarah. She's in Scotland.

6 Write sentences that mean the same. Use *must, can't* or *might / could*.

Example: I'm sure he's French.
He <u>must be French.</u>

1 I'm sure they aren't watching TV.
  They . . .
2 I'm sure she's lying.
  She . . .
3 It's possible that Joan is ill.
  Joan . . .
4 I'm sure they aren't married.
  They . . .
5 It's possible that he isn't telling the truth.
  He . . .
6 It's impossible that this painting's by Picasso.
  This . . .
7 It's possible that it's closed.
  It . . .
8 I'm sure they're angry about the delays.
  They . . .

Don't leave home without it!

7 a) In pairs. When you go on holiday, what items do you always take with you? Make a list. Then compare your list with another pair.

Example: alarm clock, torch, penknife, . . .

b) In groups of four (Pair A and Pair B). Pair A look at page 143 and Pair B at page 145.

What went wrong?

8 a) Sarah Carmichael and the receptionist are talking about the possible causes of the problem. Before you listen, whose are the ideas in brackets? Fill in the boxes with *S* (Sarah) or *R* (receptionist).

1 ☐ (I'm sure you made a mistake.)
"You .... a mistake."

2 ☐ (It's possible that you wrote the reservation on a different day.)
"You .... the reservation on a different day."

3 ☐ (It's impossible that I made a mistake about the reservation.)
"I .... a mistake about the reservation."

4 ☐ (I'm sure I didn't dream it all!)
"I .... it all!"

5 ☐ (It's possible that the travel agent booked you into another hotel.)
"Your travel agent .... you into another hotel."

6 ☐ (Perhaps you cancelled your reservation.)
"You .... your reservation."

7 ☐ (I'm sure my company changed the hotel at the last minute.)
"My company .... the hotel at the last minute."

b) 👓 80 Listen and check your answers.

c) 👓 80 What exactly did Sarah and the receptionist say? Fill in the gaps in Exercise 8a). Then listen again and check your answers.

d) In pairs. Are Sarah and the receptionist talking about the past, present or future? Read the Language Box.

Logical deduction: the past

When we make guesses (logical deductions) about the past, we use:
- *must* + *have* + past participle when we're sure that something happened or was true in the past:
  Look at that dress! It **must have cost** her a fortune!
- *might, could, may* + *have* + past participle when we think something possibly happened or was possibly true:
  I don't know where they are. They **might / could / may have gone out**.
- *can't* + *have* + past participle when we're sure something didn't happen or was impossible:
  He **can't have taken** his car. The car keys are here on the table.

Look!
- *could* + *have* + past participle = *might* + *have* + past infinitive:
  They could've / might've left this morning.
  (= I'm **not sure**. **Perhaps** this happened.)
- *couldn't* + *have* + past participle = *can't* + *have* + past participle:
  He's so kind. He couldn't have / can't have murdered her!
  (= I'm **sure that he didn't** do it.)

---

9 Are the gapped sentences (1–6) about the present or the past? Fill in the gaps with the correct form of the verbs in brackets and *must, might / could* or *can't*.

Examples: She goes on holiday three times a year. She <u>must have</u> lots of money. (have)
A: We went on safari last year.
B: Oh, that <u>must have been</u> amazing! (be)

1 A: Where's Rod gone?
   B: I'm not sure, but he .... into the village. He said he wanted to have a look round. (go)

2 A: I'm afraid Mr Butler has checked out, madam.
   B: But he .... ! He's my husband! (check out)

3 A: What's all that noise coming from room 12?
   B: Oh, the drama group .... it again. (use)

4 Terry's skiing has really improved since last year! He .... lessons before the holiday. (have)

5 You'd better phone the hotel. It's the holiday season. There .... any rooms. (not be)

6 They .... brothers! They're completely different! (be)

Pronunciation: stress in modal verbs of deduction in the past

10 a) 👓 81 Listen to sentences 1–3 and underline the stressed words / syllables.

1 She might have stolen the money.
2 They can't have known about Paul.
3 He must have left during the night.

b) 👓 81 Listen again and check your answers. Then practise saying the sentences.

Travelling light

11 **a)** In pairs. Alex is backpacking round Europe. Look at his hotel room. Use the clues in the picture to make as many guesses as you can about him. What country is he in? Where is he now? What's he doing? Where has he been? What has he done?

Examples: He could be . . .
Someone might have . . .
He can't have . . .
He must be . . .

b) Make new pairs. Take it in turns to tell each other your guesses. Are the guesses logical or can you disprove them? Who's got the highest number of logical guesses?

Grammar reference
Modal verbs of present / past deduction: page 119

Havana highlights

1 a) 🎧 82 Kate has booked a holiday to Havana with her boyfriend. She's talking to a colleague, Guy, who's already been there. Does Guy have a positive or negative opinion of places 1–3?

1 Hotel Nacional
2 Havana Café
3 The crocodile farm

b) 🎧 82 Listen again. Guy uses some of these phrases. Which does he use about the crocodile farm? the Hotel Nacional? the Havana Café? Fill in the boxes with *F* (farm), *H* (hotel) or *C* (café).

1 ☐ I wouldn't bother.
2 ☐ It's a once in a lifetime experience.
3 ☐ It's a load of rubbish.
4 ☐ It's a waste of time / money / energy.
5 ☐ You've got to see / stay / visit . . .
6 ☐ It's / It isn't worth it.
7 ☐ It's a tourist trap.
8 ☐ It's worth every penny.
9 ☐ It's a (complete) rip-off.
10 ☐ It was a letdown.
11 ☐ It's worth a visit.
12 ☐ It's / It isn't worth seeing / going to . . .

c) Which phrases in Exercise 1b) are positive? Which are negative?

2 a) 🎧 83 Derek has joined Kate and Guy. Listen to their conversation. What are they talking about? Does Derek agree with Guy?

b) 🎧 83 Listen again and fill in the gaps. Which word is stressed the most in the gapped sentences? Then read the Language Box.

1 **GUY:** The Havana Café is a complete rip-off. It's awful.
DEREK: The real Havana Café? In Cuba? Oh, it ....

2 **DEREK:** I think it's the most fantastic place I've ever been.
GUY: Oh, come on! It ....

3 **DEREK:** And all the women are so beautiful.
GUY: Oh, they ....

Contrasting opinions

When someone gives a strong opinion with a strong adjective, we can use *isn't / aren't + that + a less extreme form of the same adjective to show our different opinion. We stress *that* for emphasis:
A: It's **terrible**. **B:** Oh, it **isn't that bad**.
A: It was **boiling** every day. **B:** Oh, It **wasn't that hot**.

Look!

• In this situation, *that* means *not as* (adjective) *as you're saying*:
It's not that bad. (It's not as bad as you're saying.)

c) In pairs. Practise exchanges 1–3 in Exercise 2b).

3 a) In pairs. You've been on holiday together. One of you loved it. The other hated it. Think about the food, the places you visited / stayed in, the people you met, the weather, the activities, etc. Prepare to tell another pair of students about your holiday.

b) In groups of four. Pairs take it in turns to ask about and describe your holidays.

Example: PAIR A STUDENT 1: We've just come back from Marrakech.
PAIR B STUDENT 1: What did you think of it?
PAIR A STUDENT 2: Oh, you'd love it. The markets are amazing.
PAIR A STUDENT 1: Oh, they weren't that good. I thought they were a rip-off.
PAIR B STUDENT 2: Well, what about . . . ?

Reading for pleasure

④ Merry Christmas

1 This story is set in the office of a group of volunteers. The volunteers receive phone calls from people needing desperately to talk to someone who will listen to them without judging them in any way. What kind of people do you think might use this service?

2 🎧 84 Read and listen to the first part of the story. Then answer the questions.

1 On which day does the story take place? Where?
2 Why was the woman feeling scared?
3 What rule did she follow each time the phone rang?
4 Why do you think the caller had such difficulty in starting a conversation?

3 Now read the whole story. It starts on page 25 of *Heat wave and other stories*. Think about these questions while you read.

1 Why didn't the woman use her own name?
2 Why had Joss not eaten dinner?
3 How long had Joss been in the city?
4 How old was Joss?
5 Where was Joss staying?
6 How did the woman find out that Joss was a girl?
7 Why did Joss get angry?
8 Who did Joss say she loves?
9 Who did Joss mention that made the woman feel she was beginning to get through to Joss?
10 In what way did the woman break the rules?
11 Why had Joss run away?
12 Why did Joss ring back?

She stood at the window looking out over the street. The stores were closed, people had finished their last-minute Christmas shopping and were hurrying home. In a few hours the same people would probably be out again, showered and changed and ready to celebrate Christmas Eve in typical Australian fashion – in a bar or restaurant, or with barbecues at home by the pool, plenty of cold beer. Everyone would soon be having a good time.

"Except me," she thought to herself. "I'm here, waiting for the phone to ring. Hoping that it won't because I'm scared. I've never been on duty alone. I was mad to volunteer for this evening . . ."

The telephone rang. She let it ring four times, according to the rules. Then she picked it up.

"Hotline, may I help you?"

There was a moment's hesitation, then the line went dead.

She slowly replaced the receiver and walked back to the window. At the end of the street she could see the Harbour Bridge, the sea, a yacht . . .

The phone rang again. Again she counted four rings, then picked it up.

"Hotline, may I help you?"

Silence. She waited and then said softly, "Please let me help you."

1 Disgrace!

a) In groups of three. Judy Spike has a television show called *Disgrace* where she interviews well-known people who've been involved in a scandal. One of you is Judy Spike and the other two are a disgraced person and his / her wife / husband. Think about these questions and prepare for the interview.

1 Is the disgraced person a politician? a famous doctor? an actor? a sportsperson? the chief of police? a singer? a judge?
2 Did he / she commit a crime? have an affair? lie to the public? sell secrets to other countries?
3 Does the husband / wife forgive him / her? Is he / she here to support or to criticise? Did he / she help to commit the crime? Or did he / she tell the police?
4 What questions does Judy ask? (Use negative questions, too.)

Examples: But why did you take the money if you knew that . . . ?
Weren't you told by the police that . . . ?
Didn't you realise that so much arsenic would kill him?
Didn't you think it was strange when your wife / husband . . . ?

b) Practise your interview and then act it out for the class. The class decides if the disgraced people were innocent victims, careless or really guilty!

2 *You could be telling the truth . . .*

a) In groups. Write 6–10 sentences about the students in your group on one piece of paper. Write information that is new, interesting or surprising about your lives now and in the past. Half the sentences must be true and half must be false.

Examples: 1 Sylvie has read every Shakespeare play.
2 Marc is studying Russian.
3 Tarik went to Africa last year.
4 Marta was on TV when she was five years old.
5 Paolo owns three companies.

b) Swap sentences with another group. Decide if you think the sentences you've received might be true, can't be true, must be a lie, etc. and why.

c) Join together with the other group. Take it in turns to read the other group's sentences out and say whether you think they're true or false and why. The other group says whether you're right or wrong.

Example: B: Sentence 1 can't be true. Sylvie can't have read every Shakespeare play.
A: Why not?
B: There are too many!
A: Well, you're wrong. It's true. She has!

3 A letter to the editor

Read this letter to a local newspaper about Billy Thompson's release from prison. Fill in the gaps with the correct form of the verb in brackets or underline the correct word / phrase.

Dear Sir,

I never <u>write</u> (write) to newspapers but I feel I (<u>must</u> / might) write to you about the Billy Thompson case. He ....(1) (sentence) to one year for his crime and I can't believe that he ....(2) (release) from prison after only three months!

How can we teach our children that ....(3) (commit) crimes is wrong if the criminals ....(4) (give) sentences that are so short?

There (can / might)(5) be a lot of kids today who think that crime is a great career. It's easy money and if you ....(6) (arrest), you'll be free five minutes later.

Your article about the case filled (a whole / all)(7) page. The writer gave us (a whole / all)(8) the information about the crime, including details from a witness who ....(9) (interview) at the (place / scene)(10) of the crime. But the public seem to think Thompson's early release is great news! People (can't / mustn't)(11) be serious if they think this is right! One journalist wrote that (every / all)(12) young person steals from a shop at some time in their life, but that's not the point!

..................(13) (steal) from shops or banks or anywhere is (illegal / legal)(14) of course, but it's also (against / out of)(15) the rules of our society. You (don't have to / can't)(16) do whatever you feel like doing. It's immoral. Besides, you'll get ....(17) (arrest) and put in prison! But even prison's not really a punishment these days. Apparently, you can just sit around taking (it / them)(18) easy, playing video games – it's like a hotel with all the (comforts / things)(19) of home. Thompson must ....(20) (enjoy) his short stay there. No wonder everyone is (fiddling / cheating)(21) their taxes and breaking the law!

I don't care if Billy Thompson apologised for ....(22) (behave) so badly and promised ....(23) (be) a better person in the future. I refuse to accept his apology! This young man (must / can't)(24) have realised he was breaking the law when he did it. I'm sure his parents told him not to steal – I'm sure they warned him ....(25) (stay) out of trouble.

In fact I know they did – because I'm his father.

Yours sincerely

Tom Thompson

Look at the Word lists for Units 10–12 on pages 128–129 and check that you know all the new words.

Puzzle 4 (Units 10–12): page 121

Wavelength page

Grammar reference

The Present

Present Simple (Unit 2)

Form

Positive and negative sentences

I / You / We / They	work. / don't work.
He / She / It	works. / doesn't work.

Questions and short answers
- **Do** you work? Yes, I **do**. / No, I **don't**.
  Does she work? Yes, she **does**. / No, she **doesn't**.

Spelling: *he, she, it*
- Add -*s* to positive verbs: She live**s** in Paris.

BUT
- Add -*es* to verbs ending in -*o*, -*s*, -*sh*, -*ch*, -*x* and -*z*: go → goes, miss → misses, wash → washes, watch → watches, box → boxes, buzz → buzzes.
- Change -*y* to -*i* and add -*es* to verbs ending in a consonant + -*y*: study → studies, try → tries.

Use

General habits, routines, permanent situations
- For describing permanent situations:
  Sarah works for a law firm.
- For describing general habits and routines, often with frequency expressions and adverbs of frequency (*always, often, usually*, etc.):
  He goes to the gym **twice a week**.
  He **hardly ever** sees his parents.
  She's **always** in a bad mood.

Present Continuous (Units 2 and 9)

Form

Positive and negative sentences

I	'm / 'm not	
You / We / They	're / aren't	working.
He / She / It	's / isn't	

Questions and short answers
- **Are** you **studying**? Yes, I **am**. / No, I**'m not**.
  Is he **studying**? Yes, he **is**. / No, he **isn't**.

Spelling
- Add -*ing* to most verbs: study → studying, work → working.

BUT
- Short verbs (all one-syllable and some two-syllable verbs) ending in a vowel + a consonant, double the consonant: get → getting, travel → travelling. Don't double the consonant when the final consonant is -*y*, -*w* or -*x*: stay → staying, show → showing, mix → mixing or when there are two vowels before the final consonant: look → looking, read → reading.
  Verbs ending in -*e*, take off the -*e*: live → living.

Use

An activity happening now
- For things that are happening now:
  Listen! The couple upstairs are arguing again.

An activity happening around now
- For temporary activities that are happening around now (not necessarily at the moment of speaking):
  He's got exams soon so he's studying really hard at the moment.

Present Continuous or Present Simple?
- Amy **works** (her permanent job) for a large toy manufacturer. It's near Christmas now, so **she's working** (this is temporary) twelve hours a day.

Present Continuous with *always*
- We can use *always* with the Present Continuous to talk about things which happen very often and irritate us:
  My sister's **always** borrowing money from me!
- The opposite is *never* + Present Simple:
  You never listen to me. **NOT** ~~You're never listening~~ to me.

State verbs (Unit 2)

Form

- State verbs describe states (not activities) and are **NOT** usually used in Continuous tenses. There are three main groups of state verbs:
  Emotions and feelings: hate, love, like, want, hope, wish.
  Thinking and opinion: think, know, agree, mean, believe, understand, suppose, remember, forget, prefer.
  Having and being: have, be, come (from), own, belong, need, seem, appear, depend on.

Use

- We can use some state verbs in both Continuous and Simple tenses, but with a change in meaning:
  I **think** he's really attractive. (= opinion)
  Are you **thinking** about your holiday? (= mental activity)
  She **has** a lot of friends. (= possession)
  He**'s having** breakfast. Can he phone you back? (= activity)

The Past

Past Simple (Units 1 and 2)

Form

Positive and negative sentences

regular verbs	He	rented / didn't rent	a flat.
irregular verbs	They	bought / didn't buy	

- For Past Simple forms of irregular verbs see page 159.

Questions and short answers
- **Did** he buy it? Yes, he **did**. / No, he **didn't**.

Regular verbs: spelling
- Add -ed to most verbs: listen → listened, walk → walked.

BUT
- Add -d to verbs ending in -e: arrive → arrived, live → lived.
- With verbs ending in a consonant + -y, change -y to -i and add -ed: try → tried, worry → worried.
- Short verbs (all one-syllable and some two-syllable verbs) ending in a vowel + a consonant, double the consonant: stop → stopped, travel → travelled. Don't double the final consonant when the final consonant is -y, -w or -x: stay → stayed, show → showed, mix → mixed or when there are two vowels before the final consonant: look → looked, load → loaded.

Use

For single events that happened in the past
- They first met at a friend's party.

For past states
- My childhood was very happy.

For things that happened regularly in the past (past habits)
- She had lunch at the same café every day when she lived in Bristol.

When one action closely follows another action in the past
- We often use *when* to show which action happened first: When he got to the office, he phoned his wife.

Used to + infinitive (Unit 1)

Form

Positive and negative sentences

I / You / He	used to / didn't use to	live in France.

Questions and short answers
- **Did** he **use** to live in France? Yes, he **did**. / No, he **didn't**.

Use

Past habits and states that are finished
- For things that happened regularly / were true in the past in the past but don't happen / aren't true anymore: She used to go to yoga classes twice a week. I used to be good at maths.

With *anymore* and *any longer*
- We use *used to* + *anymore* and *any longer* to say that a situation has changed: I used to get nervous before exams but **not anymore / I don't anymore**. I used to be quite shy but **not any longer / I'm not any longer**.

Past Simple NOT *used to / didn't use to* + infinitive
- We don't use *used to* + infinitive to talk about single events, how many times something happened in the past or the duration of something in the past: He graduated three years ago. I broke my leg three times when I was a child. I studied French for two years.

Look!
- We can say how often something used to happen: I used to go to the gym twice a week.
- We use the Present Simple, not *used to*, to talk about present habits and states. He goes to yoga classes.

Would + infinitive (Unit 1)

Form / Use

Past habits
- We use *would* + infinitive for past habits or series of events to avoid repeating *used to* again and again: We **used to go** to the beach every summer when I was young. We'**d get up** really early and we'**d pack**. Then we'**d say** goodbye to the neighbours and . . .

***Used to* + infinitive NOT *would* + infinitive**
- We don't usually use *would* for states: I used to be afraid of the dark. **NOT** I'd be afraid of the dark.
- We don't usually use *would* in questions: **Did you use to** fight a lot with your brother when you were young?

Past Continuous (Unit 2)

Form

Positive and negative sentences

He	was / wasn't	travelling alone.
They	were / weren't	

Questions and short answers

- **Were** you watching TV? Yes, we **were**. / No, we **weren't**.
  Was he working? Yes, he **was**. / No, he **wasn't**.

Use

Activity in progress at a particular time in the past

- He saw a woman in the car. She **was talking** on her mobile.

An activity in progress in the past when another short activity happened

- For an activity which was in progress when another shorter single action (Past Simple) happened. Sometimes the shorter action interrupts the activity:
  I was walking along the street **when** I tripped over some rubbish.

When and _while_

- We use _when_ and _while_ to join two parts of a sentence. We can use _when_ with the Past Simple or the Past Continuous. We use _while_ with longer actions (usually the Past Continuous):
  Someone stole my wallet **while** I was looking out of the window.

Present Perfect Simple (Unit 1)

Form

Positive and negative sentences

		PAST PARTICIPLE
I / You / We / They	've / haven't	travelled much.
He / She / It	's / hasn't	

- For past participles of irregular verbs see page 159.

Questions and short answers

- **Have** you travelled much? Yes, I **have**. / No, I **haven't**.
  Has he travelled a lot? Yes, he **has**. / No, he **hasn't**.

Use

General past experiences

- For past experiences (finished actions or events in the past), but we don't say when these things happened:
  I've been to Canada.

With _ever_ and _never_

- With _ever_ (= in your whole life) and _never_ (= not in your whole life):
  Have you **ever** seen a total eclipse of the sun?
  I've **never** been to Canada.

Present result of an action

- When we're interested in the present result of an action:
  She's had a baby. (She's a mother now.)
  They've gone. (They aren't here now.)

Habits and states that began in the past and continue now

- For habits and states that began in the past and still continue / are still true in the present we use the Present Perfect Simple **NOT** the Present Simple:
  I've known him for ten years. (I still know him) **NOT** I know him for ten years.

With _for_ and _since_

- We use _for_ with a period of time and _since_ with a point in time (when the period began):
  I've known him **for** ten years.
  I've lived here **since** 1998.

Been or _gone_?

- She's **been** to Cuba. (She went and came back. She's here now.)
  She's **gone** to Cuba. (She's in Cuba now.)

Present Perfect Simple or Past Simple?

- We use the Past Simple **NOT** the Present Perfect Simple if we say when a past experience happened (_yesterday, last month, in 1997_) or give more details about the experience (_where? how? why? who? what?_):
  A: Have you ever been to Cuba?
  B: Yes, I have. I went with a friend a couple of years ago.
  A: Really? Where did you stay?
- We use the Past Simple **NOT** the Present Perfect Simple when the period of time we're talking about is now finished:
  I've worked there for two years. (And I still work there now.)
  I worked there for two years. (I don't work there anymore.)

Look!

- We can't use the Present Perfect Simple with finished times (_yesterday, last month, in 1997_) but we can use it with unfinished times (_today, this week, this year_):
  My car's broken down twice this week!

Present Perfect Continuous (Unit 5)

Form

Positive and negative sentences

I / You / We / They	've / haven't	
He / She / It	's / hasn't	been working since 7:00 a.m.

Questions and short answers
- **Have** you been working? Yes, I **have**. No, I **haven't**.
  Has he been working? Yes, he **has**. / No, he **hasn't**.

Use

An activity that began in the past and is still continuing
- She's been working on her novel for ten years. (She's still writing it.)

A recent activity that has produced present results
- For a recent activity which has produced present results you can see, hear, etc. The activity might have finished very recently or might still be continuing:
  Look at this mess! What have you been doing?
  A: Why are you crying? B: I've been arguing with my boyfriend.

Present Perfect Simple or Present Perfect Continuous?
- We use the Present Perfect Continuous to focus on the activity. We often use *How long?*:
  How long have you been working on your novel?
- We use the Present Perfect Simple to focus on completed things. We often use *How much / many?*:
  How many chapters have you written?

Look!
- Compare these questions and sentences:
  What have you been doing? (I want to know about the activity.)
  What have you done? (I want to know about the results.)
  She's been writing a novel. (The novel isn't finished.)
  She's written a novel. (The novel is finished.)

Past Perfect Simple (Unit 7)

Form

Positive and negative sentences

		PAST PARTICIPLE	
I / You / We / They / He / She / It	had / hadn't	seen	the film.

Questions and short answers
- **Had** you seen the film before? Yes, I **had**. / No, I **hadn't**.

Use

An activity that happened before another activity in the past
- We use the Past Perfect Simple to look back to a time in the past and describe an action which happened or didn't happen before that time:
  When I finally got to the restaurant, Sandra had left. (Sandra left before I arrived at the restaurant.)
  I felt very nervous because I'd never been hang gliding. (It was my first time hang gliding.)

Past Simple or Past Perfect Simple?
- When the police arrived, the burglar **escaped**. (The police arrived and then the burglar escaped.)
  When the police arrived, the burglar **had escaped**. (The burglar escaped and then the police arrived.)

Tenses in narrative

Use

Past Simple and Past Continuous (Unit 2)
- When telling a story, we use the Past Continuous to describe the longer background activity (to add interest and give background information) and we use the Past Simple to give the single events:
  I **was feeling** lonely so I **went** out into the street. People **were buying** things from street-sellers. A man **looked** at me and . . .

Past Perfect Simple (Unit 7)
- We use the Past Perfect Simple to show that an event happened before another event in the story. This makes the order of events clear and gives important background information:
  He was frightened because someone **had tried** to kill him.
  (He was frightened **at that time** because someone tried to kill him **before that time**.)

Present and future tenses (Unit 11)
- We often speak in "present time" using present and future tenses to increase the drama when we describe the story of a book / film or tell jokes:
  It's about this writer who **lives** alone on an island. One day he**'s walking** along the beach. We know he**'s going to** find . . .

The Future

- We express ideas about the future (predictions, plans, etc.) in a number of different ways. The three most common are *going to*, the Present Continuous and *will*:
  I'm going to travel when I finish university.
  I'm playing tennis with Jake tomorrow afternoon.
  I think **I'll stay** in tonight. I'm a bit tired.

Form

Going to + infinitive (Units 3 and 8)

Positive and negative sentences

I'm / I'm not	
You're / You aren't	going to have a holiday this year.
She's / She isn't	

Questions and short answers

- **Is** he going to have a holiday? Yes, he **is**. / No, he **isn't**.
  Are they going to have a party? Yes, they **are**. / No, they **aren't**.

Present Continuous (Unit 3 Day to day English)

- See page 110 for form.

Will + infinitive (Unit 8)

Positive and negative sentences

I / You / She	'll (will) / won't (will not)	see him tomorrow.

Questions and short answers

- **Will** they see him tomorrow? Yes, they **will**. / No, they **won't**.

The Future: plans, arrangements, decisions

Use

Going to + infinitive

- We use *going to* + infinitive to talk about our future plans and intentions. These are things we've thought about before:
  I'm going to take James to a restaurant for his birthday. (I've thought about this and I've decided to do it.)
  What are you going to do when the course finishes? (Have you made any plans?)
- We often use the Present Continuous NOT *going to* with the verbs *go* and *come*:
  Is she **coming** to the party? NOT USUALLY Is she ~~going to come~~ to the party?

Present Continuous

- We use the Present Continuous to talk about definite future arrangements:
  I'm having lunch with David tomorrow. (David and I have arranged this.)
  What are you doing this weekend? (What plans or arrangements have you made?)

- Sometimes there is very little difference between *going to* and the Present Continuous. We usually use the Present Continuous when we've made definite arrangements and we give details of times, dates, etc.:
  We're going to get married. (We've decided to do this but haven't decided exactly when, where, how, yet.)
  We're getting married. (We've decided on the date, booked the church, sent the invitations.)

Will + infinitive

- We use *will* + infinitive to talk about decisions we make at the moment of speaking. We haven't thought about these things before. We often use *maybe, perhaps, probably, I think, I don't think* with *will* for this meaning:
  A: What are you doing this weekend?
  B: I'm not sure. **Maybe I'll** see a film.
  (Looking at the menu.) **I think I'll** have an omelette.
  It's getting late. **I don't think I'll** wait any longer.
  NOT ~~I think I won't~~ wait any longer.

The Future: prediction

Use

Will + infinitive

- We use *will* + infinitive to make predictions about the future. These are our opinions based on what we know generally about a person, situation, etc.:
  They'll find a cure for cancer one day. (Medical research is advancing all the time. So I'm sure that a cure for cancer is possible in the future.)
  Don't ask him to the party. He won't come. (I know him. He's very shy and he hates parties.)
- We use *probably, definitely, I'm sure, I doubt if*, etc. with *will* to show degrees of certainty:
  Tigers **will definitely / I'm sure** tigers **will** become extinct.
  They**'ll probably / They may well** become extinct.

They **probably won't / I doubt if they'll** become extinct.
They **definitely won't / I'm sure they won't** become extinct.

Going to + infinitive

- We use *going to* + infinitive when we make a prediction based on present evidence / information (things that we read, see, hear, etc. now):
  Present evidence: The concert starts at 8 p.m. and it takes an hour to drive there. It's 7:30 p.m. now!
  Prediction: We're **going to be** late.

Will or *going to*?

- He'll fall. (I know him. He's very clumsy.)
  He's going to fall! (I'm looking at him now. He's dancing on a wall and I can see he's having problems with his balance.)

Relative clauses

Defining relative clauses (Unit 3)

Form / Use

- We use defining relative clauses to identify which person, thing or place we're talking about:
  A: I saw that man again yesterday.
  B: Which man?
  A: The man **who** spoke to you on the bus last week.
- We use *who* (or *that*) for people and *which* (or *that*) for things / places. In conversation we usually use *that* instead of *which / who*:
  I think this is the place **which / that** Simon was talking about.
  I need to talk to the woman **who / that** booked my flight.
- We can also use *where* for places. If we use *where*, we don't use prepositions:
  This is the house **where I lived** as a child. **OR** This is the house **which I lived in** as a child. **NOT** where I lived ~~in~~
- We use *whose* for possessives (*her, his, their,* etc.):
  That's the woman **whose** car was stolen. (That's the woman. **Her** car was stolen.)
- When *who / which / that* is the object of the clause, we can leave it out. We don't leave out *where* or *whose*:
  I think this is the place (which) Simon was talking about.
  I think this is the place where I met Simon.

Non-defining relative clauses (Unit 3)

Form / Use

- We use non-defining relative clauses to give extra information about a person or thing. We use commas to separate this clause from the main sentence:
  Mike's car, which he bought two months ago, has broken down again.
  Main sentence: Mike's car has broken down again.
  Extra information: He bought it two months ago.
- We can't use *that* in non-defining relative clauses:
  She told her boss, who hadn't heard anything about it.
  NOT She told her boss, ~~that~~ hadn't heard anything about it.

Reported speech

Reported sentences (Unit 7)

Form / Use

- We use *say* and *tell* in Reported sentences. We use an indirect object (*me*, etc.) after *tell*, **NOT** after *say*:
  He told **me** he was leaving the next day.
  He said he was leaving the next day.
- When we report what someone says, we move the main verb back one tense:

DIRECT SPEECH	REPORTED SPEECH
"I'm getting married."	He said he **was getting** married.
"I **haven't seen** her."	He said she **hadn't seen** her.
"She **lied** to me."	He told me she'**d** (she **had**) **lied** to him.

- Some modal verbs change: can → could, will → would, must → had to:

"I **can't** swim."	He told them he **couldn't** swim.

  Some modal verbs don't change: might, should, could:

"He **might** stay at home."	She said he **might** stay at home.

- Pronouns and possessive adjectives / pronouns change:

"I'm leaving."	He said **he** was leaving.
"It's **mine**."	He said it was **his**.

- Time and place references change: here → there, this → that, now → then, yesterday → the day before, today → that day, next week → the following week, last week → the previous week / the week before.

"I'm seeing her **tomorrow**."	He said he was seeing her **the next day**.
"She left three days **ago**."	He said she'd left three days **before**.

Look!
- We can use *that* after reporting verbs but we often leave *that* out in conversation:
  He told me (that) he was leaving on Monday.

Reported questions (Unit 7)

Form / Use

- We use *ask* in Reported questions.
- The word order in Reported questions is the same as for Reported sentences.
- We don't use the auxiliary *do / does* and there is no question mark.
- We can include the object but we don't have to:

DIRECT SPEECH	REPORTED SPEECH
"What **do you do**?"	She asked (me) **what I did**.
"Where **are you staying**?"	He asked (me) where **I was staying**.

- We use *if* or *whether* with *Yes / No* questions:

"**Do you have** a visa?"	She asked (me) **if / whether I had a visa**.

Reporting verbs (Unit 11)

- See page 97 for form.

Conditional sentences: *If . . .*

First Conditional (Unit 3)

Form

- We use the Present Simple in the *if* part of the sentence and *'ll (will) / won't (will not)* or *might / might not* + infinitive in the other part:
  If we don't buy the car, we'll have more money for our holiday.
  He might not find another job if he leaves this one.
  If your boss gives you a bonus this year, what will you do with the money?
- Both parts of the sentence can be positive or negative and the *if* part can come first or last in the sentence.
- We can use *unless* + a positive verb instead of *if* + negative verb. *Unless* means *if not*:
  My Mum will worry **if** I **don't go** / **unless** I **go** home soon.

Use

- We use the First Conditional for possible future situations and possible future results:
  If you don't invite her, she'll be / she might be upset.
- The First Conditional has several uses:
  Predictions: I'll be late for the party unless I leave now.
  Offers: I'll finish the report if you're too busy.
  Warnings: You'll have a heart attack if you don't take more exercise.
  Threats: I won't speak to you again if you don't apologise.
  Negotiations: If you buy the tickets, I'll pay for the drinks.

Second Conditional (Unit 6)

Form

- We use the Past Simple in the *if* part of the sentence and *would / wouldn't, could / couldn't, might / might not* + infinitive in the other part of the sentence:
  If I were rich, I **could** live anywhere I wanted. (= it would be possible to live anywhere I wanted.)
  If I had as many problems as her, I **might** get depressed. (= perhaps I'd (would) get depressed.)
  What **would** you do if you lost your job?
  If you had to choose between your best friend and your boyfriend, who **would** you choose?
- With the verb *be* we usually use *were / weren't* with all subjects, but we sometimes use *was / wasn't* with *he / she / it*, especially in conversation.

Use

- We use the Second Conditional to talk about situations in the present / future that are unlikely to happen (probably won't happen) or are unreal / impossible:
  If I had lots of money, I'd get married in a Scottish castle. (But I don't have lots of money and I'll probably never have lots of money.)
  If I were tall, I could be a model. (But I'm not tall.)

First Conditional or Second Conditional?

- If he works hard, he'll pass his exam. (I feel it's possible for him to pass, but he'll have to work hard.)
  If he worked hard, he'd pass his exam. (He doesn't work hard, so in my opinion, he's not going to pass.)

Wish + Past Simple (Unit 6)

- We use *wish* + Past Simple when we would really like a present situation or reality to be different, but this is improbable / impossible:
  I wish **my hair weren't** so curly. (But unfortunately, it is.)
  If only **I could** work flexible hours. (But unfortunately, I can't.)

Look!

- Compare these sentences:
  If I **had** more time, I **could see** my friends more often.
  I wish I **had** more time. (Because then I could see my friends more often.)
  I wish I **could see** my friends more often.

Third Conditional (Unit 8)

Form / Use

- We use the Third Conditional when we imagine different possible past situations and their results. We often use it to express regret, relief or blame.
- We use *if* + Past Perfect Simple for the imagined different past situation and *would / wouldn't, might / might not* + *have* + past participle for the imagined result:

IMAGINED PAST SITUATION	IMAGINED PAST RESULT
If I **hadn't had** a spare tyre, (Reality: I had a spare tyre.	I **would have** been late! I wasn't late. = relief)
If I **hadn't had** an affair, (Reality: I had an affair.	my husband **might not have** left me. My husband left me. = regret)
If you **hadn't forgotten** the map, (Reality: You forgot the map.	we **wouldn't have** got lost. We got lost. = blame)

Wish / If only + Past Perfect Simple (Unit 9)

Form / Use

- We use *wish / if only* + Past Perfect Simple (*had / hadn't* + past participle) to express criticism, regret and blame about past events and situations:
  I wish I'd listened to Nigel and not you! (But unfortunately I listened to you, so now I've got a problem.)
  If only I hadn't shouted at the boss. (But unfortunately I shouted at the boss, so I lost my job.)

Look!
- Compare these sentences:
  If only / I wish **I'd driven** more carefully.
  If **I'd driven** more carefully, I wouldn't have had the accident.

The Passive

The Passive (Unit 10)

Form

- We form the Passive with the correct tense of the verb *be* + past participle. We change the verb *be* to make tenses, negatives and questions.

Positive and negative sentences

		BE	PAST PARTICIPLE	
PRESENT SIMPLE	Many people	are		
PRESENT CONTINUOUS	John	isn't being		
PAST SIMPLE	She	was		
PAST CONTINUOUS	They	were being	questioned	by the police.
PRESENT PERFECT SIMPLE	I	have been		
INFINITIVE	You need to	be		
	They must			
VERB + *-ING*	I hate	being		

Use

- When the object or the action is more important than the subject (the person or thing that does the action):
  All the e-mails have been deleted.
- When the subject is obvious:
  The president was elected for a second term. (Obviously by the voters.)
- When we don't know the subject:
  Jenny was mugged twice last year.
- If we mention who or what did the action, we use the preposition *by*:
  The prize was won by a Swedish scientist.
- The Passive is more common in formal written texts (newspapers, reports, notices, etc.):
  Three people were arrested yesterday.
  Changes to the design are being made.
  Tickets must be shown at the barrier.

The Passive with *get* (Unit 10)

Form

- The verb *get* replaces *be*. We change the verb get to make tenses, negatives and questions:
  Did Steve **get** arrested?

Use

- We use the Passive with *get* in informal spoken and written English (conversations, informal letters, etc.) especially to show that something happened quickly, unexpectedly or by accident:
  I was crossing the road when I **got** hit by a car.

Look!
- We don't use the Passive with *get* for states:
  This book is loved by children. **NOT** This book gets loved by children.
- We don't usually use the Passive with *get* in the Present Perfect Simple:
  John's been attacked! **NOT** John's get attacked!

The Passive with indirect objects (Unit 10)

Use

- We use an indirect object with the Passive with verbs like *tell, speak to, give, send, inform, offer, teach (a subject), ask (a question)* to emphasise the receiver of the thing, information, gift, etc.:
  The students were asked some difficult questions.
  I was taught French when I was five years old.

Modal verbs

Form

- Modal verbs never change. They don't have an -s for *he / she / it* in the present:
  He might finish by Friday. **NOT** ~~He mights~~ finish by Friday.
- They don't have the auxiliary *do / did* in negatives, questions or short answers:
  Can you drive? **NOT** ~~Do you can~~ drive?
  I can't drive. **NOT** ~~I don't can~~ drive.
- We never use *to* after modal verbs except with *have* and *ought*:
  You should see a doctor. **NOT** You should ~~to~~ see a doctor.
  You *ought to* apologise to her.
  You *have to* wear smart clothes in this office.

- Modal verbs don't usually have past forms:
  "You **must** start exercising." → I **had to** start exercising.
- We also use *have* + past participle with modal verbs to refer to the past:
  I shouldn't have listened to you.
  He must have gone out.

Ability (Unit 4): *Can / can't, could / couldn't / was able to*

Use

Present ability: *can / can't*
- We use *can* and *can't* for present ability:
  A: Can you read Arabic? **B:** No, I **can't**, but I can speak it.

Past ability: *could / couldn't / was able to*
- When we talk about general past ability we use *could* + infinitive:
  I **could swim** very well when I was younger.
- To talk about success on one occasion we use *was able to* + infinitive:
  I was hit by a car but I wasn't badly hurt so I **was able to** walk to the hospital.

- We usually use *couldn't* in negative sentences:
  I **couldn't ride a bike** until I was twenty years old.
  I didn't have any money so I **couldn't go** with them.

Look!
- To talk about one result after difficulty or effort we use *managed to* + infinitive or *succeeded in* + verb + *-ing* (slightly more formal):
  After years of trying I finally **managed to pass / succeeded in passing** the exam.

Obligation, permission and choice (Unit 10): *must / mustn't, can / can't, have to / don't have to*

Form

Must / mustn't, can / can't
- These are modal verbs.

Have to: positive and negative sentences
- They **have to** wear suits.
  He **doesn't have to** wear a suit.

Have to: questions and short answers
- **Do** they **have to** wear suits? Yes, they **do**.
  Does she **have to** wear a suit? No, she **doesn't**.

Use

Obligation
- We use *must* in formal / written rules:
  All electronic devices **must** be turned off.
- We can use *must* or *have to* for direct orders from the speaker and for self-obligation:
  You **must** do more exercise. (Doctor to patient.)
  I **have to** stop smoking! (My order to myself.)
- We usually use *have to* to talk about rules, laws and responsibilities:
  You **have to** drive on the left in the UK. (It's the law.)
  We **have to** be home by 11:00 p.m. (It's the rule.)
  You **have to** be good at dealing with people in this job. (It's a necessary skill for the job.)
  I **have to** visit my grandmother. (She asked me to.)

No obligation
- We use *don't have to* when there's no obligation or necessity — you have a choice:
  You **don't have to** get a visa for that country.

Prohibition
- We use *can't* when a law, rule or a person says no:
  You **can't** smoke in here. (It's a no-smoking area.)
- We use *mustn't* for direct orders from the speaker.
  You **mustn't** take your sister's toys without asking. (Parent to child.)

Permission
- We use *can* when a law or rule allows it or when we give someone permission to do something:
  I **can** buy alcohol. (I'm over eighteen, so it's legal.)
  I **can** stay out as late as I like. (My parents say it's OK.)

Should / shouldn't have done (Unit 9)

Form / Use

- We use *should / shouldn't + have +* past participle to express criticism, regret and blame about the past:
  You should've brought a map!
  We shouldn't have come here.

- We use *never* to make negative ideas stronger:
  We should never have come here.

Modal verbs of present deduction (Unit 12)

Form

I / You / We / They / He / She / It	must / might / could / may / can't	know her.

Questions

- We usually use *Do you think* or modal verbs of deduction in questions.
  Could it be a forgery?
  Where do you think she might be?
  Do you think they're married?
  What do you think he's doing?

Use

- We use *must, might, could, may, can't +* infinitive to make guesses (logical deductions) about the present based on information we've got.
- When we're sure that something is true, we use *must*:
  A: I've been working on this all night. B: You **must** be exhausted!
- When we think something is possibly true, we use *might, could* or *may* (more formal):
  A: Why are all these people standing on the street over there?
  B: Well, they **might be** waiting to go into that nightclub or they **could be** waiting for someone famous to come out. They **may be** waiting for taxis.

- When we're sure that something is impossible or not true, we use *can't*:
  You **can't** be cold! It's the middle of summer!
- To talk about continuous actions, we use *must, might, may, could, can't + be +* verb + *-ing*:
  They **can't be staying** at the Ritz. They haven't got any money!

Look!
- To say that something perhaps isn't true we use *might / may not* NOT ~~couldn't~~. We don't usually contract *might not*:
  It **might not** be real gold. (= Perhaps it isn't real.)
- *Can't* is the opposite of *must*. We don't use *mustn't* to express logical deduction:
  They **can't** be man and wife. NOT They ~~mustn't~~ be man and wife.
- We don't use *can* in logical deduction:
  They **might / could / may be away**. NOT They ~~can~~ be away.

Modal verbs of past deduction (Unit 12)

Form

I / You / We / They / He / She / It	must / might / could / may / can't	have	gone out.

Questions

- We usually use *Do you think* or modal verbs of deduction in questions:
  Could they have seen me?
  Do you think he might have taken it?
  What do you think happened?
  Where do you think she's gone?

Use

- We use *must, might, could, may* and *can't + have +* past participle to make guesses (logical deductions) about the past based on information we've got.
- When we're sure that something happened or was true in the past we use *must have*:
  Jan looked really tired at work this morning. She **must have had** another bad night with the baby.

- When we think something possibly happened or was possibly true we use *might have, could have* or *may have*:
  I'm not sure where they went. They **might / could / may have** gone to Tom's.
- When we're sure something didn't happen or was impossible we use *can't have*:
  She **can't have** got married yesterday! She's already married!

Look!
- *Could have* means the same as *might have* BUT *couldn't have* means the same as *can't have*:
  I **could've / might've** left the mobile in the car.
  But he's such a nice person. He **couldn't have / can't have** said all those horrible things!

Grammar and vocabulary puzzles

Puzzle 1 (Units 1–3)

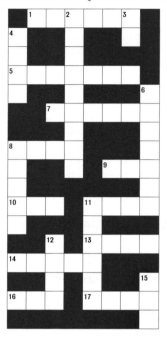

ACROSS

1 She's my best friend. I can always .... on her. (6)
5 Another word for *weird*. (7)
7 Which .... of your family are you closest to? (6)
8 If you buy that dress, you .... have enough money for new shoes. (4 contraction)
9 When .... he go on safari? (3)
10 I'm so .... – why can't I be more self-confident? (3)
11 I .... to smoke but I gave up last year. (4)
13 What do you feel .... doing tonight? (4)
14 .... are a lot of people here. (5)
16 I'm really enjoying this party. It's really .... and lively. (3)
17 Many cities have a problem with .... There are too many cars on the roads. (4)

DOWN

2 A: My name's Dan. B: .... meet you, Dan. (7, 2)
3 .... you agree with me? (2)
4 The pub was small with comfortable chairs and a log fire. It was really .... (4)
6 There was no room to dance. It was too .... (7)
8 I met a guy .... brother works in films. (5)
11 I won't buy you an ice cream .... you promise to be quiet. (6)
12 Have you ever .... to Japan? (4)
15 I went to Africa ten years .... (3)

Puzzle 2 (Units 4–6)

14 I .... I had a different job. This one's so boring. (4)
16 I was very patient and after a .... I got a great job. (5)
17 I don't like working on my own. I prefer working in a .... with other people. (4)
19 He's .... an idiot. I can't believe he did something so stupid. (4)
20 The biggest .... of my job is a company car. (4)
21 When I start working I want a well-............. job. (4)

DOWN

1 He hasn't got any parents. He's an .... (6)
2 She screamed throughout the whole concert last night. Today she's got a sore .... (6)
4 I hate sitting in the front row of a cinema. It's too close to the .... (6)
6 In your opinion, who's the .... stylish person in the world? (4)
7 Helena .... ride a horse when she was only three years old. (5)
8 Oh, what's the word? It's on the tip of my .... (6)
12 You .... to take something for that cough! (5)
14 If you .... rich, where would you live? (4)
15 Steve .... to deal with very difficult people in his job. (3)
18 Women in medieval times wore platform shoes to stop their skirts dragging in the .... (3)

ACROSS

2 A: What do you .... it is? B: I've got no idea! (5)
3 A: Are you good at maths? B: No, I'm completely .... (7)
5 Ladies and gentlemen. Tonight's .... will begin in fifteen minutes. (11)
9 It looks .... if it's moving. (2)
10 A: What's this sculpture? B: I'm not sure. I .... it's some sort of bird. (7)
11 It's .... as exciting as his earlier work. (3)
13 When did you last visit an .... gallery? (3)

Puzzle 3 (Units 7–9)

ACROSS

1 I can't believe you didn't tell anyone! You .... gone to the police! (6, 4)
4 Take your coat in .... it gets cold later. (4)
6 She asked me .... I was married. (7)
8 Come on! You only .... once! (4)
9 He .... me that he was tired. (4)
11 She wrote me a .... on the back of an envelope. (4)
12 Another way to say *I understand* is I .... *what you mean.* (3)

13 Stella's met Peter before, ... she? (5 contraction)
14 He's happy even .... he's poor. (6)
17 If .... I'd listened to Dad! Why didn't I take his advice? (4)
19 Perhaps if you'd been more polite, she .... not have got angry. (5)
20 She said she .... leaving him. (3)
22 The bride looked very calm, but the .... looked really nervous! (5)

DOWN

1 I'm .... of doing the housework all the time! (4)
2 The secretary took .... the information. (4)
3 He only married her .... her money! (3)
5 He's not happy in .... of his money and fame. (5)
7 If we .... stopped for a coffee, we wouldn't have missed the train. (5 contraction)
9 He said .... they had to leave. (4)
10 My biggest .... is that I didn't invest in the computer industry. I would have been very rich today if I had. (6)
12 I'll send you the document .... you can read it yourself. (2, 4)
15 Please be quiet! I'm .... the phone! (2)
16 Look at the time! We're .... to be late again! (5)
17 I'm sorry, he's .... at the moment. Can I take a message? (3)
18 My wife's really pleased that I get on so well with my parents-in-............... . (3)
21 What did he .... about me? (3)

Puzzle 4 (Units 10–12)

ACROSS

1 A: Where's Maria? B: I'm not sure. She .... gone to the gym. (5, 4)
4 The article was written .... a political journalist. (2)
6 Jack was .... for shoplifting last week. (8)
7 A: Who was that guy? B: It was Gerald's brother! .... you recognise him? (5 contraction)
10 I want to .... woken up at 6:30, please. (2)

11 It's a complete .... of time and money! Terrible! (5)
12 The film is .... on a famous novel. (5)
13 When I go on holiday I like to get .... from it all. (4)
14 All the computers have .... checked for viruses. (4)
15 You .... a grandmother! You look so young! (4 contraction, 2)
16 The film was set .... eighteenth-century France. (2)
17 He owns three very successful businesses. He .... making loads of money. (4, 2)

DOWN

1 Do you .... if I smoke? (4)
2 A: That was fantastic! B: Oh, come on. It wasn't .... good! (4)
3 He finally .... to sign the contract. (6)
4 I hate rude people. I don't like .... manners. (3)
5 .... the law to carry a gun in this country. (3 contraction, 7)
8 It was a Japanese film, but it was .... into English. (6)
9 A: Why did you .... to marry him? B: Because I don't love him. (6)
10 On holiday I always stay in places that are off the .... track. (6)
14 It's a good idea to have a fall............... plan when you arrange to meet someone when you are travelling. (4)

Word lists

A list of useful words from each unit (n = noun, v = verb, adj = adjective, adv = adverb, det = determiner, pron = pronoun, conj = conjunction)
/ ' / shows main stress, / , / shows secondary stress, /ə/ means that /ə/ may or may not be used.

Unit 1 It takes all sorts
acquaintance (n) /əˈkweɪntəns/
annoyed (adj) /əˈnɔɪd/
any longer (adv) /ˌeni ˈlɒŋgə/
anymore (adv) /ˌeniˈmɔː/
assertive (adj) /əˈsɜːtɪv/
attend (v) /əˈtend/
attractive (adj) /əˈtræktɪv/
bank manager (n) / ˈbæŋk ˌmænɪdʒə/
behaviour (n) /bɪˈheɪvjə/
blurb (n) /blɜːb/
boring (adj) / ˈbɔːrɪŋ/
borrow (v) / ˈbɒrəʊ/
chatty (adj) / ˈtʃæti/
colleague (n) / ˈkɒliːg/
complain (v) /kəmˈpleɪn/
confident (adj) / ˈkɒnfɪdənt/
contact (n and v) / ˈkɒntækt/
crazy (adj) / ˈkreɪzi/
crisis (n) / ˈkraɪsɪs/
deal with (v) / ˈdiːl wɪθ/
depend on (v) /dɪˈpend ɒn/
depressed (adj) /dɪˈprest/
desperate (adj) / ˈdespərət/
details (n pl) / ˈdiːteɪlz/
diagram (n) / ˈdaɪəgræm/
e-mail (n) / ˈiː meɪl/
employment agency (n) /ɪmˈplɔɪmənt
 ˌeɪdʒənsi/
engagement party (n) /ɪnˈgeɪdʒmənt ˌpɑːti/
estate agency (n) /ɪˈsteɪt ˌeɪdʒənsi/
exhausted (adj) /ɪgˈzɔːstɪd/
expert (n) / ˈekspɜːt/
favour (n) / ˈfeɪvə/
fight (n and v) /faɪt/
friendly (adj) / ˈfrendli/
gallery (n) / ˈgæləri/
generous (adj) / ˈdʒenərəs/
get away [somewhere] (v) /ˌget əˈweɪ/
get into trouble (v) /ˌget ɪntə ˈtrʌbəl/
get on [with someone] (v) /ˌget ˈɒn/
grateful (adj) / ˈgreɪtfəl/
guarantee (n) /ˌgærənˈtiː/
handsome (adj) / ˈhænsəm/
hard-working (adj) /ˌhɑːd ˈwɜːkɪŋ/
hectic (adj) / ˈhektɪk/
house-warming (adj) / ˈhaʊs ˌwɔːmɪŋ/
ignore (v) /ɪgˈnɔː/
impatient (adj) /ɪmˈpeɪʃənt/
improve (v) /ɪmˈpruːv/
insecure (adj) /ˌɪnsɪˈkjʊə/

insensitive (adj) /ɪnˈsensɪtɪv/
intelligent (adj) /ɪnˈtelɪdʒənt/
interesting (adj) / ˈɪntrɪstɪŋ/
keep calm (v) /ˌkiːp ˈkɑːm/
lazy (adj) / ˈleɪzi/
lend (v) /lend/
life-changing (adj) / ˈlaɪf ˌtʃeɪndʒɪŋ/
loan (n) /ləʊn/
lonely (adj) / ˈləʊnli/
look forward to [something] (v) /lʊk
 ˈfɔːwəd tə/
make it [somewhere] (v) / ˈmeɪk ɪt/
management (n) / ˈmænɪdʒmənt/
mean (adj) /miːn/
member (n) / ˈmembə/
memory (n) / ˈmeməri/
miserable (adj) / ˈmɪzərəbəl/
mortgage (n) / ˈmɔːgɪdʒ/
nasty (adj) / ˈnɑːsti/
nice (adj) /naɪs/
octopus (n) / ˈɒktəpəs/
organised (adj) / ˈɔːgənaɪzd/
out-going (adj) /ˌaʊt ˈgəʊɪŋ/
panic (v) / ˈpænɪk/
partner (n) / ˈpɑːtnə/
patient (adj) / ˈpeɪʃənt/
planet (n) / ˈplænɪt/
repayment (n) /rɪˈpeɪmənt/
request (n and v) /rɪˈkwest/
reschedule (v) /ˌriːˈʃedjuːl/
resolve (v) /rɪˈzɒlv/
respect (n and v) /rɪˈspekt/
[on] safari (n) /səˈfɑːri/
scientifically-proven (adj) /ˌsaɪənˌtɪfɪkli
 ˈpruːvən/
self-confident (adj) /ˌself ˈkɒnfɪdənt/
self-help (adj) /ˌself ˈhelp/
sensitive (adj) / ˈsensɪtɪv/
serious (adj) / ˈsɪəriəs/
set [something] up (v) /ˌset ˈʌp/
short notice (adj) /ˌʃɔːt ˈnəʊtɪs/
shoulder (n) / ˈʃəʊldə/
shy (adj) /ʃaɪ/
sincere (adj) /sɪnˈsɪə/
sincerely (adv) /sɪnˈsɪəli/
slave (n) /sleɪv/
sociable (adj) / ˈsəʊʃəbəl/
sort out [a problem] (v) /ˌsɔːt ˈaʊt/
spoilt (adj) /spɔɪlt/
strange (adj) /streɪndʒ/
stress (n) /stres/
stressful (adj) / ˈstresfəl/

stupid (adj) / ˈstjuːpɪd/
sweet (adj) /swiːt/
take off (v) /ˌteɪk ˈɒf/
talented (adj) / ˈtæləntɪd/
talkative (adj) / ˈtɔːkətɪv/
technique (n) /tekˈniːk/
traveller (n) / ˈtrævələ/
trust [someone] (v) /trʌst/
two-faced (adj) /ˌtuː ˈfeɪst/
unfortunately (adv) /ʌnˈfɔːtʃənətli/
unfriendly (adj) /ʌnˈfrendli/
unsociable (adj) /ʌnˈsəʊʃəbəl/
upset (adj) /ʌpˈset/
urgently (adv) / ˈɜːdʒəntli/
weird (adj) /wɪəd/
wild (adj) /waɪld/
wind down (v) /ˌwaɪnd ˈdaʊn/
worry (n and v) / ˈwʌri/

Unit 2 In the city
acceptable (adj) /əkˈseptəbəl/
alone (adj and adv) /əˈləʊn/
apricot (n) / ˈeɪprɪkɒt/
atmospheric (adj) /ˌætməsˈferɪk/
awful (adj) / ˈɔːfəl/
backdrop (n) / ˈbækdrɒp/
badly (adv) / ˈbædli/
balcony (n) / ˈbælkəni/
behave (v) /bɪˈheɪv/
brownstone (adj and n) / ˈbraʊnstəʊn/
building (n) / ˈbɪldɪŋ/
burst into tears (v) /ˌbɜːst ɪntə ˈtɪəz/
cab (n) (AmE) /kæb/
car park (n) / ˈkɑː pɑːk/
cathedral (n) /kəˈθiːdrəl/
chat (v) /tʃæt/
corner (n) / ˈkɔːnə/
cosmopolitan (adj) /ˌkɒzməˈpɒlɪtən/
damage (v) / ˈdæmɪdʒ/
delayed (adj) /dɪˈleɪd/
dirty (adj) / ˈdɜːti/
documentary (n) /ˌdɒkjʊˈmentəri/
downtown (n) (AmE) /ˌdaʊnˈtaʊn/
drunk (adj) /drʌŋk/
dust (n) /dʌst/
early (adj and adv) / ˈɜːli/
elevator (n) (AmE) / ˈelɪveɪtə/
embarrassing (adj) /ɪmˈbærəsɪŋ/
enormous (adj) /ɪˈnɔːməs/
environment (n) /ɪnˈvaɪərənmənt/
exciting (adj) /ɪkˈsaɪtɪŋ/
exhaust (n) /ɪgˈzɔːst/

expensive (adj) /ɪkˈspensɪv/
extract (n) / ˈekstrækt/
fantastic (adj) /fænˈtæstɪk/
fashionable (adj) / ˈfæʃənəbəl/
first-timer (n) /ˌfɜːst ˈtaɪmə/
fluorescent (adj) /fluəˈresənt/
fog (n) /fɒg/
fountain (n) / ˈfaʊntɪn/
fumes (n pl) /fjuːmz/
get rid of [something] (v) /get ˈrɪd əv/
get to (v) / ˈget tə/
give up (v) /ˌgɪv ˈʌp/
historic (adj) /hɪˈstɔːrɪk/
idiot (n) / ˈɪdiət/
image (n) / ˈɪmɪdʒ/
journalist (n) / ˈdʒɜːnəlɪst/
lamp-post (n) / ˈlæmp pəʊst/
landlord (n) / ˈlændlɔːd/
lift (n and v) /lɪft/
litter (n) / ˈlɪtə/
load (v) /ləʊd/
location (n) /ləʊˈkeɪʃən/
low-rent (adj) /ˌləʊ ˈrent/
lucky (adj) / ˈlʌki/
mailbox (n) (AmE) / ˈmeɪlbɒks/
mean (v) /miːn/
miss (v) /mɪs/
monument (n) / ˈmɒnjʊmənt/
nausea (n) / ˈnɔːziə/
neon sign (n) /ˌniːɒn ˈsaɪn/
nightclub (n) / ˈnaɪtklʌb/
nightmare (n) / ˈnaɪtmeə/
noise (n) /nɔɪz/
once (adv) /wʌns/
one-way street (n) /ˌwʌn weɪ ˈstriːt/
overcrowded (adj) /ˌəʊvəˈkraʊdɪd/
parking lot (n) (AmE) / ˈpɑːkɪŋ lɒt/
pavement (n) / ˈpeɪvmənt/
phone box (n) / ˈfəʊn bɒks/
police cell (n) /pəˈliːs sel/
pollution (n) /pəˈluːʃən/
popular (adj) / ˈpɒpjʊlə/
postbox (n) / ˈpəʊstbɒks/
prediction (n) /prɪˈdɪkʃən/
properly (adv) / ˈprɒpəli/
public transport (n) /ˌpʌblɪk ˈtrænspɔːt/
purse (n) /pɜːs/
queue (n and v) /kjuː/
railing (n) / ˈreɪlɪŋ/
recognise (v) / ˈrekəgnaɪz/
river (n) / ˈrɪvə/
road (n) /rəʊd/
road sign (n) / ˈrəʊd saɪn/
rooftop (n) / ˈruːftɒp/
rubbish (n) / ˈrʌbɪʃ/
shelf / shelves (n / n pl) /ʃelf, ʃelvz/
shopping centre (n) / ˈʃɒpɪŋ ˌsentə/

sidewalk (n) (AmE) / ˈsaɪdwɔːk/
sign (n) /saɪn/
skyscraper (n) / ˈskaɪˌskreɪpə/
smell (n and v) /smel/
smog (n) /smɒg/
square (n) /skweə/
statue (n) / ˈstætʃuː/
steps (n pl) /steps/
stiff (adj) /stɪf/
stool (n) /stuːl/
store (n) (AmE) /stɔː/
[be] stuck [somewhere] (adj) /stʌk/
subway (n) (AmE) / ˈsʌbweɪ/
suspicious (adj) /səˈspɪʃəs/
swear (v) /sweə/
tattoo (n) /təˈtuː/
taxi (n) / ˈtæksi/
third (adv) /θɜːd/
traffic (n) / ˈtræfɪk/
traffic jam (n) / ˈtræfɪk dʒæm/
traffic lights (n pl) / ˈtræfɪk laɪts/
tram (n) /træm/
treat [someone to something] (v) /triːt/
turn out (v) /ˌtɜːn ˈaʊt/
twice (adv) /twaɪs/
unbelievable (adj) /ˌʌnbɪˈliːvəbəl/
unload (v) /ʌnˈləʊd/
vegetarian (n) /ˌvedʒɪˈteəriən/
wrong (adj) /rɒŋ/

Unit 3 When Saturday comes
ambitious (adj) /æmˈbɪʃəs/
appetite (n) / ˈæpɪtaɪt/
aquarium (n) /əˈkweəriəm/
autograph (n) / ˈɔːtəgrɑːf/
babysitter (n) / ˈbeɪbiˌsɪtə/
banquet (n) / ˈbæŋkwɪt/
boiling (adj) / ˈbɔɪlɪŋ/
bright (adj) /braɪt/
brilliant (adj) / ˈbrɪljənt/
busy (adj) / ˈbɪzi/
butler (n) / ˈbʌtlə/
call up (v) /kɔːl ˈʌp/
cascading (adj) /kæˈskeɪdɪŋ/
casual (adj) / ˈkæʒuəl/
ceiling (n) / ˈsiːlɪŋ/
chant (n) /tʃɑːnt/
choice (n) /tʃɔɪs/
circus (n) / ˈsɜːkəs/
clip (n) /klɪp/
colourful (adj) / ˈkʌləfəl/
comfortable (adj) / ˈkʌmftəbəl/
consequence (n) / ˈkɒnsɪkwəns/
convince (v) /kənˈvɪns/
cool (adj) /kuːl/
cool off (v) /ˌkuːl ˈɒf/

cosy (adj) / ˈkəʊzi/
credits (n pl) / ˈkredɪts/
crowded (adj) / ˈkraʊdɪd/
crunch (v) /krʌntʃ/
dark (adj) /dɑːk/
delicious (adj) /dɪˈlɪʃəs/
dilemma (n) /dɪˈlemə/
dimly-lit (adj) /ˌdɪmli ˈlɪt/
elderly (adj) / ˈeldəli/
elegant (adj) / ˈelɪgənt/
excellent (adj) / ˈeksələnt/
fan (v) /fæn/
fiancé / fiancée (n) /fiˈɒnseɪ/
film script (n) / ˈfɪlm skrɪpt/
folder (n) / ˈfəʊldə/
freezing (adj) / ˈfriːzɪŋ/
fun (adj) /fʌn/
furious (adj) / ˈfjʊəriəs/
generation (n) /ˌdʒenəˈreɪʃən/
get ready (v) /get ˈredi/
greasy (adj) / ˈgriːsi/
guess (n and v) /ges/
hilarious (adj) /hɪˈleəriəs/
huge (adj) /hjuːdʒ/
incredible (adj) /ɪnˈkredɪbəl/
inspire (v) /ɪnˈspaɪə/
jazz (n) /dʒæz/
juicy (adj) / ˈdʒuːsi/
lean out (v) /ˌliːn ˈaʊt/
ledge (n) /ledʒ/
leisure (n) / ˈleʒə/
lipstick (n) / ˈlɪpstɪk/
literally (adv) / ˈlɪtərəli/
lively (adj) / ˈlaɪvli/
lizard (n) / ˈlɪzəd/
loads (n pl) /ləʊdz/
lush (adj) /lʌʃ/
make-up (n) / ˈmeɪk ʌp/
modern (adj) / ˈmɒdn/
muscle (adj) / ˈmʌsəl/
negotiation (n) /nɪˌgəʊʃiˈeɪʃən/
noisy (adj) / ˈnɔɪzi/
out-of-work (adj) /ˌaʊt əv ˈwɜːk/
packed (adj) /pækt/
portion (n) / ˈpɔːʃən/
posh (adj) /pɒʃ/
proud (adj) /praʊd/
quiet (adj) / ˈkwaɪət/
relaxed (adj) /rɪˈlækst/
reputation (n) /ˌrepjʊˈteɪʃən/
reserve (v) /rɪˈzɜːv/
ruin (v) / ˈruːɪn/
scared (adj) /skeəd/
shadow (n) / ˈʃædəʊ/
shark (n) /ʃɑːk/
simple (adj) / ˈsɪmpəl/
smart (adj) /smɑːt/

smoky (adj) / ˈsməʊki/
solve (v) /sɒlv/
spacious (adj) / ˈspeɪʃəs/
special effects (n pl) /ˌspeʃəl ɪˈfekts/
starving (adj) / ˈstɑːvɪŋ/
strange-looking (adj) / ˈstreɪndʒ ˌlʊkɪŋ/
sweaty (adj) / ˈsweti/
terrified (adj) / ˈterɪfaɪd/
threat (n) /θret/
tiny (adj) / ˈtaɪni/
tip (n) /tɪp/
traditional (adj) /trəˈdɪʃənəl/
unless (conj) /ʌnˈles/
unusual (adj) /ʌnˈjuːʒuəl/
warning (n) / ˈwɔːnɪŋ/
waterfall (n) / ˈwɔːtəfɔːl/
welcoming (adj) / ˈwelkəmɪŋ/
wonderful (adj) / ˈwʌndəfəl/
wrestler (n) / ˈreslə/

Unit 4 How do you do that?
ability (n) /əˈbɪləti/
abuse (n) /əˈbjuːs/
act (n) /ækt/
additional (adj) /əˈdɪʃənəl/
advertising agency (n) / ˈædvətaɪzɪŋ
  ˌeɪdʒənsi/
agency (n) / ˈeɪdʒənsi/
alcoholism (n) / ˈælkəhɒlɪzəm/
annual (adj) / ˈænjuəl/
applicant (n) / ˈæplɪkənt/
application form (n) /ˌæplɪˈkeɪʃən fɔːm/
apply [for something] (v) /əˈplaɪ/
aspect (n) / ˈæspekt/
astronaut (n) / ˈæstrənɔːt/
attraction (n) /əˈtrækʃən/
audience (n) / ˈɔːdiəns/
background (n) / ˈbækɡraʊnd/
bill (v) / ˈbɪl/
bodyguard (n) / ˈbɒdiɡɑːd/
bonus (n) / ˈbəʊnəs/
booking (n) / ˈbʊkɪŋ/
breakthrough (n) / ˈbreɪkθruː/
career ladder (n) /kəˈrɪə ˌlædə/
cartoon (n) /kɑːˈtuːn/
challenge (n) / ˈtʃælɛndʒ/
childhood (n) / ˈtʃaɪldhʊd/
childlike (adj) / ˈtʃaɪldlaɪk/
classic (n) / ˈklæsɪk/
comedian (n) /kəˈmiːdiən/
comedy (n) / ˈkɒmədi/
concerning (prep) /kənˈsɜːnɪŋ/
concrete jungle (n) /ˌkɒŋkriːt ˈdʒʌŋɡəl/
conference facilities (n pl) / ˈkɒnfərəns
  fəˌsɪlətiz/
consider (v) /kənˈsɪdə/

convenience (n) /kənˈviːnjəns/
course (n) /kɔːs/
creative (adj) /kriˈeɪtɪv/
criticism (n) / ˈkrɪtɪsɪzəm/
curiosity (n) /ˌkjʊəriˈɒsɪti/
current (adj) / ˈkʌrənt/
Curriculum vitae (n) /kəˌrɪkjʊləm ˈviːtaɪ/
dancer (n) / ˈdɑːnsə/
decade (n) / ˈdekeɪd/
decision (n) /dɪˈsɪʒən/
definitely (adv) / ˈdefɪnətli/
demanding (adj) /dɪˈmɑːndɪŋ/
destiny (n) / ˈdestɪni/
divorce (n) /dɪˈvɔːs/
dynamic (adj) /daɪˈnæmɪk/
employment agency (n) /ɪmˈplɔɪmənt
  ˌeɪdʒənsi/
enclose (v) /ɪnˈkləʊz/
enjoyable (adj) /ɪnˈdʒɔɪəbəl/
entertain (v) /ˌentəˈteɪn/
enthusiastic (adj) /ɪnˌθjuːziˈæstɪk/
extremely (adv) /ɪkˈstriːmli/
fabulous (adj) / ˈfæbjʊləs/
fail (v) /feɪl/
failure (n) / ˈfeɪljə/
fluent (adj) / ˈfluːənt/
formula (n) / ˈfɔːmjʊlə/
genius (n) / ˈdʒiːniəs/
glory (n) / ˈɡlɔːri/
hopeless [at] (adj) / ˈhəʊplɪs/
hot-air balloon (n) /ˌhɒt ˈeə bəˌluːn/
impersonal (adj) /ɪmˈpɜːsənəl/
impress (v) /ɪmˈpres/
independence (n) /ˌɪndɪˈpendəns/
influence someone (v) / ˈɪnfluəns
  ˌsʌmwʌn/
ingredient (n) /ɪnˈɡriːdiənt/
inspiration (n) /ˌɪnspɪˈreɪʃən/
interviewer (n) / ˈɪntəvjuːə/
invention (n) /ɪnˈvenʃən/
inventor (n) /ɪnˈventə/
joke (n) /dʒəʊk/
light bulb (n) / ˈlaɪt bʌlb/
literate (adj) / ˈlɪtərət/
manage [to] (v) / ˈmænɪdʒ/
marital status (n) / ˈmærɪtl ˌsteɪtəs/
masterpiece (n) / ˈmɑːstəpiːs/
microphone (n) / ˈmaɪkrəfəʊn/
natural gift (n) /ˌnætʃərəl ˈɡɪft/
pain (n) /peɪn/
patent (v) / ˈpeɪtnt/
pay rise (n) / ˈpeɪ raɪz/
perk (n) /pɜːk/
perspiration (n) /ˌpɜːspɪˈreɪʃən/
persuade (v) /pəˈsweɪd/
photocopier (n) / ˈfəʊtəʊˌkɒpiə/
physical (adj) / ˈfɪzɪkəl/

poverty (n) / ˈpɒvəti/
pressure (n) / ˈpreʃə/
productive (adj) /prəˈdʌktɪv/
qualification (n) /ˌkwɒlɪfɪˈkeɪʃən/
referee (n) /ˌrefəˈriː/
represent (v) /ˌreprɪˈzent/
reptile (n) / ˈreptaɪl/
responsibility (n) /rɪˌspɒnsɪˈbɪləti/
responsible [for] (adj) /rɪˈspɒnsɪbəl/
screen (n) /skriːn/
security (n) /sɪˈkjʊərəti/
senior (adj) / ˈsiːniə/
signature (n) / ˈsɪɡnətʃə/
skill (n) /skɪl/
stage (n) /steɪdʒ/
stage management (n) /ˌsteɪdʒ
  ˈmænɪdʒmənt/
stand-in (n) / ˈstænd ɪn/
stand-up comic (n) /ˌstænd ʌp ˈkɒmɪk/
status (n) / ˈsteɪtəs/
struggle (v) / ˈstrʌɡəl/
submarine commander (n) / ˈsʌbməriːn
  kəˌmɑːndə/
succeed [in] (v) /səkˈsiːd/
suitability (n) /ˌsuːtəˈbɪləti/
suitable (adj) / ˈsuːtəbəl/
switch off (v) /ˌswɪtʃ ˈɒf/
take care [of something / someone] (v)
  /teɪk ˈkeər/
talent (n) / ˈtælənt/
team (n) /tiːm/
timetable (n) / ˈtaɪmˌteɪbəl/
tragedy (n) / ˈtrædʒədi/
useless [at] (adj) / ˈjuːslɪs/
vacancy (n) / ˈveɪkənsi/

Unit 5 Culture vultures
abstract (adj) / ˈæbstrækt/
achieve (v) /əˈtʃiːv/
actually (adv) / ˈæktʃuəli/
aisle (n) /aɪl/
amazing (adj) /əˈmeɪzɪŋ/
apparently (adv) /əˈpærəntli/
architect (n) / ˈɑːkɪtekt/
attendant (n) /əˈtendənt/
author (n) / ˈɔːθə/
avant-garde (adj) /ˌævɒŋ ˈɡɑːd/
back issue (n) /ˌbæk ˈɪʃuː/
back row (n) /ˌbæk ˈrəʊ/
backstage (n) /ˌbækˈsteɪdʒ/
ballet (n) / ˈbæleɪ/
box office (n) / ˈbɒks ˌɒfɪs/
brave (adj) /breɪv/
complex (n) / ˈkɒmpleks/
complicated (adj) / ˈkɒmplɪkeɪtɪd/
compose (v) /kəmˈpəʊz/
composer (n) /kəmˈpəʊzə/

concert (n) / ˈkɒnsət/
constant (adj) / ˈkɒnstənt/
contestant (n) /kənˈtestənt/
cultural object (n) /ˌkʌltʃərəl ˈɒbdʒɪkt/
culture (n) / ˈkʌltʃə/
defend (v) /dɪˈfend/
design (v) /dɪˈzaɪn/
director (n) /dɪˈrektə/
disappointed (adj) /ˌdɪsəˈpɔɪntɪd/
disease (n) /dɪˈziːz/
drums (n pl) /drʌmz/
entertaining (adj) /ˌentəˈteɪnɪŋ/
entrance (n) / ˈentrəns/
everyday (adj) / ˈevrɪdeɪ/
exact (adj) /ɪgˈzækt/
exhibit (n) /ɪgˈzɪbɪt/
exhibition (n) /ˌeksɪˈbɪʃən/
experimental (adj) /ɪkˌsperɪˈmentl/
fame (n) /feɪm/
famous (adj) / ˈfeɪməs/
far (adj) /fɑː/
film (n) /fɪlm/
film director (n) / ˈfɪlm daɪˌrektə/
fragile (adj) / ˈfrædʒaɪl/
front row (n) /ˌfrʌnt ˈrəʊ/
giant (adj and n) / ˈdʒaɪənt/
gig (n) /gɪg/
guitarist (n) /gɪˈtɑːrɪst/
hard (adj) /hɑːd/
hero (n) / ˈhɪərəʊ/
impressive (adj) /ɪmˈpresɪv/
inability (n) /ˌɪnəˈbɪləti/
installation (n) /ˌɪnstəˈleɪʃən/
interval (n) / ˈɪntəvəl/
knowledge (n) / ˈnɒlɪdʒ/
leather (adj) / ˈleðə/
librarian (n) /laɪˈbreərɪən/
literature (n) / ˈlɪtərətʃə/
nearly (adv) / ˈnɪəli/
nervous (adj) / ˈnɜːvəs/
never-ending (adj) /ˌnevər ˈendɪŋ/
novel (n) / ˈnɒvəl/
obvious (adj) / ˈɒbvɪəs/
opera (n) / ˈɒpərə/
ordinary (adj) / ˈɔːdənəri/
painter (n) / ˈpeɪntə/
painting (n) / ˈpeɪntɪŋ/
parade (n) /pəˈreɪd/
penicillin (n) /ˌpenɪˈsɪlɪn/
performance (n) /pəˈfɔːməns/
philosopher (n) /fɪˈlɒsəfə/
philosophy (n) /fɪˈlɒsəfi/
photographer (n) /fəˈtɒgrəfə/
photography (n) /fəˈtɒgrəfi/
play (n) /pleɪ/
playwright (n) / ˈpleɪraɪt/
poet (n) / ˈpəʊɪt/

poetry (n) / ˈpəʊɪtri/
portrait (n) / ˈpɔːtrɪt/
predictably (adv) /prɪˈdɪktəbli/
presenter (n) /prɪˈzentə/
print (n and v) /prɪnt/
print maker (n) / ˈprɪnt meɪkə/
prize (n) /praɪz/
programme (n) / ˈprəʊgræm/
publisher (n) / ˈpʌblɪʃə/
quiz show (n) / ˈkwɪz ʃəʊ/
record producer (n) / ˈrekɔːd prəˌdjuːsə/
reference book (n) / ˈrefərəns bʊk/
remote (control) (n) /rɪˌməʊt kənˈtrəʊl/
score (n) /skɔː/
sculptor (n) / ˈskʌlptə/
sculpture (n) / ˈskʌlptʃə/
secret (n) / ˈsiːkrɪt/
self-promotion (n) /ˌself prəˈməʊʃən/
series (n) / ˈsɪəriːz/
skilful (adj) / ˈskɪlfəl/
slightly (adv) / ˈslaɪtli/
snob (n) /snɒb/
so (adv) /səʊ/
sort [of] (n) /sɔːt/
spirit (n) / ˈspɪrɪt/
spiritual (adj) / ˈspɪrɪtʃuəl/
stimulation (n) /ˌstɪmjʊˈleɪʃən/
stuff (n) /stʌf/
such (pre det) /sʌtʃ/
television presenter (n) / ˈteləˌvɪʒən prɪˌzentə/
tower (n) /taʊə/
unsuccessful (adj) /ˌʌnsəkˈsesfəl/
useful (adj) / ˈjuːsfəl/
venue (n) / ˈvenjuː/
visitor (n) / ˈvɪzɪtə/
visual (adj) / ˈvɪʒuəl/
vulture (n) / ˈvʌltʃə/
website (n) / ˈwebsaɪt/
well-known (adj) /ˌwel ˈnəʊn/
whisper (v) / ˈwɪspə/
writer (n) / ˈraɪtə/

Unit 6 Skin deep
afford (v) /əˈfɔːd/
ankle (n) / ˈæŋkəl/
appearance (n) /əˈpɪərəns/
aristocrat (n) / ˈærɪstəkræt/
arsenic (n) / ˈɑːsənɪk/
audition (n and v) /ɔːˈdɪʃən/
authentic (adj) /ɔːˈθentɪk/
baggy (adj) / ˈbægi/
beehive (n) / ˈbiːhaɪv/
belt (n) /belt/
blouse (n) /blaʊs/
boots (n pl) /buːts/
bother (v) / ˈbɒðə/
brand-new (adj) /ˌbrænd ˈnjuː/

buckle (n) / ˈbʌkəl/
busk (v) /bʌsk/
button (n) / ˈbʌtn/
category (n) / ˈkætəgəri/
caviar (n) /ˌkævɪˈɑː/
chalky (adj) / ˈtʃɔːki/
champagne (n) /ʃæmˈpeɪn/
checkout (n) / ˈtʃekaʊt/
checked (adj) /tʃekt/
clinic (n) / ˈklɪnɪk/
cloth (n) /klɒθ/
[item of] clothing (n) / ˈkləʊðɪŋ/
clumsy (adj) / ˈklʌmzi/
cold (n) /kəʊld/
collar (n) / ˈkɒlə/
corset (n) / ˈkɔːsɪt/
cough (n) /kɒf/
customary (adj) / ˈkʌstəməri/
deadly (adj) / ˈdedli/
decay (n) /dɪˈkeɪ/
delicate (adj) / ˈdelɪkət/
diet (n) / ˈdaɪət/
dishonest (adj) /dɪsˈɒnɪst/
divine (adj) /dɪˈvaɪn/
drag (v) /dræg/
dress (n) /dres/
enamel (n) /ɪˈnæməl/
eyebrow (n) / ˈaɪbraʊ/
faint (v) /feɪnt/
fashion (n) / ˈfæʃən/
film premiere (n) / ˈfɪlm ˌpremieə/
fit (n and v) /fɪt/
flared (adj) /fleəd/
fortune (n) / ˈfɔːtʃən/
frame (n) /freɪm/
genie (n) / ˈdʒiːni/
gloves (n pl) /glʌvz/
goat (n) /gəʊt/
grapefruit (n) / ˈgreɪpfruːt/
greetings card (n) / ˈgriːtɪŋz kɑːd/
hairstyle (n) / ˈheəstaɪl/
hang (v) /hæŋ/
hangover (n) / ˈhæŋəʊvə/
headache (n) / ˈhedeɪk/
hearing (n) / ˈhɪərɪŋ/
heels (n pl) /hiːlz/
hiccups (n pl) / ˈhɪkʌps/
high (adj) /haɪ/
icon (n) / ˈaɪkɒn/
immortal (adj) /ɪˈmɔːtl/
impractical (adj) /ɪmˈpræktɪkəl/
influential (adj) /ˌɪnfluˈenʃəl/
jacket (n) / ˈdʒækɪt/
jeans (n pl) /dʒiːnz/
jog (v) /dʒɒg/
juice (n) /dʒuːs/
jumper (n) / ˈdʒʌmpə/

knee (n) /ni:/
laces (n pl) /leɪsɪz/
landscape (n) / 'lændskeɪp/
lead (n) /led/
lifestyle (n) / 'laɪfstaɪl/
light up (v) /ˌlaɪt 'ʌp/
liquid (n) / 'lɪkwɪd/
magnificent (adj) /mæg'nɪfɪsənt/
mango (n) / 'mæŋgəʊ/
medieval (adj) /ˌmedi'i:vəl/
mess (n) /mes/
millennium (n) /mɪ'leniəm/
mini-dress (n) / 'mɪni dres/
mistake (n) /mɪ'steɪk/
model (n and v) / 'mɒdl/
mud (n) /mʌd/
musician (n) /mju:'zɪʃən/
nosebleed (n) / 'nəʊzbli:d/
ointment (n) / 'ɔɪntmənt/
operation (n) /ˌɒpə'reɪʃən/
overheat (v) /ˌəʊvə'hi:t/
pale (adj) /peɪl/
paranoia (n) /ˌpærə'nɔɪə/
passion (n) / 'pæʃən/
patterned (adj) / 'pætənd/
peasant (n) / 'pezənt/
performer (n) /pə'fɔ:mə/
personality (n) /ˌpɜ:sə'næləti/
pig (n) /pɪg/
pinch (v) /pɪntʃ/
pin-striped (adj) / 'pɪn straɪpt/
plain (adj) /pleɪn/
plaster (n) / 'plɑ:stə/
plastic surgery (n) /ˌplæstɪk 'sɜ:dʒəri/
platform shoe (n) /ˌplætfɔ:m 'ʃu:/
pocket (n) / 'pɒkɪt/
polo-neck [jumper] (n) /ˌpəʊləʊ nek/
portable (adj) / 'pɔ:təbəl/
possession (n) /pə'zeʃən/
powder (n) / 'paʊdə/
[the] press (n) /pres/
privacy (n) / 'prɪvəsi/
pumice stone (n) / 'pʌmɪs stəʊn/
puppy (n) / 'pʌpi/
raw (adj) /rɔ:/
respectable (adj) /rɪ'spektəbəl/
revolutionary (adj) /ˌrevə'lu:ʃənəri/
rinse (v) /rɪns/
rotting (adj) / 'rɒtɪŋ/
scarf (n) /skɑ:f/
selection (n) /sɪ'lekʃən/
shave (v) /ʃeɪv/
shiny (adj) / 'ʃaɪni/
shirt (n) /ʃɜ:t/
short-sleeved (adj) /ˌʃɔ:t 'sli:vd/
shoulder pad (n) / 'ʃəʊldə pæd/
showcase (n) / 'ʃəʊkeɪs/

sight (n) /saɪt/
singer (n) / 'sɪŋə/
skin (n) /skɪn/
skinny (adj) / 'skɪni/
skirt (n) /skɜ:t/
sleeve (n) /sli:v/
sleeveless (adj) / 'sli:vlɪs/
smooth (v) /smu:ð/
sore throat (n) /ˌsɔ: 'θrəʊt/
soul (n) /səʊl/
stall (n) /stɔ:l/
stick (v) /stɪk/
stitches (n pl) / 'stɪtʃɪz/
stomachache (n) / 'stʌməkeɪk/
straighten (v) / 'streɪtn/
strappy (adj) / 'stræpi/
striped (adj) /straɪpt/
stylish (adj) / 'staɪlɪʃ/
sunburn (n) / 'sʌnbɜ:n/
suntan (n) / 'sʌntæn/
tanned (adj) /tænd/
taste (n) /teɪst/
tax (n) /tæks/
tease (v) /ti:z/
therapy (n) / 'θerəpi/
throughout (adv) /θru:'aʊt/
tie (n) /taɪ/
tight (adj) /taɪt/
tilt (v) /tɪlt/
top (n) /tɒp/
top-class (adj) /ˌtɒp 'klɑ:s/
touch (n) /tʌtʃ/
trainers (n pl) / 'treɪnəz/
trick (n and v) /trɪk/
trolley (n) / 'trɒli/
tropical (adj) / 'trɒpɪkəl/
trousers (n pl) / 'traʊzəz/
T-shirt (n) / 'ti: ʃɜ:t/
ugly (adj) / 'ʌgli/
unattractive (adj) /ˌʌnə'træktɪv/
underwear (n) / 'ʌndəweə/
urine (n) / 'jʊərɪn/
video artist (n) / 'vɪdiəʊ ˌɑ:tɪst/
villa (n) / 'vɪlə/
vitamin (n) / 'vɪtəmɪn/
waist (n) /weɪst/
weight (n) /weɪt/
wig (n) /wɪg/
wish (n and v) /wɪʃ/
witch (n) /wɪtʃ/
worn (adj) /wɔ:n/
youthful (adj) / 'ju:θfəl/

Unit 7 Can we talk?
afterwards (adv) / 'ɑ:ftəwədz/
anyway (adv) / 'eniweɪ/
arrest (v) /ə'rest/

attach (v) /ə'tætʃ/
attack (v) /ə'tæk/
babysit (v) / 'beɪbisɪt/
brake (n) /breɪk/
call back (v) /ˌkɔ:l 'bæk/
calmly (adv) / 'kɑ:mli/
cancel (v) / 'kænsəl/
cashier (n) /kæ'ʃɪə/
charge [someone with a crime] (v)
   /tʃɑ:dʒ/
charity (n) / 'tʃærəti/
coldly (adv) / 'kəʊldli/
con (v) /kɒn/
con-artist (n) / 'kɒn ˌɑ:tɪst/
connection (n) /kə'nekʃən/
crash (v) /kræʃ/
crew (n) /kru:/
cure (n and v) /kjʊə/
[be] cut off (adj) /ˌkʌt 'ɒf/
delete (v) /dɪ'li:t/
document (n) / 'dɒkjʊmənt/
drama (n) / 'drɑ:mə/
dramatic (adj) /drə'mætɪk/
envelope (n) / 'envələʊp/
episode (n) / 'epɪsəʊd/
eventful (adj) /ɪ'ventfəl/
extension (n) /ɪk'stenʃən/
extras (n pl) / 'ekstrəz/
[at] first (adv) /fɜ:st/
get back [to someone] (v) /ˌget 'bæk/
get through [to someone] (v) /ˌget 'θru:/
glamorous (adj) / 'glæmərəs/
go off (v) /ˌgəʊ 'ɒf/
gun (n) /gʌn/
hang up (v) /ˌhæŋ 'ʌp/
however (adv) /haʊ'evə/
imagine (v) /ɪ'mædʒɪn/
innocent (adj) / 'ɪnəsənt/
instantly (adv) / 'ɪnstəntli/
insured (adj) /ɪn'ʃʊəd/
irritated (adj) / 'ɪrɪteɪtɪd/
irritation (n) /ˌɪrɪ'teɪʃən/
jewellery (n) / 'dʒu:əlri/
jury (n) / 'dʒʊəri/
later (adv) / 'leɪtə/
lawyer (n) / 'lɔ:jə/
life savings (n pl) /ˌlaɪf 'seɪvɪŋz/
lifetime (n) / 'laɪftaɪm/
look up [information] (v) /ˌlʊk 'ʌp/
luck (n) /lʌk/
luckily (adv) / 'lʌkɪli/
mask (n) /mɑ:sk/
maze (n) /meɪz/
mechanic (n) /mɪ'kænɪk/
Member of Parliament (n) /ˌmembər əv
   'pɑ:ləmənt/
memory (n) / 'meməri/

middle-aged (adj) /ˌmɪdl 'eɪdʒd/
misfortune (n) /mɪs'fɔːtʃən/
miss out [something] (v) /ˌmɪs 'aʊt/
mobile phone (n) /ˌməʊbaɪl 'fəʊn/
old-fashioned (adj) /ˌəʊld 'fæʃənd/
plot (n) /plɒt/
put [someone] through (v) /ˌpʊt 'θruː/
recently (adv) / 'riːsəntli/
ring [someone] up (v) /ˌrɪŋ 'ʌp/
robbery (n) / 'rɒbəri/
sentence (v) / 'sentəns/
shock (n) /ʃɒk/
sunny (adj) / 'sʌni/
take down [information] (v) /ˌteɪk 'daʊn/
then (adv) /ðen/
trendy (adj) / 'trendi/
typical (adj) / 'tɪpɪkəl/
tyre (n) /taɪə/
venture (n) / 'ventʃə/
victim (n) / 'vɪktɪm/
voter (n) / 'vəʊtə/
wallet (n) / 'wɒlɪt/
while (conj) /waɪl/

Unit 8 Life, death and the universe
anniversary (n) /ˌænɪ'vɜːsəri/
argue (v) / 'ɑːgjuː/
blame (n) /bleɪm/
blood (n) /blʌd/
campaign (n) /kæm'peɪn/
career change (n) /kə'rɪə ˌtʃeɪndʒ/
clone (n and v) /kləʊn/
criminal (n) / 'krɪmɪnəl/
determined (adj) /dɪ'tɜːmɪnd/
disagree (v) /ˌdɪsə'griː/
drain (n) /dreɪn/
edge (n) /edʒ/
efficient (adj) /ɪ'fɪʃənt/
electricity (n) /ɪˌlek'trɪsəti/
evidence (n) / 'evɪdəns/
explode (v) /ɪk'spləʊd/
explosion (n) /ɪk'spləʊʒən/
extinct (adj) /ɪk'stɪŋkt/
fancy (v) / 'fænsi/
fine (n) /faɪn/
forefather (n) / 'fɔːˌfɑːðə/
gadget (n) / 'gædʒɪt/
gamble (v) / 'gæmbəl/
get off with (v) /get 'ɒf wɪð/
heart attack (n) / 'hɑːt əˌtæk/
immoral (adj) /ɪ'mɒrəl/
in case (conj) /ɪn 'keɪs/
interrupt (v) /ˌɪntə'rʌpt/
march (v) /mɑːtʃ/
microscope (n) / 'maɪkrəskəʊp/
microwave (n) / 'maɪkrəweɪv/

opinion (n) /ə'pɪnjən/
otherwise (adv) / 'ʌðəwaɪz/
ozone layer (n) / 'əʊzəʊn ˌleɪə/
pathetic (adj) /pə'θetɪk/
pioneer (n) /ˌpaɪə'nɪə/
poster (n) / 'pəʊstə/
practical (adj) / 'præktɪkəl/
private investigator (n) /ˌpraɪvət
  ɪn'vestɪgeɪtə/
probably (adv) / 'prɒbəbli/
regret (n and v) /rɪ'gret/
relief (n) /rɪ'liːf/
robot (n) / 'rəʊbɒt/
rope (n) /rəʊp/
second-hand (adj) /ˌsekənd 'hænd/
[be] sick (adj) /sɪk/
side effect (n) / 'saɪd ɪˌfekt/
silly (adj) / 'sɪli/
spicy (adj) / 'spaɪsi/
sport (n) /spɔːt/
survive (v) /sə'vaɪv/
technical support (n) /ˌteknɪkəl sə'pɔːt/
torch (n) /tɔːtʃ/
transmit (v) /trænz'mɪt/
treat (v) /triːt/
undoubtedly (adj) /ʌn'daʊtɪdli/
unemployed (adj) /ˌʌnɪm'plɔɪd/
vacation (n) (AmE) /və'keɪʃən/
vacuum cleaner (n) / 'vækjuəm ˌkliːnə/
vision (n) / 'vɪʒən/
waterproof (adj) / 'wɔːtəpruːf/
well-informed (adj) /ˌwel ɪn'fɔːmd/
well-qualified (adj) /ˌwel 'kwɒlɪfaɪd/
whale hunting (n) / 'weɪl ˌhʌntɪŋ/
wimp (n) /wɪmp/
zone (n) /zəʊn/

Unit 9 It's a family affair
admiration (n) /ˌædmə'reɪʃən/
admission (n) /əd'mɪʃən/
afford (v) /ə'fɔːd/
aggressive (adj) /ə'gresɪv/
album (n) / 'ælbəm/
alley (n) / 'æli/
Alsatian (n) /æl'seɪʃən/
although (conj) /ɔːl'ðəʊ/
answering machine (n) / 'ɑːnsərɪŋ
  məˌʃiːn/
appropriate (adj) /ə'prəʊprɪət/
architecture (n) / 'ɑːkɪtektʃə/
argument (n) / 'ɑːgjʊmənt/
[be] attracted to (v) /ə'træktɪd tə/
automatically (adv) /ˌɔːtə'mætɪkli/
awe-inspiring (adj) / 'ɔː ɪnˌspaɪərɪŋ/
balloon (n) /bə'luːn/
barely (adv) / 'beəli/
become (v) /bɪ'kʌm/

benefit (n) / 'benəfɪt/
best man (n) /ˌbest 'mæn/
birthday (n) / 'bɜːθdeɪ/
bouquet (n) /bu'keɪ/
bride (n) /braɪd/
bridegoom / groom (n) / 'braɪdgruːm,
  -grʊm, gruːm, grʊm/
bridesmaid (n) / 'braɪdzmeɪd/
bruise (n) /bruːz/
budget (n) / 'bʌdʒɪt/
burst in (v) /ˌbɜːst 'ɪn/
cake (n) /keɪk/
calorie (n) / 'kæləri/
candelabra (n) /ˌkændə'lɑːbrə/
candle (n) / 'kændl/
candlelight (n) / 'kændl-laɪt/
celebrate (v) / 'seləbreɪt/
celebration (n) /ˌselə'breɪʃən/
century (n) / 'sentʃəri/
cereal (n) / 'sɪərɪəl/
ceremony (n) / 'serəməni/
chat show (n) / 'tʃæt ʃəʊ/
cheer up (v) /ˌtʃɪər 'ʌp/
chemical (n) / 'kemɪkəl/
clenched (adj) /klentʃd/
clue (n) /kluː/
conservative (adj) /kən'sɜːvətɪv/
contrast (n) / 'kɒntrɑːst/
corn (n) /kɔːn/
couple (n) / 'kʌpəl/
cupboard (n) / 'kʌbəd/
daring (adj) / 'deərɪŋ/
decorate (v) / 'dekəreɪt/
decorations (n pl) /ˌdekə'reɪʃənz/
despite (prep) /dɪ'spaɪt/
diary (n) / 'daɪəri/
disaster (n) /dɪ'zɑːstə/
disastrous (adj) /dɪ'zɑːstrəs/
dysfunctional (adj) /dɪs'fʌŋkʃənəl/
elephant (n) / 'elɪfənt/
embodied [in] (adj) /ɪm'bɒdid/
equipment (n) /ɪ'kwɪpmənt/
even though (prep) / 'iːvən ˌðəʊ/
fan (n) /fæn/
fanatic (n) /fə'nætɪk/
fed up [with someone / something] (adj)
  /ˌfed 'ʌp/
firework (n) / 'faɪəwɜːk/
flooded (adj) / 'flʌdɪd/
gang up (v) /ˌgæŋ 'ʌp/
ghost (n) /gəʊst/
gift (n) /gɪft/
gossip (n) / 'gɒsɪp/
guest (n) /gest/
guidance (n) / 'gaɪdəns/
haunted (adj) / 'hɔːntɪd/
honeymoon (n) / 'hʌnimuːn/
host (n) /həʊst/

identification (n) /aɪˌdentɪfɪˈkeɪʃən/
inaccurate (adj) /ɪnˈækjʊrət/
ingenuity (n) /ˌɪndʒəˈnjuːəti/
in order to (prep) /ɪn ˈɔːdə tə/
in spite of (prep) /ɪn ˈspaɪt əv/
invest (v) /ɪnˈvest/
jealous (adj) /ˈdʒeləs/
jet liner (n) /ˈdʒet ˌlaɪnə/
keep [someone] company (v) /ˌkiːp ˈkʌmpəni/
laboratory (n) /ləˈbɒrətri/
landmark (n) /ˈlændmɑːk/
legend (n) /ˈledʒənd/
maid of honour (n) /ˌmeɪd əv ˈɒnə/
manners (n pl) /ˈmænəz/
mascara (n) /mæˈskɑːrə/
maturity (n) /məˈtʃʊərəti/
memorable (adj) /ˈmemərəbəl/
minister (n) /ˈmɪnɪstə/
mixture (n) /ˈmɪkstʃə/
monkey (n) /ˈmʌŋki/
mysterious (adj) /mɪˈstɪəriəs/
nerves (n pl) /nɜːvz/
newborn baby (n) /ˌnjuːbɔːn ˈbeɪbi/
newly-married (adj) /ˌnjuːli ˈmærid/
nightie (n) /ˈnaɪti/
nutritious (adj) /njuːˈtrɪʃəs/
observatory (n) /əbˈzɜːvətəri/
obtain (v) /əbˈteɪn/
occasion (n) /əˈkeɪʒən/
paradise (n) /ˈpærədaɪs/
parents-in-law (n pl) /ˈpeərənts ɪn ˌlɔː/
party (n) /ˈpɑːti/
passerby (n) /ˌpɑːsəˈbaɪ/
peer (n) /pɪə/
plunge (n and v) /plʌndʒ/
powerful (adj) /ˈpaʊəfəl/
present (n) /ˈprezənt/
propose (v) /prəˈpəʊz/
raindrop (n) /ˈreɪndrɒp/
rebel (v) /rɪˈbel/
relation (n) /rɪˈleɪʃən/
relative (n) /ˈrelətɪv/
relieved (adj) /rɪˈliːvd/
reunion (n) /riːˈjuːnjən/
satisfaction (n) /ˌsætɪsˈfækʃən/
savoury (adj) /ˈseɪvəri/
script (n) /skrɪpt/
scriptwriter (n) /ˈskrɪptˌraɪtə/
server (n) /ˈsɜːvə/
sewing machine (n) /ˈsəʊɪŋ məˌʃiːn/
share (v) /ʃeər/
shrine (n) /ʃraɪn/
skydiving (n) /ˈskaɪdaɪvɪŋ/
soap opera (n) /ˈsəʊp ˌɒpərə/
spectacular (adj) /spekˈtækjʊlə/
speech (n) /spiːtʃ/

stained glass (n) /ˌsteɪnd ˈglɑːs/
stare (v) /steə/
statement (n) /ˈsteɪtmənt/
stretch limo (n) /ˌstretʃ ˈlɪməʊ/
surfing gear (n) /ˈsɜːfɪŋ ɡɪə/
symbol (n) /ˈsɪmbəl/
take [someone's] side (v) /ˌteɪk ˈsaɪd/
tear (n) /tɪə/
teenage (adj) /ˈtiːneɪdʒ/
teenager (n) /ˈtiːneɪdʒə/
toast (n) /təʊst/
toaster (n) /ˈtəʊstə/
trill (v) /trɪl/
truck (n) /trʌk/
tune (n) /tjuːn/
turkey (n) /ˈtɜːki/
unexpected (adj) /ˌʌnɪkˈspektɪd/
unforgettable (adj) /ˌʌnfəˈɡetəbəl/
unsigned (adj) /ˌʌnˈsaɪnd/
untraceable (adj) /ʌnˈtreɪsəbəl/
vase (n) /vɑːz/
voice mail (n) /ˈvɔɪs meɪl/
wedding (n) /ˈwedɪŋ/
weigh (v) /weɪ/
weep (v) /wiːp/
windscreen (n) /ˈwɪndskriːn/

Unit 10 What's going on?

[in] addition (adv) /əˈdɪʃən/
admit (v) /ədˈmɪt/
also (adv) /ˈɔːlsəʊ/
although (conj) /ɔːlˈðəʊ/
annoying (adj) /əˈnɔɪ-ɪŋ/
anti-social (adj) /ˌænti ˈsəʊʃəl/
apologise (v) /əˈpɒlədʒaɪz/
break into (v) /ˌbreɪk ˈɪntə/
breaking the speed limit (n) /ˌbreɪkɪŋ ðə ˈspiːd ˌlɪmɪt/
broadcast (n) /ˈbrɔːdkɑːst/
bug (n) /bʌɡ/
burden (n) /ˈbɜːdn/
burglary (n) /ˈbɜːɡləri/
capitalism (n) /ˈkæpɪtl-ɪzəm/
cardboard (adj) /ˈkɑːdbɔːd/
charming (adj) /ˈtʃɑːmɪŋ/
cheat (n and v) /tʃiːt/
chew (v) /tʃuː/
coffin (n) /ˈkɒfɪn/
comment (n and v) /ˈkɒment/
conduct (v) /kənˈdʌkt/
[in] contrast (adv) /ˈkɒntrɑːst/
corruption (n) /kəˈrʌpʃən/
council (n) /ˈkaʊnsəl/
cruise (n) /kruːz/
dangerous (adj) /ˈdeɪndʒərəs/
demonstrator (n) /ˈdemənstreɪtə/
descend [into] (v) /dɪˈsend/

downside (n) /ˈdaʊnsaɪd/
drink-driving (n) /ˌdrɪŋk ˈdraɪvɪŋ/
dropping litter (n) /ˌdrɒpɪŋ ˈlɪtə/
duty (n) /ˈdjuːti/
effective (adj) /ɪˈfektɪv/
erupt (v) /ɪˈrʌpt/
exotic (adj) /ɪɡˈzɒtɪk/
faith (n) /feɪθ/
fare-dodging (n) /ˈfeə ˌdɒdʒɪŋ/
fiddling taxes / expenses (n) /ˌfɪdlɪŋ ˈtæksɪz, ɪkˈspensɪz/
firstly (adv) /ˈfɜːstli/
flood (n) /flʌd/
forge (v) /fɔːdʒ/
forgery (n) /ˈfɔːdʒəri/
fraud (n) /frɔːd/
fraudster (n) /ˈfrɔːdstə/
frustrating (adj) /frəˈstreɪtɪŋ/
funeral (n) /ˈfjuːnərəl/
furthermore (adv) /ˌfɜːðəˈmɔː/
government (n) /ˈɡʌvənmənt/
grave (n) /ɡreɪv/
hamster (n) /ˈhæmstə/
hibernate (v) /ˈhaɪbəneɪt/
hitting (n) /ˈhɪtɪŋ/
horn (v) /hɔːn/
hurl (v) /hɜːl/
illegal (adj) /ɪˈliːɡəl/
impress (v) /ɪmˈpres/
in conclusion (adv) /ɪn kənˈkluːʒən/
insect (n) /ˈɪnsekt/
inspector (n) /ɪnˈspektə/
interview (n and v) /ˈɪntəvjuː/
investigation (n) /ɪnˌvestɪˈɡeɪʃən/
irritating (adj) /ˈɪrɪteɪtɪŋ/
jaywalking (n) /ˈdʒeɪwɔːkɪŋ/
[be] knocked down (adj) /ˌnɒkt ˈdaʊn/
law (n) /lɔː/
licence (n) /ˈlaɪsəns/
lie (n and v) /laɪ/
loot (v) /luːt/
make up (v) /ˌmeɪk ˈʌp/
moreover (adv) /mɔːˈrəʊvə/
necessary (adj) /ˈnesəsəri/
on the other hand (adv) /ɒn ði ˈʌðə hænd/
overreact (v) /ˌəʊvəriˈækt/
paralysed (adj) /ˈpærəlaɪzd/
peaceful (adj) /ˈpiːsfəl/
power cut (n) /ˈpaʊə kʌt/
prayer (n) /preə/
promote (v) /prəˈməʊt/
protest (n) /ˈprəʊtest/
queue-jumping (n) /ˈkjuː ˌdʒʌmpɪŋ/
rare (adj) /reə/
recommend (v) /ˌrekəˈmend/
release (v) /rɪˈliːs/

remind (v) /rɪˈmaɪnd/
riot (n) /ˈraɪət/
riot gear (n) /ˈraɪət gɪə/
rule (n) /ruːl/
safety (n) /ˈseɪfti/
scandal (n) /ˈskændl/
secondly (adv) /ˈsekəndli/
self-employed (adj) /ˌself ɪmˈplɔɪd/
selfish (adj) /ˈselfɪʃ/
sexism (n) /ˈseksɪzəm/
shoplifting (n) /ˈʃɒpˌlɪftɪŋ/
sibling (n) /ˈsɪblɪŋ/
smacking (n) /ˈsmækɪŋ/
speeding (n) /ˈspiːdɪŋ/
stealing (n) /ˈstiːlɪŋ/
strike (v) /straɪk/
summarise (v) /ˈsʌməraɪz/
summit meeting (n) /ˈsʌmɪt ˌmiːtɪŋ/
supply (n) /səˈplaɪ/
survey (n) /ˈsɜːveɪ/
suspect (n) /ˈsʌspekt/
suspect (v) /səˈspekt/
thirdly (adv) /ˈθɜːdli/
tolerance (n) /ˈtɒlərəns/
tragic (adj) /ˈtrædʒɪk/
trap (v) /træp/
trial (n) /ˈtraɪəl/
violence (n) /ˈvaɪələns/
virus (n) /ˈvaɪərəs/
witness (n) /ˈwɪtnɪs/
wreck (v) /rek/

Unit 11 The silver screen
action film (n) /ˈækʃən fɪlm/
adventure film (n) /ədˈventʃə fɪlm/
agree (v) /əˈgriː/
animated (adj) /ˈænɪmeɪtɪd/
anxious (adj) /ˈæŋkʃəs/
awfully (adv) /ˈɔːfəli/
blockbuster (n) /ˈblɒkˌbʌstə/
bow (n) /baʊ/
can't stand (v) /ˌkɑːnt ˈstænd/
cellar (n) /ˈselə/
chartbuster (n) /ˈtʃɑːtˌbʌstə/
cigar (n) /sɪˈgɑː/
classic (adj) /ˈklæsɪk/
confused (adj) /kənˈfjuːzd/
confusion (n) /kənˈfjuːʒən/
crime (n) /kraɪm/
crow (n) /krəʊ/
critic (n) /ˈkrɪtɪk/
dead (adj) /ded/
dub (v) /dʌb/
emotion (n) /ɪˈməʊʃən/
entertain (v) /ˌentəˈteɪn/
fantasy (n) /ˈfæntəsi/
foyer (n) /ˈfɔɪeɪ/

frightening (adj) /ˈfraɪtn-ɪŋ/
funny (adj) /ˈfʌni/
gory (adj) /ˈgɔːri/
gripping (adj) /ˈgrɪpɪŋ/
horror film (n) /ˈhɒrə fɪlm/
independent (adj) /ˌɪndɪˈpendənt/
luggage (n) /ˈlʌgɪdʒ/
merchandise (n) /ˈmɜːtʃəndaɪz/
monster (n) /ˈmɒnstə/
mood (n) /muːd/
musical (adj and n) /ˈmjuːzɪkəl/
ocean (n) /ˈəʊʃən/
permission (n) /pəˈmɪʃən/
plot (n) /plɒt/
popcorn (n) /ˈpɒpkɔːn/
predictable (adj) /prɪˈdɪktəbəl/
producer (n) /prəˈdjuːsə/
rainbow (n) /ˈreɪnbəʊ/
realistic (adj) /ˌrɪəˈlɪstɪk/
request (n) /rɪˈkwest/
review (n) /rɪˈvjuː/
romance (n) /rəʊˈmæns/
romantic (adj) /rəʊˈmæntɪk/
romantic comedy (n) /rəʊˌmæntɪk
  ˈkɒmədi/
sad (adj) /sæd/
scary (adj) /ˈskeəri/
scene (n) /siːn/
science fiction (adj) /ˌsaɪəns ˈfɪkʃən/
screenplay (n) /ˈskriːnpleɪ/
search (v) /ˈsɜːtʃ/
servant (n) /ˈsɜːvənt/
sexy (adj) /ˈseksi/
shocking (adj) /ˈʃɒkɪŋ/
show off (v) /ˌʃəʊ ˈɒf/
slam (v) /slæm/
softy (n) /ˈsɒfti/
soundtrack (n) /ˈsaʊndtræk/
star (n) /stɑː/
stud (adj and n) /stʌd/
stunt (n) /stʌnt/
subtitles (n pl) /ˈsʌbˌtaɪtlz/
surreal (adj) /səˈrɪəl/
suspense (n) /səˈspens/
teeniest (adj) /ˈtiːniəst/
tense (adj) /tens/
terrifying (adj) /ˈterɪfaɪ-ɪŋ/
theory (n) /ˈθɪəri/
thriller (n) /ˈθrɪlə/
trailer (n) /ˈtreɪlə/
unaware (adj) /ˌʌnəˈweər/
usher (n) /ˈʌʃə/
war film (n) /ˈwɔː fɪlm/
western (n) /ˈwestən/
whole (adj) /həʊl/

Unit 12 Taking off
backpacker (n) /ˈbækpækə/
backpacking (n) /ˈbækpækɪŋ/
blistering (adj) /ˈblɪstərɪŋ/
breathtaking (adj) /ˈbreθˌteɪkɪŋ/
careless (adj) /ˈkeələs/
check out (v) /ˌtʃek ˈaʊt/
chilling out (n) /ˌtʃɪlɪŋ ˈaʊt/
companion (n) /kəmˈpænjən/
compromise (n) /ˈkɒmprəmaɪz/
crocodile (n) /ˈkrɒkədaɪl/
disgrace (n) /dɪsˈgreɪs/
explore (v) /ɪkˈsplɔː/
fallback plan (n) /ˈfɔːlbæk ˌplæn/
goal (n) /gəʊl/
guilty (adj) /ˈgɪlti/
hair parting (n) /ˈheə ˌpɑːtɪŋ/
handle (n) /ˈhændl/
hassle (v) /ˈhæsəl/
hesitation (n) /ˌhezɪˈteɪʃən/
highlight (n) /ˈhaɪlaɪt/
incompatible (adj) /ˌɪnkəmˈpætɪbəl/
itinerary (n) /aɪˈtɪnərəri/
logical (adj) /ˈlɒdʒɪkəl/
long-haul (adj) /ˈlɒŋhɔːl/
mosquito (n) /məˈskiːtəʊ/
occupied (adj) /ˈɒkjʊpaɪd/
off the beaten track (adj) /ˌɒf ðə ˌbiːtn
  ˈtræk/
orchestra (n) /ˈɔːkɪstrə/
potentially (adj) /pəˈtenʃəli/
receiver (n) /rɪˈsiːvə/
reservation (n) /ˌrezəˈveɪʃən/
rip-off (n) /ˈrɪp ɒf/
scenery (n) /ˈsiːnəri/
sights (n pl) /saɪts/
soak (v) /səʊk/
softly (adv) /ˈsɒftli/
souvenir (n) /ˌsuːvəˈnɪə/
spare (adj) /speə/
street trader (n) /ˈstriːt ˌtreɪdə/
tacky (adj) /ˈtæki/
take it easy (v) /ˌteɪk ɪt ˈiːzi/
tie the knot (v) /ˌtaɪ ðə ˈnɒt/
underestimate (v) /ˌʌndərˈestɪmeɪt/
volunteer (n) /ˌvɒlənˈtɪə/
waste (n) /weɪst/
whine (v) /waɪn/
yacht (n) /jɒt/

Information for pair and group work

Unit 11 Conversations, Exercise 1, page 98

STUDENT A PART 2

a) Look at Student B's pictures. Answer Student B's questions with one of the responses (f–j).

f) Excuse me.
g) Don't worry about it. / Never mind.
h) Cheers.
i) Congratulations!
j) Sorry!

b) Check your responses with another pair.

Unit 3, Exercise 9c), page 25

PAIR A

a) You're both in the same dilemma and you don't know what to do.

> You're engaged to someone but you've fallen in love with someone else.

Discuss possible solutions to your problem and the advantages and disadvantages of each solution.

b) When you finish, go back to Exercise 9d), page 25.

Unit 4, Exercise 4, page 33

STUDENT A

a) Fill in the gaps with true information about your childhood.

> **Childhood**
> 1 My .... taught me how to ride a bike.
> 2 I used to love ....
> 3 I was always good at ....
> 4 I couldn't ....
> 5 The person who influenced me the most was probably my ....

b) When you finish, write a question for each sentence. Then go round the class, ask other students your questions and try to find someone who is similar to you for each question.

Example: My brother taught me how to ride a bike.
> A: Who taught you how to ride a bike?
> B: My older brother.
> A: So did mine. How long did it take?

Unit 9 *DYR?* Units 7–9, Exercise 2a), page 82

STUDENT C

a) Read your paragraph. Do you think it's at the beginning, middle or end of the story? Read it until you can tell your part of the story without looking at it.

> Suddenly the stranger pulled out a gun. "Give me all the money!" he said. Jed gave the man the money – he didn't want a fight! Then Jemima saw a policeman at the end of the alley. They ran to the policeman as the thief ran the other way. "Stop that man!" they shouted. "He's taken our 500 dollars!" The policeman looked at them. "500 dollars? You aren't from here, are you?" he asked. "Can I see some identification?" "But he's got my wallet. He took everything! And he's escaping! Do something!" said Jed. But by then the thief was miles away. "Oh, forget it," said Jemima. "No identification and no money, huh?" said the policeman. "Well you two are under arrest!"

b) When you finish, go back to Exercise 2b), page 82.

Unit 9, Exercise 7, page 75

PAIR A

a) Look at the picture. What are the man and woman thinking? Write as many sentences as you can with *should / shouldn't have done* and *wish / if only* + Past Perfect Simple. Don't say what your situation is. Just give clues in your sentences.

Example: WOMAN: You should have brought a better map.

b) When you finish, take it in turns to read your sentences to your group of eight. The group guesses what your situation is.

Unit 2, Exercise 15, page 19

PAIR A

a) You're going to make up a short story about something that happened in a city. Choose eight of the pictures and phrases from the table to use in your story.

b) Think about questions 1–3, make notes on your story. If you use a picture, you don't have to use the exact word for what is shown in the picture – it can be something connected with the picture. If you use a phrase, it must be exactly as it's written. Use the Past Simple and Past Continuous.

Example: picture: phrase: eventually we saw

We were all standing under one **umbrella**. OR It **was raining** very hard. **Eventually we saw** a taxi. We **were getting** into the taxi when a man **came** up to us and . . .

1 Where did it happen? In a church? at a station? on a rooftop?
2 When did it happen? In the evening? the middle of the night?
3 Who was involved? How many people? How did the story end? How did the people feel in the end?

c) When you finish, practise telling your story to each other.

d) Make a group of four with Pair B and tell them your story. You can use your notes to help you but don't read your story! When you finish, check Pair B's answers. Did they tick the eight pictures / phrases you used?

e) Look at page 137 and listen to Pair B's story. Tick the pictures / phrases they use.

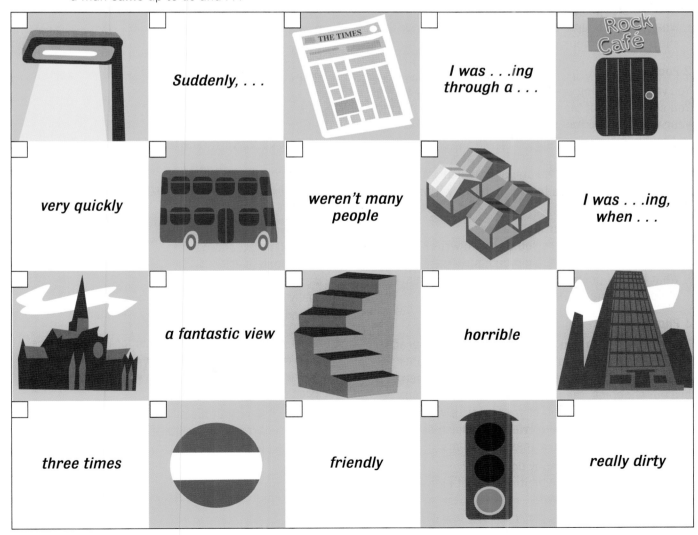

Unit 6 *DYR?* Units 4–6, Exercise 2c), page 56

PAIR B

You're artists / performers and you really want to work at the Arts Café. Choose two of the people (1–4), one for each of you. Help each other change your past experience so that it looks much more impressive. Don't tell complete lies, but exaggerate the good points so that Valerie and Mallory will give you a chance!

1 Painter

You're a struggling painter. You went to art college but you haven't had any exhibitions of your work yet. Every Sunday you go to the park and hang your paintings on the railings for tourists to buy. One of your paintings is also hanging in the local hospital. Your mother bought it from you and then gave it to the hospital as a gift. Think about these questions.

- What type of work do you do? Why is it important?
- Where have you had exhibitions?
- What kind of people come to your exhibitions?
- What kind of people buy your work? Is your work on show in any famous places?

2 Poet

You've been writing poetry since you were very young. You spend a lot of time in cafés, getting inspiration for your work. You've had some of your work published – in greetings cards! So far you've had one poetry reading event in your local café. The people in the café didn't understand and the manager asked you to leave. Perhaps your work was too revolutionary. Think about these questions.

- Where do you get your inspiration?
- What kind of poetry are you trying to write?
- Where has your poetry been published?
- What kind of poetry events have you had? What kind of people come to them?

3 Photographer

You really want to make it as an artistic photographer, but at the moment you're a portrait photographer in a shopping centre. You take photos of people when they are out shopping, then try to sell them the photos. You've had one exhibition of your work. It was in your mother's house and about twenty of your mother's friends came. Think about these questions.

- What kind of photography do you do?
- Where have you had exhibitions? What kind of people come to them?
- Is your work on show in any famous places?
- What kind of people buy your work?

4 Dancer

You did ballet classes as a teenager until the teacher told your parents you were too clumsy. Your parents wouldn't pay for any more lessons after that. However, you were allowed to dance in the school's performance of *Swan Lake* before you left. After you left school you bought a portable CD player and since then you've been busking in streets all over the place – inventing the dances as you do them. Think about these questions.

- What kind of dance do you perform?
- What inspires you to dance?
- Where have you performed? What famous places?
- What famous dancers have you performed with?

Unit 11 Conversations, Exercise 1, page 98

STUDENT B PART 1

a) Look at Student A's pictures. Answer Student A's questions with one of the responses (a–e).

a) Bless you!
b) That sounds interesting.
c) You're welcome.
d) Excuse me.
e) That's OK.

b) When you finish, look at Part 2, page 142.

Unit 4, Exercise 4, page 33

STUDENT B

a) Fill in the gaps with true information about your schooldays.

Schooldays
1 I did well at ....
2 I was hopeless at ....
3 I was really interested in ....
4 I really hated ....
5 I learned most from my .... teacher.

b) When you finish, write a question for each sentence. Then go round the class, ask other students your questions and try to find someone who is similar to you for each question.

Example: I did well at biology.
  A: Did you do well at biology at school?
  B: Yes, I did.
  A: So did I. Why did you like it?

Unit 2 Conversations, Exercise 8, page 21

STUDENT C

As you listen to Students A and B, tick the phrases you hear. Remember to stop them after three minutes! Then report to Students A and B, telling them what phrases they used, how natural they sounded, etc.

Student A: Speaker	
Hesitating (giving himself / herself time to think)	Um. Hmm. I mean . . . The thing is . . .
Checking the listener understands	You know? Do you know what I mean? Right? OK?

Student B: Listener	
Showing interest	Really? Oh yeah?
Checking information	Do you mean . . . ? So . . . ?
Encouraging / showing you're listening	I see. Mm-hm. Uh-huh. Yeah. Right.
Agreeing	I know. Absolutely. Sure. Right.
Echoing	Echo questions Repeating key words Further question Further statement
Exclamations	I can imagine! What a / an . . . That's (so) . . . I know (exactly) what you mean! That's right! No way!

Unit 5, Exercise 5b), page 41

ALL STUDENTS

Check your answers.

1 William Shakespeare
2 Julia Roberts
3 Gustave Eiffel
4 Agatha Christie
5 Michelangelo
6 Ringo Starr
7 Leonardo da Vinci
8 Kiri Te Kanawa
9 Antonio Vivaldi
10 Elvis Presley

Unit 3, Exercise 9c), page 25

PAIR B

a) You're both in the same dilemma and you don't know what to do.

Someone you work with is trying to get your job. You've found out some damaging information about this person. You don't know whether to give this information to your boss.

Discuss possible solutions to your problem and the advantages and disadvantages of each solution.

b) When you finish, go back to Exercise 9d), page 25.

Unit 10, Exercise 10, page 87

STUDENT B

Say sentences 1 and 2 about yourself to the other students. They're going to ask you as many negative questions as possible to find out if you're telling the truth. Answer their questions and defend your sentences for as long as you can.

Example: B: My boyfriend / girlfriend and I have got a perfect relationship.
A: What?! Haven't you ever had a row?
B: Sometimes, but we've always made up afterwards.
C: But haven't you ever . . . ? Isn't there . . . ? Aren't you . . . ? Didn't you . . . ?

1 My boyfriend / girlfriend and I have got a perfect relationship.
2 I'm always really organised.

Unit 10, Exercise 6, page 85

STUDENT A / PAIR A

a) The order of the news broadcast hasn't been decided yet. You think your story should go first. Read the notes about the story and invent the details. How can you make it the best and most exciting story of the day? Have you got any film? Interviews?

Your story involves an animal. Is it a rare animal seen somewhere unusual? Is it a dangerous animal that has escaped from somewhere? Is it a child's strange pet? Is it an insect or exotic spider? Something else?

b) In groups of four (Students A, B, C and D) or eight (Pairs A, B, C and D). You're in the meeting. Work fast to decide the order of the news items.

Unit 4, Exercise 4, page 33

STUDENT C

a) Fill in the gaps with true information about your natural abilities.

Natural abilities
1 People say I'm good at ....
2 I'm useless at ....
3 I can .... really well.
4 I take after my mother / father. She / He is / was very ....
5 I really admire people who are good at ....

b) When you finish, write a question for each sentence. Then go round the class, ask other students your questions and try to find someone who is similar to you for each question.

Example: People say I'm good at drawing.
    A: Do people say you're good at drawing?
    B: Well, my mother does.
    A: So does mine. Do you think you're good?

Unit 5, Exercise 11, page 43

PAIR B

a) Prepare for the meeting.
- You would like a statue of someone from the visual arts (a painter, sculptor, photographer, etc.). The person can be living or dead.
- Make a list of six reasons why your idea should be chosen.
- Make a list of things people might say against your choice so you can defend it.

Examples: Advantages: He's done some of the best . . .
    Disadvantages: His work isn't as important as . . .

b) In groups. Pairs take it in turns to present your ideas to the group and explain why it's the best choice. Discuss each pair's idea and agree on one idea.

Example: He's / She's / It's much more . . . than . . . And that's really important because . . .

Unit 9, Exercise 7, page 75

PAIR B

a) Look at the picture. What are the man and woman thinking? Write as many sentences as you can with *should / shouldn't have done* and *wish / if only* + Past Perfect Simple. Don't say what your situation is. Just give clues in your sentences.

Example: MAN: You shouldn't have worn that dress!

b) When you finish, take it in turns to read your sentences to your group of eight. The group guesses what your situation is.

Unit 9 *DYR?* Units 7–9, Exercise 2a), page 82

STUDENT A

a) Read your paragraph. Do you think it's at the beginning, middle or end of the story? Read it until you can tell your part of the story without looking at it.

"Big Daddy's Truck Bargains" was offering exactly the truck they wanted for only 500 dollars – all the money they had! They didn't think twice. They walked to the city in two days, with 500 dollars in Jed's pocket. When they arrived, Jemima realised that she didn't have the exact address. She hadn't written it down. She knew it was near the church but they didn't have a map. "Well," said Jed. "We'll ask someone." So he stopped a passerby. "Excuse me, sir. We've got 500 dollars in cash and we want to buy a truck, but we don't know where "Big Daddy's Truck Bargains" is!" "No problem," said the stranger. "I'll take you." And he led them down a dark alley.

b) When you finish, go back to Exercise 2b), page 82.

Unit 4, Exercise 8c), page 35

PAIR A

a) You work for the Dynamic Jobs agency. You're going to interview Pair B and offer each student one of the jobs (1–3). Look at each job. What skills do the applicants need? What are the good and bad aspects of the job?

dynamic jobs

① astronaut
② swimwear model
③ head of Greenworld environmental organisation

b) Swap application forms with Pair B. Look at the forms. Write 8–10 questions to ask each student to help you decide which job to offer him / her.

Examples: In your last job did you . . . ?
You don't like working in a team. Why's that?
So, having new challenges is important to you. How do you feel about . . .ing?
Are you good at working with people?
Have you ever worked with animals?
Have you got any fears? spiders? heights?

c) Interview each student in Pair B. Don't say what your three jobs are until after the interviews!

d) Now swap roles. You're the applicants and Pair B interview you.

e) Decide on which jobs to offer each student in Pair B. Then tell Pair B which jobs you chose and why.

Unit 5 Conversations, Exercise 5, page 47

TEAM A

a) You're going to play "Your time's up!". Write four more questions like questions 1–4 for Team B to answer. (You must know the answers!)

1 Which detective lived at 221b Baker Street, London? (Answer: Sherlock Holmes)
2 Who discovered penicillin? (Answer: Alexander Fleming)
3 What was President John F. Kennedy's middle name? (Answer: Fitzgerald)
4 What's the phrasal verb (two words) which means *stop doing something*? (Answer: *give up*)

b) Then look at the rules of the game on page 138.

Unit 3, Exercise 9c), page 25

PAIR C

a) You're both in the same dilemma and you don't know what to do.

You want to be an actor / singer but your parents want you to be a lawyer / doctor.

Discuss possible solutions to your problem and the advantages and disadvantages of each solution.

b) When you finish, go back to Exercise 9d), page 25.

Unit 10, Exercise 10, page 87

STUDENT A

Say sentences 1 and 2 about yourself to the other students. They're going to ask you as many negative questions as possible to find out if you're telling the truth. Answer their questions and defend your sentences for as long as you can.

Example: A: I'm totally fit and healthy. I only eat healthy food.
B: What?! Don't you ever have a bag of crisps?
A: No! Never! They're really bad for you.
C: But haven't you ever . . . ? Isn't there . . . ? Aren't you . . . ? Didn't you . . . ?

1 I'm totally fit and healthy. I only eat healthy food.
2 I'm a very calm person and I love everybody.

Unit 6 *DYR?* Units 4–6, Exercise 2c), page 56

PAIR A

a) You're Valerie and Mallory. You're looking for top-class artists and performers. You're going to interview two artists / performers (a painter, photographer, dancer or poet). Think of questions to ask about their past experience and art. Make sure they're being honest about their past experience.

Examples: **How long** have you been . . .ing?
How many exhibitions have you had / times have you performed?
Have you ever published any of your work? been on televison? **Where? When?**
Who taught you to . . . / has influenced you?
When did you start performing?
What made you become . . . ?
Tell us about your . . .
Can you give us an example of your poetry / dance now?

b) When you finish, go back to Exercise 2d), page 56.

Unit 5, Exercise 11, page 43

PAIR C

a) Prepare for the meeting.

- You would like a modern, abstract sculpture (not a statue) that represents the spirit of art and culture. Design your sculpture and give it a title.
- Make a list of six reasons why your idea should be chosen.
- Make a list of things people might say against your choice so you can defend it.

Examples: Advantages: This is very important because . . .
Disadvantages: Some people won't like it because . . .

b) In groups. Pairs take it in turns to present your ideas to the group and explain why it's the best choice. Discuss each pair's idea and agree on one idea.

Example: He's / She's / It's much more . . . than . . . And that's really important because . . .

Unit 10, Exercise 10, page 87

STUDENT C

Say sentences 1 and 2 about yourself to the other students. They're going to ask you as many negative questions as possible to find out if you're telling the truth. Answer their questions and defend your sentences for as long as you can.

Example: c: I'm completely satisfied with my life.
A: What?! Don't you want to change anything?
c: No, I don't. Everything is perfect.
B: But haven't you ever . . . ? Isn't there . . . ? Aren't you . . . ? Didn't you . . . ?

1 I'm completely satisfied with my life.
2 I have a perfect memory.

Unit 1, Exercise 10a), page 9

STUDENT B

Fill in the boxes (1–4) on page 9 with information about your life.

Box 1: write the name of a person you work or study with that you really like.
Box 2: write the month of your best friend's birthday.
Box 3: write the name of an acquaintance you don't like very much or that you'd like to know better.
Box 4: write the name of a place that has happy memories for you.

Unit 9 *DYR?* Units 7–9, Exercise 1c), page 82

STUDENT C

a) Read the script for the soap opera several times until you can remember all the information. Then think about the changes you need to make to report what the script says.

Example: Marlene said that she had some important news . . .

SCENE 4

Charlene is making coffee in her kitchen as Marlene enters.

MARLENE: Charlene – I've got some important news.
CHARLENE: Is it about Janie and Bobby?
MARLENE: Er . . . yeah. How did you know?
CHARLENE: I didn't know. I guessed. Well, what's the story?
MARLENE: Basically, Janie and Bobby wanted to start a new business selling surfing gear. They needed money and they couldn't wait. So they took it from under old Mrs Palmer's bed. They didn't know she had a weak heart.
CHARLENE: Well. Where are they?
MARLENE: I don't know. They disappeared when Mrs Palmer died.

---

b) When you finish, go back to Exercise 1d), page 82.

Unit 10, Exercise 6, page 85

STUDENT B / PAIR B

a) The order of the news broadcast hasn't been decided yet. You think your story should go first. Read the notes about the story and invent the details. How can you make it the best and most exciting story of the day? Have you got any film? Interviews?

Your story is a tragic human interest story with a lesson. What happened to the people involved and what can the incident teach us? Who is responsible? The council? government? Does it ask bigger questions about living together in society? Who have you interviewed about it? Are they angry?

b) In groups of four (Students A, B, C and D) or eight (Pairs A, B, C and D). You're in the meeting. Work fast to decide the order of the news items.

Unit 5 Conversations, Exercise 4c), page 47

The capital of Iceland is Reykjavík.

Unit 2, Exercise 15, page 19

PAIR B

a) You're going to make up a short story about something that happened in a city. Choose eight of the pictures and phrases from the table to use in your story.

b) Think about questions 1–3, make notes on your story. If you use a picture, you don't have to use the exact word for what is shown in the picture – it can be something connected with the picture. If you use a phrase, it must be exactly as it's written. Use the Past Simple and Past Continuous.

Example: picture: phrase: eventually we saw

We were all standing under one **umbrella**. OR It **was raining** very hard. **Eventually we saw** a taxi. We **were getting** into the taxi when a man **came** up to us and . . .

1 Where did it happen? In a church? at a station? on a rooftop?
2 When did it happen? In the evening? the middle of the night?
3 Who was involved? How many people? How did the story end? How did the people feel in the end?

c) When you finish, practise telling your story to each other.

d) Make a group of four with Pair A. Look at page 131 and listen to Pair A's story. Tick the pictures / phrases they use.

e) Tell Pair A your story. You can use your notes to help you remember but don't read your story! When you finish, check Pair A's answers. Did they tick the eight pictures / phrases you used?

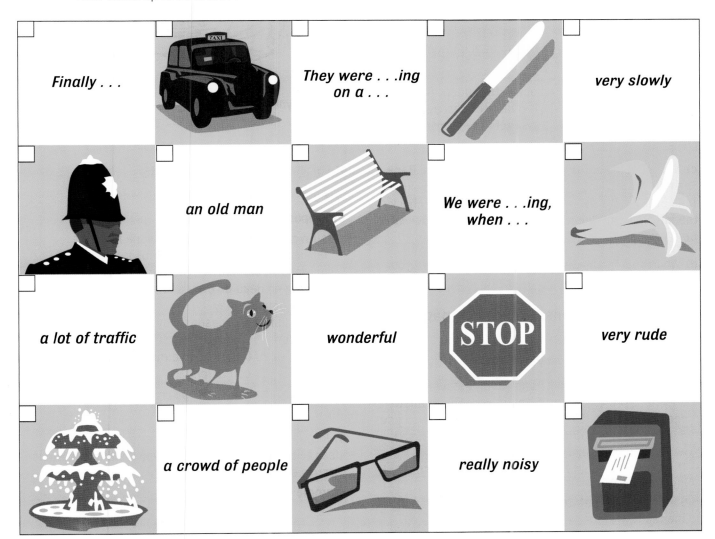

Unit 7, Exercise 13, page 62

STUDENT A

a) You're two different people who want to speak to John Burns at Burns Enterprises. You're going to phone Student B and leave two messages. Read the information and invent the messages.

1 You're John's mother / father. You've rung several times in the last week. It's someone's birthday next week and you don't know what to buy or do.
   - Whose birthday is it?
   - What do you want him to do? Phone you? Come and see you? Buy something? Organise something?
   - How can he contact you?

2 You're Leopold Gantry. Your company, Gantry and Son, hasn't received the things you ordered six weeks ago. This is the second time this has happened.
   - What were the things?
   - What do you want to do? Cancel the order? Give them another week?
   - Do you want him to phone you back? Meet you?
   - How can he contact you?

b) In AB pairs. Sit back-to-back with Student B. Phone Burns Enterprises and leave your two messages. Make sure the secretary (Student B) gets the information right each time.

c) Now you're a secretary at the Globe National Bank. The person Student B wants to speak to isn't available. Take Student B's two messages. Remember to check the information. Begin *Globe National Bank. How can I help you?*

d) When you finish, compare your messages. Do your notes include the important information?

Unit 5 Conversations, Exercise 5, page 47

ALL STUDENTS

Follow these rules and play the game.

- One Team A student asks one Team B student a question. The student has got 10 seconds to answer.
- The student gets 50 points for a correct answer and 5 points for each different hesitation phrase used while he / she thinks.
- Then one Team B student asks one Team A student a question.
- Continue until both teams' questions are finished. The team with the highest score wins.

Unit 9, Exercise 7, page 75

PAIR D

a) Look at the picture. What are the man and woman thinking? Write as many sentences as you can with *should / shouldn't have done* and *wish / if only* + Past Perfect Simple. Don't say what your situation is. Just give clues in your sentences.

Example: WOMAN: I wish we'd brought more food.

b) When you finish, take it in turns to read your sentences to your group of eight. The group guesses what your situation is.

Unit 5, Exercise 11, page 43

PAIR D

a) Prepare for the meeting.

- You would like a statue of someone from the classical world of words and music (a writer, composer, poet, playwright, etc.). The person can be living or dead or even a character from a famous book or play.
- Make a list of six reasons why your idea should be chosen.
- Make a list of things people might say against your choice so you can defend it.

Examples: Advantages: He's such a talented . . .
Disadvantages: He isn't as famous as . . .

b) In groups. Pairs take it in turns to present your ideas to the group and explain why it's the best choice. Discuss each pair's idea and agree on one idea.

Example: He's / She's / It's much more . . . than . . .
And that's really important because . . .

Unit 7, Exercise 5, page 59

PAIR A

a) Read this story. Then answer questions 1–8.

To Horseface, with love

Geoffrey Dickens, a Member of Parliament in England, had a problem when he went to a party to meet some of his voters. There was a very unattractive woman at the party who followed him everywhere he went. He was trying to talk to "his public" but every time he turned around, there she was again – asking him stupid questions. He couldn't escape! By the end of the party he was very irritated.

A few days later he received a letter from her. His irritation disappeared when he finished reading her letter, because at the end of the letter, after her name, she had written "Horseface". The poor woman obviously knew about her disadvantages but she could laugh about them. Geoffrey liked that. So he sent her the photo she had asked for and he added a short personal note: "To Horseface, with best wishes, Geoffrey Dickens."

However, he had a terrible shock later when his secretary asked him about the letter. "It was from that ugly woman at the party," the secretary said. Then he added, "I wrote 'Horseface' after her name so you'd know which one she was."

(adapted from *The One Hundred Stupidest Things Ever Done*)

1 Which two methods of communication are used in the story?
2 Who was Geoffrey Dickens?
3 Where was he when he met the woman?
4 Why was he irritated by the end of the party?
5 Why did he smile when he finished reading the woman's letter? What did he think she had done?
6 What did he write on the photo he sent to her?
7 Why did he have a terrible shock when he spoke to his secretary about the woman later?
8 How do you think Geoffrey felt?

b) Practise telling your story to each other. Use the Past Simple and the Past Perfect Simple. Make sure you don't forget any important details.

c) Each make a new pair with one student from Pair B. Tell your story clearly, as many times as necessary. Don't look at the book! Then ask questions 1–8. When you finish, listen to the student from Pair B's story and answer the questions.

Unit 9 *DYR?* Units 7–9, Exercise 1c), page 82

STUDENT D

a) Read the transcript of the phone call several times until you can remember all the information. Then think about the changes you need to make to report what the transcript says.

Example: She said that she was really bored with her job, her life . . .

SERENA: I'm so bored . . . with my job . . . my life . . . everything. If I don't do something soon, I'll go crazy. I want a complete change!
TANYA: What do you mean? What are you going to do?
SERENA: Well, for a start, I've decided to leave my job.
TANYA: What?! Do you know what you're doing? Your job's fantastic! And it pays so well.
SERENA: Yeah, I know . . . but money isn't everything. I've wanted to leave for ages . . . I might go on a little adventure.
TANYA: What do you mean?
SERENA: Well, I don't know . . . but I saw a really interesting ad in the paper yesterday. This guy is looking for a female travelling companion . . .
TANYA: Are you serious?! Are you going?
SERENA: Well, I don't know yet. I'm thinking about it . . .

b) When you finish, go back to Exercise 1d), page 82.

Unit 9 *DYR?* Units 7–9, Exercise 2a), page 82

STUDENT B

a) Read your paragraph. Do you think it's at the beginning, middle or end of the story? Read it until you can tell your part of the story without looking at it.

Jed and Jemima were old farmers who lived in a tiny wooden house in the hills, a long way from the nearest city. One day, Jemima was at the market talking to all her friends when she realised she was late. Really late! She had to get home in time to make Jed's tea because Jed **had** to have his meal at six exactly. He got really furious if it was just one minute late! She jumped into their old truck and drove home as fast as she could. It really wasn't safe – Jed was always promising to fix the brakes but he hadn't done them yet. Well, of course, poor Jemima crashed that truck! She was fine but the truck was in pieces.

b) When you finish, go back to Exercise 2b), page 82.

Unit 7, Exercise 5, page 59

PAIR B

a) Read this story. Then answer questions 1–8.

An unexpected e-mail

A businessman, Mr Harold Shore, went on a short business trip to Bermuda. The flight was terrible and he arrived at his hotel very late. His wife was going to join him the following day, so as soon as he arrived at the hotel he sent her a short e-mail.

His wife had recently changed her e-mail address. Harold made a mistake with her new address and the e-mail went to Mrs Joy Elkson, eighty-two years old. Mrs Elkson's husband, Henry, had died a few months before and she lived alone. She had bought her computer as a new interest after Henry's death and she used e-mail and the Internet every day. When she opened Harold's e-mail and read it, she immediately fainted.

Some time later Mrs Elkson's daughter found her mother lying on the floor near her computer. The computer was on with the e-mail message still on the screen. It read:

Darling,

It was a terrible journey but I eventually arrived safely. I am waiting for your arrival tomorrow.
By the way, it's as hot as hell down here.

Love,

H

1 Which method of communication is the story about?
2 Where was Harold Shore?
3 Why was he there?
4 Why did he arrive late?
5 Who did he send an e-mail to and why?
6 Who did Harold Shore's e-mail go to? What had Harold Shore done? Why had he done it?
7 Why did Mrs Elkson live alone? What had happened?
8 What happened when Mrs Elkson read Harold Shore's e-mail? Why?

b) Practise telling your story to each other. Use the Past Simple and the Past Perfect Simple. Make sure you don't forget any important details.

c) Each make a new pair with one student from Pair A. Listen to his / her story and answer his / her questions. When you finish, tell your story clearly, as many times as necessary. Don't look at the book! Then ask questions 1–8.

Unit 7, Exercise 13, page 62

STUDENT B

a) First you're going to be a secretary and Student A is going to leave two messages with you. Then you're going to be two different people who want to speak to Danielle Taylor at the Globe National Bank. You're going to phone Student A and leave two messages. Read the information and invent your messages.

1 You're Rory Jago. You're a very important client of the bank. You want to change the time and place of a meeting with Ms Taylor next week.
   • Why do you want to change it?
   • When was the meeting? When do you want it to be?
   • How can she contact you?

2 You're an old friend. You haven't seen Danielle for a long time. You're in town at the moment and you would love to see her.
   • Why are you in town? For how long?
   • Where would you like to meet? When?
   • How can she contact you?

b) In AB pairs. Sit back-to-back with Student A. You're a secretary at Burns Enterprises. The person Student A wants to speak to isn't available. Take Student A's two messages. Remember to check the information. Begin *Burns Enterprises. How can I help you?*

c) Now phone the Globe National Bank and leave your two messages. Make sure the secretary (Student A) gets the information right each time.

d) When you finish, compare your messages. Do your notes include the important information?

Unit 9, Exercise 12, page 77

PAIR A

a) You're a newly-married couple who chose one of the weddings in Exercise 11. Unfortunately something went wrong. You're going to be interviewed for a daytime TV chat show. Think about questions 1–6 and prepare your story.

1 Which wedding did you choose and why?
2 What was the ceremony like?
3 How did you feel?
4 What did you wear?
5 What was the best moment?
6 What went wrong?

b) In groups of four (Pair A and Pair B). Take it in turns to act out your interview for the class.

Unit 9 *DYR?* Units 7–9, Exercise 1c), page 82

STUDENT A

a) Read the letter several times until you can remember all the information. Then think about the changes you need to make to report what the letter says.

Example: He said that he loved her and . . .

> Darling,
>
> I love you. I've never felt like this about anyone. I don't want to have an office love affair. I need you with me forever. I can't stand the idea of sharing you with another man – even if he is your husband. I want you to run away with me to the USA. I worked in New York years ago and I've still got a lot of contacts there. I know we can start a new life together. All we need is love.
>
> Yours forever,
>
> Stan
>
> PS What is your favourite flower? Where were you born? We've still got so much to learn about each other.

b) When you finish, go back to Exercise 1d), page 82.

Unit 10, Exercise 6, page 85

STUDENT C / PAIR C

a) The order of the news broadcast hasn't been decided yet. You think your story should go first. Read the notes about the story and invent the details. How can you make it the best and most exciting story of the day? Have you got any film? Interviews?

> Your story is the result of months of investigation by political journalists. It's not dramatic or violent but it's very important. Is it about a danger to the public? corruption? the health service? public transport? drugs? crime? Something else? Who have you interviewed about it?

b) In groups of four (Students A, B, C and D) or eight (Pairs A, B, C and D). You're in the meeting. Work fast to decide the order of the news items.

Unit 8, Exercise 1c), page 66

12 years. Man first walked on the moon in 1969.

Unit 5, Exercise 11, page 43

PAIR A

a) Prepare for the meeting.

- You would like a statue of someone from popular culture (an actor / actress, model, famous singer, DJ, film director, etc.). The person can be living or dead.
- Make a list of six reasons why your idea should be chosen.
- Make a list of things people might say against your choice so you can defend it.

Examples: Advantages: She's a really talented . . .
Disadvantages: She isn't as important as . . .

b) In groups. Pairs take it in turns to present your ideas to the group and explain why it's the best choice. Discuss each pair's idea and agree on one idea.

Example: He's / She's / It's much more . . . than . . . And that's really important because . . .

Unit 9, Exercise 7, page 75

PAIR C

a) Look at the picture. What are the man and woman thinking? Write as many sentences as you can with *should / shouldn't have done* and *wish / if only* + Past Perfect Simple. Don't say what your situation is. Just give clues in your sentences.

Example: MAN: I wish I'd read the instructions.

b) When you finish, take it in turns to read your sentences to your group of eight. The group guesses what your situation is.

Unit 9, Exercise 12, page 77

PAIR B

a) You're presenters for a daytime TV chat show. You're going to interview a newly-married couple who chose one of the weddings in Exercise 11. Unfortunately something went wrong. Read questions 1–6 and write five more questions to ask the couple about their wedding experience.

1 Which wedding did you choose and why?
2 What was the ceremony like?
3 How did you feel?
4 What did you wear?
5 What was the best moment?
6 What went wrong?

b) In groups of four (Pair A and Pair B). Take it in turns to act out your interview for the class.

Unit 4, Exercise 4, page 33

STUDENT D

a) Fill in the gaps with true information about your learned skills.

Learned skills
1 My .... taught me how to swim.
2 I know how to ....
3 I've had .... lessons. (subject? sport?)
4 I learned how to .... when I was ....
5 I'd like to learn how to ....

b) When you finish, write a question for each sentence. Then go round the class, ask other students your questions and try to find someone who is similar to you for each question.

Example: My dad taught me how to swim.
    A: Who taught you how to swim?
    B: My dad, when we were on holiday.
    A: So did mine. How old were you?

Unit 1, Exercise 10a), page 9

STUDENT A

Fill in the boxes (1–4) on page 9 with information about your life.

Box 1: write the name of the family member you're closest to, apart from your parents.
Box 2: write the name of the place where you met someone who is important to you.
Box 3: write down the last present you gave someone.
Box 4: write the name of a person you work or study with that you don't like.

Unit 11 Conversations, Exercise 1, page 98

STUDENT B PART 2

a) Show Student A pictures 6–10. Ask how you can respond in these situations.

Example: 6 Someone says "Cheers!".
    B: What do you say when someone says "Cheers!"?

b) Check your responses with another pair.

Someone says "Cheers".

Someone is angry with you for being late.

Someone has just passed his / her driving test.

You're trying to get the waiter's attention.

Someone apologises for a mistake and you want to make him / her feel better about it.

Unit 4, Exercise 8c), page 35

PAIR B

a) You work for the Dynamic Jobs agency. You're going to interview Pair A and offer each student one of the jobs (1–3). Look at each job. What skills do the applicants need? What are the good and bad aspects of the job?

dynamic jobs dj

① submarine commander
② head of the reptile house at the city zoo
③ dancer at Disco Loco

b) Swap application forms with Pair A. Look at the forms. Write 8–10 questions to ask each student to help you decide which job to offer him / her.

Examples: In your last job did you . . . ?
You don't like working in a team. Why is that?
So, having new challenges is important to you. How do you feel about . . .ing?
Are you good at working with people?
Have you ever worked with animals?
Have you got any fears? spiders? heights?

c) You're the applicants. Pair A will interview you.

d) Now swap roles and interview each student in Pair A. Don't say what your three jobs are until after the interviews!

e) Decide on which jobs to offer each student in Pair A. Then tell Pair A which jobs you chose and why.

Unit 3, Exercise 9c), page 25

PAIR D

a) You're both in the same dilemma and you don't know what to do.

A friend of yours has met someone, fallen in love with someone and got engaged. It all happened very fast. You don't know your friend's new fiancé / fiancée very well but you don't like him / her. You know he / she has a really bad reputation.

Discuss possible solutions to your problem and the advantages and disadvantages of each solution.

b) When you finish, go back to Exercise 9d), page 25.

Unit 12, Exercise 7b), page 103

PAIR A

a) Read these pieces of holiday advice. Try to guess what the missing object / noun is. Use *It could be . . . , It might be . . . , It can't be . . . , It must be . . .*

Examples: It must be a knife.
It might be a kind of hat.

1 Soak a cotton .... in cold water and tie it round your neck to keep cool in the heat.
2 Don't forget to put .... on your hair parting!
3 If you're going to a hot country, don't pack your things in .... It'll attract mosquitoes, which love dark areas. If you have any, keep it away from your bed at night!
4 Tie a brightly coloured .... to the handle of your suitcase or backpack for easy identification among all the similar luggage at the baggage collection.
5 Wear .... when looking at street traders' goods. They won't be able to see what you're looking at and so won't try to hassle you into buying it.

(adapted from *The Guardian*)

b) In groups of four (Pair A and Pair B). Tell Pair B your idea / ideas for the missing words in sentences 1–5. Pair B will tell you the answers if you can't guess.

c) Listen to Pair B telling you what they think the missing objects are in their sentences (a–e). Look at Pair B's missing objects and tell them if their guesses are right.

local newspaper
library
frisbee
pair of socks
underwear

d) In your same groups of four. Do you take any of the things listed on holiday?

Unit 10, Exercise 10, page 87

STUDENT D

Say sentences 1 and 2 about yourself to the other students. They're going to ask you as many negative questions as possible to find out if you're telling the truth. Answer their questions and defend your sentences for as long as you can.

Example: D: I'm completely honest.
　　　　A: What? Haven't you ever told a little lie?
　　　　D: No! Never!
　　　　B: But haven't you ever . . . ? Isn't there . . . ? Aren't you . . . ? Didn't you . . . ?

1 I'm completely honest.
2 I'm completely satisfied with my job.

Unit 9 *DYR?* Units 7–9, Exercise 2a), page 82

STUDENT D

a) Read your paragraph. Do you think it's at the beginning, middle or end of the story? Read it until you can tell your part of the story without looking at it.

So they had to buy a new one. Old Pa Welbeck at the local store had a truck for sale. He wanted 800 dollars for it and wouldn't take a cent less. It didn't matter if you were old friends or not! And no, he would **not** accept a little money every week. And he wouldn't accept chickens or corn – just cash! Jed and Jemima found it hard to save that much. They had to buy food, beer and cigarettes and neither of them wanted to give up smoking or drinking! Not for a truck! So the weeks went by and they didn't save much. Then one day Jemima heard an advertisement on the radio for "Big Daddy's Truck Bargains" in the city.

b) When you finish, go back to Exercise 2b), page 82.

Unit 5 Conversations, Exercise 5, page 47

TEAM B

a) You're going to play "Your time's up!". Write four more questions like questions 1–4 for Team A to answer. (You must know the answers!)

1 Who was the first man to walk on the moon? (Answer: Neil Armstrong)
2 What's the American English word for *taxi*? (Answer: *cab*)
3 What's the longest river in the world? (Answer: the Nile)
4 What's the first name of the little boy in the cartoon comedy series "The Simpsons"? (Answer: Bart)

b) Then look at the rules of the game on page 138.

Unit 11 Conversations, Exercise 1, page 98

STUDENT A PART 1

a) Show Student B pictures 1–5. Ask how you can respond in these situations.

Example: 1 You want to get past someone.
　　　　A: What do you say when you want to get past someone?

b) When you finish, look at Part 2, page 130.

You want to get past someone.

Someone apologises for standing on your toe.

Someone says thank you to you.

Someone you've met tells you what his / her job is.

Someone sneezes.

Unit 10, Exercise 6, page 85

STUDENT D / PAIR D

a) The order of the news broadcast hasn't been decided yet. You think your story should go first. Read the notes about the story and invent the details. How can you make it the best and most exciting story of the day? Have you got any film? Interviews?

> Your story is about a famous person. Who is the famous person? What happened? You've got some not very clear photos of the event taking place which were taken from a long way away. The famous person has refused to make any comment. Have you found someone else to interview?

b) In groups of four (Students A, B, C and D) or eight (Pairs A, B, C and D). You're in the meeting. Work fast to decide the order of the news items.

Unit 9 *DYR?* Units 7–9, Exercise 1c), page 82

STUDENT B

a) Read the e-mail several times until you can remember all the information. Then think about the changes you need to make to report what the e-mail says.

Example: He asked if we could meet on Thursday . . .

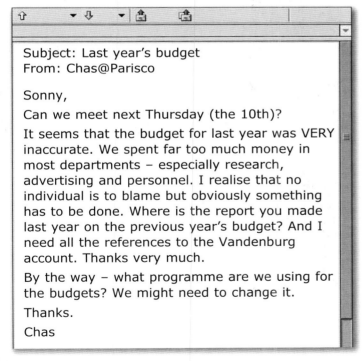

Subject: Last year's budget
From: Chas@Parisco

Sonny,

Can we meet next Thursday (the 10th)?

It seems that the budget for last year was VERY inaccurate. We spent far too much money in most departments – especially research, advertising and personnel. I realise that no individual is to blame but obviously something has to be done. Where is the report you made last year on the previous year's budget? And I need all the references to the Vandenburg account. Thanks very much.

By the way – what programme are we using for the budgets? We might need to change it.

Thanks.

Chas

b) When you finish, go back to Exercise 1d), page 82.

Unit 12, Exercise 7, page 103

PAIR B

a) Read these pieces of holiday advice. Try to guess what the missing object / noun is. Use *It could be . . .*, *It might be . . .*, *It can't be . . .*, *It must be . . .*

Examples: It must be a knife.
It might be a kind of hat.

a) Always carry a .... with the title showing so people won't know you're a tourist.

b) In a new town or city, always visit the .... You can find information about local events and history and there's a comfortable chair to sit in when you're tired.

c) Essential item: a .... You can lean on it to write. You can prepare food on it and eat off it. You can even play with it and make friends!

d) Wherever you go, take a spare .... They don't take up much space and wet, cold or blistering feet can really ruin your day.

e) Don't take all your best .... Take your worst and throw it away instead of bringing it home. You don't have to look like a film star!

(adapted from *The Guardian*)

b) In groups of four (Pair A and Pair B). Listen to Pair A telling you what they think the missing objects are in their sentences (1–5). Look at Pair A's missing objects and tell them if their guesses are right.

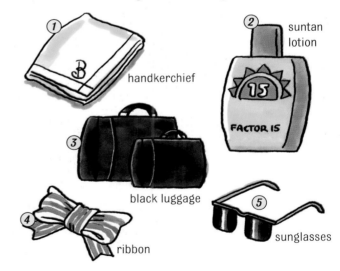

c) Tell Pair A your idea / ideas for the missing words in sentences a–e. Pair A will tell you the answers if you can't guess.

d) In your same groups of four. Do you take any of the things listed on holiday?

Key to Grammar and vocabulary puzzles

Puzzle 1 (Units 1–3)

ACROSS

1 depend
5 strange
7 member
8 won't
9 did
10 shy
11 used
13 like
14 there
16 fun
17 smog

DOWN

2 pleased to
3 do
4 cosy
6 crowded
8 whose
11 unless
12 been
15 ago

Puzzle 2 (Units 4–6)

ACROSS

2 think
3 useless
5 performance
9 as
10 suppose
11 not
13 art
14 wish
16 while
17 team
19 such
20 perk
21 paid

DOWN

1 orphan
2 throat
4 screen
6 most
7 could
8 tongue
12 ought
14 were
15 has
18 mud

Puzzle 3 (Units 7–9)

ACROSS

1 should have
4 case
6 whether
8 live
9 told
11 note
12 see
13 hasn't
14 though
17 only
19 might
20 was
22 groom

DOWN

1 sick
2 down
3 for
5 spite
7 hadn't
9 that
10 regret
12 so that
15 on
16 going
17 out
18 law
21 say

Puzzle 4 (Units 10–12)

ACROSS

1 might have
4 by
6 arrested
7 didn't
10 be
11 waste
12 based
13 away
14 been
15 can't be
16 in
17 must be

DOWN

1 mind
2 that
3 agreed
4 bad
5 it's against
8 dubbed
9 refuse
10 beaten
14 back

Recording scripts

Recording 1

WOMAN: Um, excuse me, but er are you American?

MAN: Er, yes, I am.

W: Oh. Are you from New York?

M: Well, er, Boston actually, but I've lived in New York for the last three years.

W: Oh, well, I know it sounds funny, but have we met before?

M: Er, no, no, we haven't.

W: Now are you sure? Because you know I've got the feeling I've met you somewhere. Er have you ever been to India?

M: Er, no, I haven't.

W: Oh. Um, have you travelled much?

M: Well, yes, a bit.

W: Oh, um, where have you been?

M: Well, Europe . . . Africa . . .

W: Africa? Ooh, when did you go there?

M: Two years ago.

W: Oh did you go on safari?

M: Yes, er, I did.

W: That's it! I knew it! You're the one . . .

Recording 4

1 BETH: Yeah, I'm really glad you came. . . . Yeah, it was a good party. . . . Tony? Yeah, he's a bit strange, isn't he? Did you hear what he said to me? . . . No! I don't know him. I've only met him once or twice. He's a friend of a friend. Clive — you know Clive? . . . Hmm, yeah, well they went to university together.

2 B: Oh, every time she rings it's a different problem. . . . Yeah, I know. And now she's split up with her boyfriend, so she wants to come round all the time and wants us to go out. I mean, she doesn't realise I've got a life of my own. Of course I love her, but I don't want to see her all the time. . . . Yeah, it's driving me crazy. But she's been like this since we were kids. But Mum and Dad haven't helped. They've always given her anything she wanted. She's quite spoilt. She just expects everyone to jump when she needs them.

3 B: Yeah, we're really close. I can talk to her about anything. She's like a sister to me. I mean, we've known each other since we were at primary school. . . . Exactly. I know I can always depend on her. If I ever have a problem I know she'll be there for me, for advice or, you know, just a shoulder to cry on.

4 B: Oh, he's so sweet. I know we've only been together for two months but I've never felt like this before. I think I'm in love. . . . Yeah, but it's strange. I mean,

we've got nothing in common. He hates all the films I like, the music I like. . . . Yeah, really! But you know what they say — opposites attract!

5 B: No, we don't really get on. She's a bit, um, you know, difficult. And I don't trust her. I think she wants my job! She's always so serious when Mr Clark comes in. You know, "Oh, I was reading a really good book about management at the weekend." Ugh, it makes me sick!

Recording 6

1 MAN 1: I don't really think anybody needs this kind of book, um, because . . . you, you can't control what other people feel. You can't make other people fall in love with you. It doesn't matter how many techniques you learn or, um, whatever book you read, you can't actually control other people. Um, and do you even get a money back guarantee if you . . . if you don't fall in love? Or you don't make someone fall in love with you? How does that work?

2 WOMAN 1: This book I think I could really use. In my job, I find it quite stressful at times trying to do a lot of different things at once. Er, I find myself running around . . . and, and I need to be really organised . . . and I need to keep my head straight because if I let the stress get to me then I'm not going to do a very good job.

3 WOMAN 2: I worry too much about people's feelings and therefore when they ask me to do a favour for them, or if they want to meet up and I feel I don't really have time, I always find myself saying yes and even when I'm saying it I know what my heart is really saying is no. So this book would make my life so much simpler. It would give me the confidence to know what to say and how to deal in these situations . . . with these situations.

Recording 7

DOCTOR JESSE: So, Farrah, you really think that my book has helped you?

FARRAH: Oh yes, Doctor. There's no doubt in my mind. Well, these days, I fe. . .

DR J: In what way?

F: Sorry. Well, these days I feel like a new woman! And it's all because of your fabulous book.

DR J: Thanks, Farrah. So just how has my book changed your life?

F: Well, these days I think about me! I didn't use to pay attention to my needs,

but now I listen to myself. And more importantly — my husband and my kids listen to me, too.

Recording 8

FARRAH: . . . more importantly — my husband and my kids listen to me, too.

DR J: But it wasn't always like that.

F: No. Er. Oh, I . . . I used to come home from work, and they would tell me what to cook for supper! And I'd cook it! Then I'd wash the dishes and clean the house and I wouldn't finish until midnight or later. I used to feel like a slave!

DR J: And did they use to help you?

F: Uh-uh. No sir. No way. My husband used to come home and eat his dinner in front of the TV and then he'd just go to bed. My kids were the same. I used to tell them to help round the house but they'd just ignore me. Nobody took me seriously. I used to hear a little voice in my head which said: "Say no! Don't do it!" but I didn't use to listen to it — until I read your book!

DR J: But now?

F: Now everything is different. I used to be depressed but not anymore. My husband respects me. My kids listen to me and try to help. They used to fight a lot, you know? But they don't any longer. We're all much happier together. We love each other. Yes, I certainly think it's all thanks to your book.

DR J: Well, thank you, Farrah.

F: Oh no, Doctor, thank you.

Recording 10

JOURNALIST: Er, excuse me, do you live here?

ROSS: Um, yes, yes, I do. I live right above that café.

J: Oh, right! Fantastic. Um, so do you mind if I ask you a few questions?

R: Well, I'm in a bit of a hurry but . . . er, yeah, all right.

J: So, so what's it like living here in Soho? The heart of London. A friendly, cosmopolitan community right in the centre of this historic city . . .

R: Is this for TV?

J: Er, no. Radio.

R: Oh, well, anyway er — I hate it here. It's awful. I'm thinking about moving, in fact.

J: Oh. Why's that?

R: Well, the thing is, fashionable places attract fashionable people, right? I, I understand that. But this place is becoming too popular! It's just so overcrowded! I mean I get up at six every morning for work! But do the people round here care? Oh no! People come here and they just sit in the pavement cafés all night. All the bars stay open until three or four in the morning. I mean it's just noise! All the time! And er at the moment it's really bad. I'm working on a very important project for some American clients. Er I'm working twelve or thirteen hours a day and I swear I'm not getting more than four or five hours' sleep a night!

J: Er, but there must be a good side to living here?

R: Oh sure! Oh sure! Everybody thinks it's so exciting here! You know, er my friends say to me: "It must be so atmospheric!" – but would you like to live in an expensive, noisy, twenty-four-hour disco?

J: Well I . . .

R: And it's so dirty! Look around you! All these people are eating and drinking in my street – but do you think they'll take their rubbish home with them? Ha! And there's a lot of crime, too . . .

J: Hmm, yeah, those kids over there look a bit suspicious. What are they doing to that car?

R: Hey! That's my car! Oi! You! Get away from there! Hey! I'm watching you! See what I mean? Believe me – it's just getting worse and worse!

J: Um, so, er . . . how long have you lived here then?

R: Me? Oh, er I moved in about a month ago. Yeah, I was really lucky. I got this low-rent flat . . .

Recording 12

ELLIE: Well, Adam, my boyfriend, treated me to a weekend in Amsterdam for my thirtieth birthday, you know, a romantic weekend. Um, we–his brother knew this really nice little family hotel in a nice part of Amsterdam. We were looking forward to getting away. Anyway, the weekend came, um we got to the airport, got on the plane. Everything was OK. Um, then there was this announcement. The plane was delayed, um, we, we were just stuck there for about an hour. So we were sitting there, when my boyfriend suddenly remembered something. We had to phone this hotel if we were going to arrive after eleven p.m. You know, um to, to let them know. But we couldn't. We were stuck in the plane. Well, finally we arrived in Amsterdam. It was after eleven p.m. and we just got a taxi to the hotel, and well, when we got there, we rang the bell. No answer. We rang again, several times . . . nothing. It was about er twelve now, I guess. So we finally

gave up and oh, we just walked round the streets looking for another hotel but everywhere was full. Oh it was unbelievable! And I was getting really tired and miserable, and then it started to rain, you know. It oh just got worse and worse. Anyway, at oh um about half past two in the morning, we were walking down this back street when we saw a small light. It was the police station. So we went in and well asked them what to do. But they just said there were no rooms in Amsterdam. It was some big um public holiday but we could stay there, in the police station. So, we did. I mean we had no choice oh and we were both so tired by that time. But all the police cells were full of drunk young guys, you know, um big holiday, and the policeman was nice but because most of them were English, it was so embarrassing! So we had to sleep on these plastic chairs in the reception area with these oh really bright fluorescent lights. Ugh! It was awful. The phone was ringing all the time and they were bringing people in all night and . . . Oh anyway, the next morning we both felt terrible, um really stiff. But we found our hotel and it was really nice. But we were so tired we just slept until the evening. The whole day. But we did have Saturday night in Amsterdam so it kind of turned out all right in the end.

Recording 13

1 STUDENT 1: Hello, how are you?

STUDENT 2: Er fine, thanks. And you?

S1: Fine, thanks. And you?

S2: Fine, thanks. And you?

S1: Er, fine, thanks. And you?

S2: Fine, thanks. And you?

S1: Fine, thanks. And you?

S2: Fine, thanks. And you?

S1: Fine, thanks. And you?

S2: Fine, thanks. And you?

2 JEAN: Hi, Dave! How are you?

DAVE: Ooh, well, not too good actually, Jean. I've had a bad back over the last couple of days and I just can't seem to get rid of it. Of course the doctor says not to worry but then they always do, don't they?

J: Oh, yeah, I . . .

D: And my head's a bit strange . . .

J: Yeah, I . . .

D: I can't really explain . . .

J: I . . .

D: It's a sort of nausea, but in the head, not the stomach, do you know what I mean?

J: It's . . .

D: And I can't sleep these days . . .

J: Oh dear, look at the time! Bye, Dave!

D: Ooh and my feet . . .

Recording 14

ANTONIO: . . . And just travelling round Europe. I've been in London about three weeks now.

CLARA: Really?

A: Yeah. And it's just so different, you know?

C: Yeah.

A: Yeah, you know, the people . . .

C: Hmm.

A: . . . The atmosphere.

C: Absolutely.

A: I mean, I come from this tiny village, um, about three hundred kilometres from São Paulo.

C: Uh-huh.

A: And London is just so, I mean, so big.

C: Yeah, yeah, I know.

A: You know, there are cinemas . . .

C: Mm-hm.

A: . . . Theatres, music. Everybody's rushing everywhere . . .

C: Yeah, yeah.

A: . . . doing something. People never stop here.

C: Do you mean you don't like it?

A: No, no, no, I love it. It's really exciting. There's always something to do. There's always something going on. Do you know what I mean?

C: Yeah, yeah. So you don't miss Brazil, then?

A: No, well, only when I think about it. The sun, maybe . . .

C: Oh, yes, that definitely . . .

Recording 15

CLARA: I really like London – I've been here about eleven times, I think.

ANTONIO: Eleven times? This is my first time here.

C: Really? When I first came here I couldn't speak any English at all so I felt really er lost all the time.

A: I know exactly what you mean.

C: Mmm. I used to come to this café – right here – for lunch most days because my school was near here.

A: Your school? Were you studying English?

C: Well, trying to. I thought I could go from nothing to perfect English in two months!

A: Two months? That's impossible!

C: I know that now! Anyway, it was my first day at the school and I was having lunch here and there was a guy sitting where you are. And every time I looked at him, he was looking at me. As if he was um checking something.

A: That's strange. Was he a student from your school?

C: No, no. I didn't know him. Anyway, he

suddenly got up and left, just like that, and I thought: "He's a thief!" And I checked in my bag and sure enough – my purse was gone!

A: Gone? Did you go after him?

C: Well, I stood up and started to run after him out of the café and I wanted to shout: "Stop thief!" but I didn't know "thief" in English, so I was shouting: "Stop bad man! Stop bad man!" and the waiter caught me by the arm because he thought I was trying to leave without paying. I tried to explain but he just got angry and told me to pay.

A: Did he? What an idiot!

C: Oh no, no, I can understand now, but then I just felt so completely alone.

A: Yeah. I can imagine!

C: I just sat down and burst into tears. All I had was my bus pass and about one pound twenty in change. I couldn't even pay for my lunch.

A: That's terrible. What did you do?

C: Well, I phoned my flatmate to ask her to come into town and to bring me some money and she said: "Oh, Clara! Hi! I knew you'd phone!" and I asked why and she said: "Because you left your purse here when you went to school this morning with all your money in it!"

A: No way! Really? How did you feel?

C: Embarrassed! And so stupid! But, you know, happy, too.

A: Yeah! "Stop bad man!"

C: Please! Don't . . .

Recording 16

FRIEND 1: Do you remember the guy we were talking to at Sam's party?

FRIEND 2: Do you mean the guy whose best friend is a film director . . . said he could get us into films?

F1: Yeah, well Jay and I went to that bar he told us about on Saturday – it was Jay's birthday.

F2: That's incredible! I was there on Thursday! It was some stupid office party. They were looking for somewhere that was modern, you know, cool. At least, I think it was the same bar. It's the bar that's got a lizard hanging from the ceiling? Right?

F1: Yeah.

F2: So what did you think of it?

F1: Well, it was OK but it was really crowded, difficult to get a drink and quite noisy and smoky, too.

F2: Oh, it must be different during the week – I mean it was busy but not really crowded when we were there. Besides, it's quite spacious. I thought it was quite relaxed, and I liked the mix of people. Some smart, some casual, just having a drink. Some straight from the office –

like us. Some of the records which the DJ put on were a bit . . .

F1: Too loud? Yeah, I know! So were you sitting in the restaurant bit?

F2: Well, we were sitting in the upstairs part which has those enormous windows. Is that what you mean?

F1: Yeah, that looked nice.

F2: Yeah, our boss reserved a big corner table there. According to him, it's the part where all the media people sit! Our waiter, who was an out-of-work actor, was really funny. But I didn't see anyone famous. Oh, except I saw that guy who's in that beer ad. You know, the guy with the little dog?

F1: Oh right, yeah.

F2: Oh, and there was also . . .

Recording 17

ALISON: I'm going home.

STEPHANIE: Why? We've only been here an hour. There are loads more shops. Come on.

A: No, Stephanie. That's it. If I stay here, I'll spend all my money.

S: So what?

A: Well you know I'm saving for my holiday. If I spend any more, I won't have enough for Spain.

S: Oh well, we could just window-shop.

A: I can't window-shop! You know that. Unless I leave right now, I'll spend it all.

S: Well, what are you going to do then?

A: I don't know. But I'm not going to ruin my holiday just because you can't stop shopping.

S: Oh I can stop! There! I've stopped! I'm going to have a drink. Are you coming? Oh come on. Just one quick drink at the pub.

A: Oh sure. If we go to the pub, I'll be there all night.

S: Well, I'm going. If Tom's working on the bar, I might get a couple of free drinks. Who knows?

A: Oh, well, if they're free . . .

Recording 18

1 WIFE: Oh, look at the time! I don't believe it!

HUSBAND: Well, they started late.

W: But I told the babysitter we'd be home by one o'clock!

H: You're joking! Well I don't want to leave yet.

W: Well, if we stay longer, we'll have to pay her more.

H: What do you mean?

W: She charges by the hour.

H: Well, that's OK. This is good. I want to stay.

W: But the thing is we've never used her before. She might get a bit nervous if we come home late the first time.

H: Oh, she'll be all right. Stop worrying!

W: Mmm. Yeah, all right . . .

H: Carol, you're not listening to the best jazz musicians in the country. What's the point of coming out if you don't enjoy yourself?

W: Yeah, you're right. I know, but . . . Oh look – I'm going to phone her. I'm just going to check that she's fine and the kids are OK.

H: OK. Tell her we'll be back by two thirty at the latest.

2 ABIGAIL: . . . After two years together . . . but I . . . Oh, um – cappuccino?

FRIEND: Yeah, fine.

A: Two cappuccinos, and a slice of double chocolate Boston cheesecake, please.

F: Wow! You are depressed.

A: I know, I'm eating to forget. I've got to do something to stop thinking about Jason.

F: Look, this is stupid. Why don't you just phone him? You'll feel better if you talk to him. And who knows? If you both talk about the problems, you might get back together.

A: Exactly. And I'm not sure that I want to get back together with Jason. That's the problem. If we start going out together again, the same thing will happen again . . .

F: So you're going to sit at home every night, feeling miserable and waiting for him to phone you. Just so you can tell him to leave you alone. Oh really Abi, what are you going to do?

A: Mmm! Right now I'm going to eat this cheesecake. Then we can talk about Jason.

F: You need help, Abigail.

Recording 19

ANGIE: What do you feel like doing tonight?

MARTY: I don't know, Angie. What do you feel like doing?

A: Well, we have to do something. It's Saturday night. I don't want to go bowling like last Saturday. How about calling up that girl we met at the movies about a month ago?

M: Which one was that?

A: That girl that was sitting in front of us with the little friend.

M: Oh, yeah.

A: We took them home all the way out in Brooklyn. Her name was Mary Feeney. What do you say? Do you think I ought to give her a ring?

M: It's five o'clock already, Angie. She's probably got a date by now.

A: Well, let's call her up. What can we lose?

M: I didn't like her, Angie. I don't feel like calling her up.

A: Well, what do you feel like doing tonight?

M: I don't know. What do you feel like doing?

A: Well, we're back to that, huh? I say to you: "What do you feel like doing tonight?" And you say to me: "I don't know, what do you feel like doing?" Well, I'll tell you what I feel like doing. I feel like calling up Mary Feeney. She likes you.

Recording 20

RAE: OK, so we're both working every single second of the day next Monday, so, let's say Tuesday, half past four?

BRETT: Sorry, Rae. Impossible. I'm playing golf with Sellers and Company. How about Wednesday morning, say ten fifteen?

R: Out of the question. I'm flying to Washington at nine! What do you say to half past four Wednesday afternoon?

B: A big no no, my friend.

R: And half past four Wednesday morning?

B: Um, nope. I'm sleeping until six thirty. How about Thurs. . .

R: Don't even think about Thursday!

B: Right! Hmm. Friday's really . . . er w–e–l–l. What are you doing on Friday from twelve thirty until one? Maybe a quick lunch?

R: Ouch! The boss is giving a presentation on plastics – right through until five. How does six fifteen until seven Friday evening look?

B: Friday evening. Hey, er oh . . . yeah. I'm not doing anything after six p.m. I'm all yours!

R: Oh! Wait! Darn it! Sorry! I'm meeting Mary at the airport at six twenty. Where are you spending the weekend? Maybe on Sunday we could . . .

Recording 22

MARK: I know things were a bit different in those days. Quite different, really. Er before my mum and dad got married – and people used to get married much younger in the fifties than they do now – my mum and dad were . . . what? Twenty? Twenty-one? Anyway, before that my mum says she used to spend hours getting ready to go out. I mean maybe girls still do but she says, you know, she'd start about six. Wash her hair, then she'd take literally an hour to get dressed and then she'd do her hair and her make-up. Really paint her face, not just a bit of lipstick. No-one does that now, do they? So my dad used to come

round, this was a Saturday night, no-one ever used to go out in the week in those days! Nowadays people go to clubs and that any night they want, but then . . . Anyway, Dad'd come round about half past seven and they'd walk to the bus stop – no-one had cars then – and they'd go to this dance hall and, dance. Not to records – there was a live band. And at midnight the place would close and my dad would walk my mum home, because there didn't use to be any buses after about eleven. Rock and roll, eh?

Recording 23

MRS WELLORF: We've just been a bit concerned about Lucy's progress at school, so we really don't know whether to continue at all because . . .

PROFESSOR BLUNT: Ah, Mrs Wellorf. There's no doubt that you should continue. Lucy is making wonderful progress. Aren't you, Lucy?

LUCY: Dunno.

PB: Fabulous! She's so honest.

MR WELLORF: But do you seriously think that she is genius material?

PB: Absolutely! I have her report here, and er, it's, it's very interesting. Um, she makes me think of the genius Martha Graham . . .

MRS W: The dancer? Really?

PB: Oh yes. Lucy loves to run and dance and move, just like Martha Graham. And um like Martha Graham, she's not very good at mathematics. Mathematics isn't really one of her stronger points. In fact, she dances during the mathematics lessons. A sign of genius.

MR W: Um, OK, er, but how about her other basic subjects . . . er, reading, writing?

PB: Um, yes, well, um she's quite good at writing, um, not too enthusiastic, perhaps and er her reading is perhaps not um, um, b–b–b–b–but, did you know that Picasso himself was hopeless at reading? Hopeless! His assistants had to deal with all of his letters, business documents, you know . . .

MR & MRS W: Oh, really?

PB: Yes, but he was extremely good at artistic work, of course. There are always two sides, you see.

MRS W: Oh, so do you mean she's good at painting?

PB: Um, she's not bad at drawing, I think. Look, she's drawing on my desk now!

MR & MRS W: Oh, well done, Lucy!

PB: Er, yes. But um perhaps her genius will really develop in a different direction. Mahatma Ghandi, for example, had no artistic talent, but he was very

good at communicating and dealing with people, you see.

MR W: So Lucy's good with people? Er, she's got a lot of friends?

PB: W–e–l–l, um, how many is "a lot"? Anyway, Einstein was useless at making friends, terrible with people! But obviously he had the most amazing mind . . .

MRS W: So she's like a mixture of Martha Graham, Einstein, Picasso and Ghandi?

PB: S–s–she's a little more um angry and er physical than Ghandi perhaps, but um yes, in a way.

MR W: So we're not wasting our money sending her to your school?

PB: Oh, dear me no! No, no, no, no! It's simply a question of discovering her personal strengths and developing them. But, um with genius, you must be patient.

MRS W: Well, thank you so much, Professor Blunt.

MR W: Um yes, and here's our cheque for next year. Thank you very much for everything.

PB: Er she's worth every penny. Aren't you, Lucy?

L: Dunno.

PB: She's so sweet – brilliant conversationalist . . .

Recording 24

1 FRANK: Running a club, well, it's a really demanding job. I have to take care of everything. Um, but I've got a lot of experience and I think these days I'm quite good at dealing with people. I mean, when you're on stage, doing a comedy act, you have to deal with people all the time. You have to take criticism, which is really difficult, especially if the criticism is coming from some idiot at the back who's shouting at you and not listening. Um you can't get angry with the audience. You have to think on your feet and quickly say something funny so the others will listen to you and not him. Sometimes I don't know why I do it. I mean, it's so stressful. But, on a good night, it's fantastic. There's nothing like it. I mean, I think I've got a natural talent for comedy but there is a lot of pressure. I have to write new material every day. I'm always reading the papers, thinking up ideas, watching people, taking notes. Um you can't use the same jokes again and again – so I never really switch off, you know. But um I love the freedom. Nobody tells me what to talk about. I don't have to get up early – no timetable. I can wear what I want, which is great. Of course there's no job security, and I might earn more if

I worked for a company . . . in the er marketing department of some multinational . . . global . . . er I-don't-know-what, but um I couldn't just sit in an office waiting to get an annual pay rise, because for me, this isn't really a job. It's just what I am.

2 ALAN: Well, I'm, er, responsible for making sure that we get new clients and of course, that we keep the ones we've got. There's a lot of stress. I'm under pressure to succeed, but that's the job. I spend half my working day on the phone or writing e-mails and the rest in meetings or with clients where I have to look smart because I'm representing the company. I mean I don't have to wear a tie, unless I want to, but definitely smart. Um, before I started, one of the attractions was the money, obviously. And it's true, if you're lucky, it's very well-paid. I travel all over the world and I get all those perks, like a car, regular bonuses, long holidays. But I work long hours, too. Basically I have to be available all the time. I have to stay in meetings till two in the morning sometimes, or work all weekend. I can't go home just because it's five o'clock. You have to work in a team here, too. People depend on me, I depend on them. You have to get on well with your colleagues. And your clients because if I lose them I might lose my job. But I mean, er, I think I'm quite good at working with people. Um, you have to deal with problems, too, and make decisions quickly. When you work for an advertising agency, everything's fast but I can work under pressure, so it's OK. It's never boring, you know – work hard, play hard. I don't think there's another job I'd prefer. I really enjoy doing what I do.

Recording 26

1 MARIO: Um, I have to sit next to the aisle because my legs are very, um, very long, you know?

ZARA: It's OK, Mario. We're sitting in the front row.

M: Ah. OK . . .

ANNOUNCER: Ladies and gentlemen, will you please take your seats. This evening's performance will begin in five minutes.

2 MAN 1: Whoa! Hey! Hello, Dorking! Are you ready to rock and roll! Please welcome to the stage, Axilla!

3 ATTENDANT 1: Who's in charge of these children? Please tell them not to climb on the exhibits! Oi! Get down from there! That's ten thousand years old!

4 MAN 2: This is so stupid! The presenter knows nothing about it? Turn it over.

WOMAN 1: You turn it over. You've got the remote.

M2: No, I haven't. You've got it.

W1: I haven't got it. You had it a minute ago. You're probably sitting on it . . .

5 MAN 3: Er, excuse me . . .

LIBRARIAN: Ssssh!

M3: Er, have you got back issues of *The Times*?

L: Sorry?

M3: Um, have you got . . . ?

L: Ssssh! Please!

M3: All right, um, sorry. I was looking for back issues . . .

L: Tobacco?

M3: Um, no, I was, er, trying to locate . . .

6 WOMAN 2: Er, excuse me. Who did this sculpture? I can't see the artist's name anywhere.

ATTENDANT 2: That's modern art, that is . . .

W2: Er, yes, I know. But I um can't find the name of the sculptor anywhere. Do you . . .

A2: That's not real art. My four-year-old daughter could do that . . .

W2: Yes, perhaps, but, er oh dear . . .

Recording 27

ZARA: How long have we got? About fifteen minutes?

MARIO: Yes, I think so. So, are you enjoying it?

Z: Yeah, I think it's great! I can't wait for the ending! How about you?

M: Um, to be honest, I'm a bit lost. It's all rather complicated.

Z: OK. What do you want to know?

M: Well, er, Sarah and John were married, right?

Z: Yeah.

M: And Rebecca and John were having an affair.

Z: Yeah, that's right.

M: OK, so, who phoned Sarah that night?

Z: Rebecca!

M: Ah! I thought so. And what did she say?

Z: She told her everything, but Sarah already knew about the affair. She found the letter on . . .

M: On the table, in the kitchen! Right! Right! OK. But who wrote the letter? Rebecca or John?

Z: John wrote it. But he was killed before he could send it.

M: Oh, I see. Well, who killed John?

Z: Terry, his br . . .

M: Oh, his brother. OK. I get that. But what made him do that?

Z: Well, we don't know yet – that's the question. What did Terry find out that day? And who told him?

M: OK! Right. I think I've got it now.

Z: So, shall we go back in? Have you finished your drink?

M: Er, yeah, yeah . . .

Recording 28

MALLORY: Oh! Val! Come here! Just look at this! Fantastic, don't you think?

VALERIE: Hmm, John Frank.

M: I just love his work.

V: Hmm, what's it called? No! Don't tell me! It's er *Child in Time* no, er, no, no, *Wing* . . . just *Wing*.

M: Let's see, um, it's called *Black on White*.

V: Oh, Of course! Well, it's a bit more experimental than his other work, slightly less ordinary. It's all right.

M: What do you mean "all right"?!

V: Well, I mean "all right". I prefer this one by Yi Mo, you know, that Chinese artist. She's such an amazing painter. Just look at the way she uses colour. It's so black! Her style is a lot freer than Frank's.

M: Oh, how can you say that?! His style is much more exciting.

V: Well, I'm sorry. I don't agree. It really does nothing for me. The whole thing is just so obvious.

M: Oh, you're such a snob, Val, just because Mo is more famous. I think Frank is far more talented than any artist at this exhibition. And this is a modern masterpiece.

V: Oh! Now you've gone too far! It's far less interesting than Mo's work. Look at this! Have you ever seen anything like this before?

M: Well, I suppose it isn't quite as boring as some of her other stuff, um, perhaps it's nearly as interesting as some of Frank's early work. No! No, it's just boring . . . obvious . . .

Recording 30

NIGEL: . . . so I came here to New York to live where Warhol lived and to be er an artist, man.

DUNCAN: Right! So what have you been doing?

N: What've . . . well, I've been, um, I've been creating art, man.

D: Er, art?

N: Yeah, I've been, er, I've been er making films.

D: Oh yeah? Really? Can I see one?

N: Well I, I haven't finished a whole film, er, I've been er, I've been busy. I mean, er, I've been writing a novel, too!

D: Oh, fantastic. How much have you written?

N: Well, um, nothing um, really, yet, but er well I've thought of a fantastic title.

D: Oh, right. Let's see, is it called *I'm So Useless*? I mean, I don't believe you, Nigel! You never change!

N: No, no, come on. I mean I haven't got much time, man! Yeah. I've been going out! You know – I've been exploring New York! I need ideas, man, artistic stimulation!
D: Where have you been?
N: Um well, I've been to lots of places.
D: Have you been to the Museum of Modern Art?
N: Huh! I mean, have I been to . . . ? Well, er, no, not yet, but well it's, er, I'm, I've been working on a series of portraits . . .

Recording 31

MAN: Hmm, so, what about this one?
WOMAN: Oh, I like it. It looks er warm. What do you think it is?
M: Hmm, I've got no idea what it is. I suppose it's some sort of animal.
W: Oh, it doesn't look like an animal to me. I think it's meant to be two people.
M: People? Hmm.
W: Yeah, see? This is the man. It looks as if he's whispering, telling her a secret or something . . .
M: Oh, yeah. That looks like a giant ear . . .
W: No, that's her head . . .
M: Hmm, maybe. No, wait. Maybe they're two hands. They might be holding something.
W: Hmm.
M: So, what is it anyway? Have a look.
W: Oh, er . . . oh, *Moon Head*. Hah! See? I was right.
M: Well, you got the head bit right. Oh, I want a coffee.
W: Oh, yeah, me too. Where's the café?
M: Er, I think it's down on the first floor.

Recording 33

QUIZMASTER: Thank you. Thank you. So, it's all or nothing, then. The ten-second big one! For a possible 10,000 pounds! Hey, hey. Are you ready, Geoff?
GEOFF: Um, yes.
Q: OK, for ten thousand pounds, in ten seconds, what is the capital of Iceland?
G: Oh! Oh! Um it's er, oh no, no, no. Hang on, hang on. Let me think. Don't tell me, don't tell me . . .
Q: I can't tell you.
G: Ssh, oh it's um . . .
Q: Five seconds, Geoff.
G: Ssssh. Oh, it's on the tip of my tongue. It's er . . . Oh! I know it, I know it. It, it starts with G, I mean, there's a G in it.
Q: Time's up, Geoff, I'm sorr . . .
G: Ssssssh, wait a minute! Let me see. Oh, I know it's . . .
Q: Er sorry, Geoff. Er that's it.
G: No, no, no, no, no, wait a minute, um just a second. It's um, oh Os . . . , oh no, that's er that's Sweden. I know it.

Q: I'm sorry Mr Cook, that's it, we're all out of time.
G: No! Hold on, um oh, Iceland, Iceland, Iceland. It's, it's something like Chakyak, er, oh, or um, Chakyak. Chekooyak! Chikayak!
Q: OK. That's it! Security! Security!
G: No, no, no! I've nearly got it! Is it Copenhagen?

Recording 34

1 AMY: Well, in the early 90s I was living in London . . .
MAN: Mm-hm.
A: And I, er, was in a pub one night and I met this guy who was training at the Vidal Sassoon hair salon.
M: Oh.
A: And he asked me if I would go in one day to do a sort of a hair fashion show modelling thing.
M: Yeah.
A: He just wanted to do my hair.
M: Cool.
A: I thought OK, that would be fun, so I went in and anyway he took my hair and teased it up into this big beehive that just sat up on the top of my head.
M: Fantastic!
A: It was hilarious – it was just this big mess of hair all teased up sitting up there.
M: And you didn't like it? Or . . . ?
A: Well, it wasn't "me" really. I mean it definitely isn't what I would do to my hair in the morning. Anyway it was very funny. Um, at the end of the day he asked me if I wanted to keep it or if I wanted to lose it.
M: Yeah . . .
A: And I thought, well, I'm never ever going to look this way again, so I decided to keep it.
M: Right.
A: And I was the strangest person in the London Tube for a day.
M: Well, that's one way of getting attention anyway.
A: Yeah, well, it . . . it worked!
2 TIM: Hmm, well, I've always wanted a leather jacket, a black leather jacket. And I wanted something that looked really authentic, really . . .
WOMAN: Uh-huh . . .
T: . . . sort of worn. Sort of film-starish . . .
W: Uh-huh . . .
T: You know, so, I'd heard from people that you could buy things like this a . . . down at the Portobello Market in London . . .
W: Oh . . . yeah.
T: Er, so I went down there with a few friends and we had a great time just going to all the stalls trying on all the

jackets. There were hundreds and hundreds to choose from. Er, so I found one and it just looked fantastic. It was er, a really, really excellent fit . . . Um . . .
W: Uh-huh.
T: . . . it was sort of . . . looked very worn . . . just the perfect look I wanted. something . . .
W: Great!
T: . . . that could go with everything.
W: Yeah . . .
T: So, I bought that there and then. And I've loved it ever since.

Recording 35

RYAN: Wow! I wish I could live on an island like that. Isn't that amazing?
TINA: Mmm. What's the magazine?
R: Oh, it's *Scene*.
T: Oh, let's have a look.
R: Hmm, they've got divorced again.
T: Mmm, and look . . . look at her lips!
R: Yeah!
T: No, I mean look how plastic she looks. She's had so many operations.
R: No . . .
T: Yeah, yeah . . . look . . . look, look there . . .
R: Hmm, yeah. I see what you mean.
T: Well, if I had loads of money, I'd have plastic surgery.
R: Really?
T: Well, not as many times as her, but yeah, definitely. In fact I'd just love to have money. I mean, look at her, look at those clothes, look at her lifestyle, all those parties, film premieres, amazing-looking men. It's not fair!
R: Well, yeah, sure. I wish I didn't have to work. I wish I had more money, but I mean . . . Would you really like to be that famous?
T: Yeah, yes, please. Oh, don't give me that "Yeah, but would you really be happy?" rubbish. If I were famous, I could have anything I wanted. Of course I'd be happy.
R: Not necessarily. Look at all the therapy those people have had and broken marriages . . . paranoia. Would you really be happy if you had everything? I mean you wouldn't have to work for anything.
T: Great! I hate working.
R: Oh, be serious. People would follow you everywhere. You wouldn't have any privacy. Just think, photographers would camp outside your house if they thought they could get a photo. People would think you were public property! Are you telling me that wouldn't bother you?
T: Look! I wouldn't care what people thought if I had that much money.
R: Oh, yes you would. You'd be miserable! You'd hate it!

T: No, I wouldn't. Look. If it weren't fun, people wouldn't want it. OK, sure, if I were in the public eye all the time, it might get depressing sometimes, er, the stress and everything. But if I got depressed, I'd just er have some champagne . . . buy another house . . .

R: Oh, you're useless.

Recording 37

TONY: Well, I'm an actor, and er, when I was just starting out this friend of mine told me about this ad in the paper . . . looking for people to appear in a TV commercial. So, I phoned the agency to er arrange an interview. And the woman I spoke to told me: "Oh you should have a good chance of getting this job – a strong young man like you." Of course, um you know, this was over the phone and the woman had only heard my voice. And I er panicked a bit, because I'm actually very skinny! I told my friend about it and he told me that Christopher Reeve had put on several jumpers when he auditioned for *Superman*, so he just advised me to do the same and put on lots of jumpers. So when the day came, I put on about five jumpers, one on top of the other and I went along to the interview. Only this was in June and it can get really hot here in Spain in June. And I er had to wait for ages for my interview. I mean, you know, there were lots of people there. And I was sitting there, in all those jumpers, and finally, I just got overheated and I fainted in the interview room. Um, but the funny thing is it turned out they were hiring all kinds of people. They didn't have to be big guys or anything so all those jumpers were just a waste of time. But anyway I did get the job in the end.

Recording 40

1 MAN: If I had to have one, I would have my surname, which is Wong, in Chinese, because I think Chinese characters look very beautiful and I think I would have it on the top of my right arm.

2 WOMAN: If I had to have one, I suppose I would have a flower and the flower would be green and red, and it would be quite small, quite delicate and . . . hmm . . . I think I would have it on my ankle because I love shoes, I love sandals, um, in the summer, and I think that would kind of fit quite nicely with the, with the type of sort of strappy sandals that I like to wear.

Recording 41

JOURNALIST: So er, you're calling it the Art Café. Is that right?

VALERIE: Arts Café.

J: Er, yeah, right, um, hmm . . . what are you planning to have, er, in the way of arts?

V: Well, we want this place to be a showcase for hot young talent. You know writers, painters, visual arts and performing arts.

J: I see, er, so are you going to have live music?

V: Oh, yes, jazz, classical . . .

J: And er, yeah, and singers?

V: Oh, no! This isn't karaoke, darling! We want poetry, dance, art!

MALLORY: Oh Val, you're such a snob!

J: Er, yeah, um, so if you have live music, what about dance?

M: Oh, definitely! We hope to show the best of modern dance.

J: But I mean, the audience . . . the people who come to the café. They won't dance? You haven't got a dance floor?

V & M: Ugh! No, no, no. No dancing.

J: Er, right, OK. Um well, what about art? I mean, you know, visual arts, er painting . . .

V: Oh, well, we're going to have regular exhibitions, I mean artists can use us to sell their work . . . painting, sculpture, video installations. I mean only modern, experimental stuff. There are so many exciting artists around at the moment. And we want to set up a photographic gallery as well.

M: And don't forget our poetry evenings, Val. I want this place to be full of writers, poets, intellectuals. I've just got to have creative stimulation!

V: Yes, otherwise he goes into a deep depression and just eats chocolate for days . . .

M: Val! Don't be awful! I can't help it! I'm a very sensitive person.

J: Er, speaking of food . . . what kind?

V: Oh! Our menu is divine! World cuisine! We've got a fantastic chef! He's Mongolian, actually!

J: So, er are you interviewing people at the moment?

V: Oh, yes! We want the right sort of performers . . . top-class. We want to attract quality customers so we simply must provide quality entertainment. Do you see?

J: Um, yes . . .

M: Yeah! People will come here to feed their souls . . . and their stomachs.

V: Oh, you're a poet, Mal!

M: Oh, Val.

J: Er well, um so that's about it really.

V: Well, you must come to our grand opening. I mean, of course, as our guest.

J: Er, yeah, yeah, yeah . . . thanks. Yeah, looking forward to it.

Recording 42

FELIX: . . . And told him not to be late this time. So Tony got to the restaurant at nine . . . incredible for him. You know what he's like . . . always late and then he took a taxi home and I went . . .

FRIEND: Er, sorry? Um, a taxi? What?

FELIX: Oh! Sorry! He'd forgotten his wallet – typical of him!

F: Oh, right. Mm-hmm.

FELIX: So anyway, Tony finally got back to the restaurant at about, oh, I don't know . . . about ten o'clock? And he started screaming at the manager! He was so angry. I mean he was . . .

F: Wait! Hold on. The manager? Why did he . . . ?

FELIX: Oh, sorry. The manager had given our table to someone else! Unbelievable! So I said to Tony, I said: "Tony why don't we go and have an Indian instead . . . "

Recording 44

1 SECRETARY 1: Good morning. Prime Sales. How can I help you?

MR PEARSON: Hello. Could I speak to Mr Gibson, please? That's Gibson in Marketing, not the Gibson in Sales.

S1: I'm sorry. Mr Gibson is out at the moment. Can I take a message?

MR P: Er, yes. Could you tell him Jack Pearson rang?

S1: How do you spell that, please?

MR P: P–E–A–R–S–O–N. Now, we had a meeting planned for Monday at eleven thirty, but I'm going to be out of town in Madrid for four days next week, so I want to change the meeting to Friday, if that's possible. At the same time. And it'll have to be in room seven oh six, as room seven oh four isn't free on Fridays.

S1: Er, OK, so that's Mr Pearson, on Friday, at eleven thirty, room seven oh six.

MR P: That's right. If there's any problem, just tell him to phone my secretary.

S1: Right. OK.

MR P: Thanks very much.

2 CLAIRE: Yeah, hello?

JASON: Hi, Sally? This is Jason. Look, did I . . .

C: This isn't Sally. It's Claire. Sally's out somewhere.

J: Oh. Right. Um, could you tell her Jason rang? It's about a book she's got. Only it's my book and I need it as soon as possible, for an exam. Anyway, I think she's got it. I'm sure I lent . . .

C: What's it called?

J: *Intellectual Capital*. I can't remember the author.

C: OK. So, what do you want her to do?

J: Well, could she bring it to my flat? She knows the address. I'll be in all evening, studying, or she could phone if that's a problem.

C: OK. Has she got your number?

J: I think so. But it's 987253 – just in case.

C: OK. I'll tell her.

J: Great, thanks. Bye then.

C: Yeah, bye.

3 SECRETARY 2: Jones and Peters.

MR JONES: Oh, hi, Steve. Is my wife there?

S2: Hello, Mr Jones. No, I'm afraid she's in a meeting.

MR J: Oh, right. That's OK. Just tell her I rang, and um, er, I might ring her later this afternoon.

S2: So you don't want her to phone you?

MR J: No, no, no. That's fine. I'll ring her. Or I'll see her at home. It's not important, really.

S2: OK. Fine. Bye.

MR J: Bye then.

4 ANSWERPHONE: *(Beeeeeep)*

WOMAN: Jane? Pick up if you're there. Jane? Oh, OK. It's nothing really. It's Jill. It's about the cinema tonight. Are you going? I need to know. Ring me, would you, when you get this. I'll probably be in. Um, unless I'm out. Er, OK. Bye then.

5 ANSWERPHONE: *(Beeeeeep)*

MAN: Hello. This is Stan Baker, and I'm calling from Coffer Enterprises. That's C–O–F–F–E–R, in Liverpool, obviously – I mean you know us, we, um, right, anyway, this is the third message I've left this week. I hope this is the right number. Anyway I'd be most grateful if Martin Sands in the Sales Department could get back to me as soon as possible on 08706 21730 extension, er, nine. Um, before ten tomorrow, Thursday, would be best, ten in the morning, that is. It's regarding order number 614ZX. There seems to be, oh, I'll explain when we, er, it's quite important. Thank you very much.

Recording 46

PROFESSOR KARL: Brrr. Look at those clouds! There's going to be a terrible storm tonight! What a way to begin the year!

MAX: Professor! Are you listening to anything I'm saying? I'm talking about the future of medicine and you're only interested in . . . in the weather!

PK: Sorry, I . . . but it's just . . . I can't believe that . . .

M: Oh I'm not saying it will happen tomorrow. But it will happen! Medicine is changing all the time! Every day scientists understand more about the human body.

PK: Hmm, well, we'll see about that.

M: No! No! Look! The microscope! The microscope has improved enormously in recent years – we can now see into the very blood in your veins! We can . . .

PK: Perhaps, but . . .

M: And the hundreds of hours I've spent in this room over this microscope have produced . . . this!

PK: And what, exactly, is that?

M: It's a chemical mixture. A medicine so strong that I believe it may be the most important discovery of our time. When doctors realise the power it has why, it'll . . . it . . .

PK: Where's that smoke coming from? That's going to explode!

M: Yes! Yes! Exactly! An explosion across the world of medicine! The scientific community will . . .

PK: No, you fool! I mean it's going to explode! Look at it!

M: Wha . . .? *(BOOM!)* Ha! Can you imagine any disease surviving that?! Professor? Professor? Professor . . .

Recording 47

1 MAN 1: Aggh!!! Wow! Oh that was close!

WOMAN 1: Are you all right?

M1: Oh, er, yes. I er . . . I can't believe it. Just a few seconds. If I hadn't stopped to . . . to read this poster, it would have hit me!

W1: I know! You're very lucky.

M1: Oh, oh, it makes me feel sick to think about it!

2 MAN 2: Oh, this is all my fault. I've been so stupid, so very, very stupid. Ten years of marriage down the drain. How could I forget our anniversary? After everything that's happened? How could I do it? Maybe if I'd bought her some . . . some flowers or something, she might not have done this.

3 WOMAN 2: Oh! What?! I don't believe it! Oh! This is all Alice's fault! If I hadn't stopped to buy her a present, this wouldn't have happened! She can pay the fine! Oh really! I was only in the shop for two minutes. These people are so pathetic. Why aren't they out catching the real criminals? Oh, there's a police officer. Um, excuse me! Um, Officer!

Recording 49

KATH: You should do that!

ALAN: Huh! You must be joking!

K: Go on, be a sport!

A: You can't be serious!

K: Oh, come on. It'll be a laugh. It'll be fun!

A: Yeah, that's easy for you to say. You're not going to be on the stage!

K: Huh! Believe me, if I could sing, I'd be up there right now! Come on! You only live once!

A: No! No way! I'm not going to get up . . .

K: Oh, don't be such a wimp. Really, I mean what have you got to lose?

A: Are you joking? What about my reputation? I mean it's all right for you . . .

K: Reputation? Um, there are only about nine people in here, and nobody's listening anyway.

A: I know that, but I've told you. I really don't want to do it.

K: P–l–e–a–s–e. Just have a go. I'll pay for the meal.

A: OK.

Recording 51

GEORGE: Oh honestly! No, I mean Bernard, you can't seriously believe that it's right? What about qualifications? All those years that people spend studying and . . .

BERNARD: No, no. Hold on, George – I only said I think it's OK in some situations. I think if you can do the job . . .

G: Yes, but what about the other people? The people who don't have parents or uncles in the business? If you ask me, it's just unfair and immoral . . .

B: Yeah, all right. I see what you mean, but if somebody in your family can help you, by giving you a good start, then as far as I'm concerned, you'd be stupid not to take it.

G: Yes, stupid. But honest!

B: Oh, come on, George. This is the real world. The thing is, if everybody else is going to be immoral, then, you can't be the only one who goes through life living . . . .

G: But really, come on, all those well-qualified people out there, unemployed, while some twenty-year-old gets a brilliant job because her daddy knows the director. You really think that's right?

B: Well, as I said, if she can do the job, then it doesn't matter exactly how she got it, does it?

G: No, I'm sorry, I disagree completely!

Recording 52

1 MOTHER: . . . which obviously surprised him. And then he said to me . . .

TIMMY: Mummy!

MOTHER: Timmy! Why aren't you playing with the others?

T: Mummy. I feel sick. I want to go home.

M: Oh well, it's your own fault. You shouldn't have eaten so much cake. Honestly! He's been nothing but trouble all day. I should have left him at home.

AUNT: But darling, it is a children's party.

M: Oh, yes. I suppose you're right.

2 WIFE 1: Where were you? You should have been here.

HUSBAND 1: Yes, I know, I know. I wish I'd been here. But, why didn't you phone me?

W1: Oh for goodness sake, Jeremy! I was having a baby!

H1: Oh, I know darling, I know, and a very sweet one, too. So is it a boy or a girl? Do you know . . . ?

3 HUSBAND 2: What is that supposed to be? That's not music.

WIFE 2: Well, you shouldn't have asked the children to organise it, dear.

H2: Yeah, I wish I hadn't asked them.

W2: Really?

H2: No, look at them. They're having a lovely time. And anyway, how often do we celebrate twenty-five years of marriage?

W2: Oh, Harry . . .

4 BRIDE: I should never have listened to you . . . a circus wedding! What a stupid, stupid idea! If only we'd done what Mummy and Daddy said . . . a simple ceremony in a country church . . .

GROOM: I know – I'm sorry. It was the fireworks. They shouldn't have been so close to the house but oh, er, at least it's . . . unforgettable.

B: Darling, the house is on fire, there are elephants in the garden, and my mother has been attacked by a monkey. Yes, it's unforgettable, and . . . this was supposed to be the happiest day of my life. Oh, if only I'd married Nigel.

G: Nigel? N–N–N–Nigel who? Darling . . .

Recording 53

INTERVIEWER: You had some kind of cultural difference thing at your wedding, didn't you, Martin?

MARTIN: Er no – well yes. It was quite funny actually. Um, we got home after the honeymoon, and you know, we're in our new home and trying to see what things we already had and what we had to buy . . .

I: What you could afford after the . . .

M: Yeah, yeah. We still had to get a lot of things for the house. So we were just going through, I mean looking back at what we'd got from people. You know, what the families, my family and my wife, Ana's, what they'd given us. For the wedding. Wedding presents . . . gifts. So that was when I really saw this huge difference between the way the Spanish, I mean what the Spanish think is an appropriate present and the English, you know, what we normally give to each other. Even close family. So we're sitting at the kitchen table and Ana's trying to make a list . . . get things straight . . . and she says something like: "And my aunts gave us £300 each, that's £1200.

My cousin, er, who I haven't seen for about ten years and didn't even come to the wedding sent us £200, and, er . . . what about your brother? What did we get from your brother?" And I say: "Um . . . a toaster." And she writes that down, but I got a bit embarrassed. But it's perfectly normal as a wedding present in England – you give practical things for the house . . . but it just sounds so . . . a toaster . . . from my closest family! And there she is talking about all this money. It was quite funny . . .

Recording 54

1 MAN: Well, you know, um, I'm one of three and I . . . I think three's a bad number because you always get two people sort of ganging up against a third . . . so I'd say two is a good number, or er, four if you're . . . if you've got a lot of money, then and you can afford it, then four, I'd say, but . . . two.

2 WOMAN 1: Well, I left home when I was eighteen to go to college. And that worked really well for me. I felt like I was at the right level of maturity in terms of being able to manage my life and needing a bit of freedom. You always need guidance from your parents and, and from your . . . from your . . . peers but I think once you've . . . once you've sort of crossed, say, seventeen years old, I think it's an OK time to leave home and . . . and try living on your own. Knowing always that you can rely on your parents to . . . to help you out of a bad situation, if you get yourself into one.

3 WOMAN 2: I think children – teenagers – should rebel against their parents. I think it's . . . it's a natural thing. I don't think it should have to be very, um, aggressive, or a nasty period er, of, of development. I think it should be done in a positive way.

Recording 55

NANCY: M-u-u-um, Sid didn't tell me that Tom phoned, and I needed to . . .

MOTHER: Now, now, now, maybe he just forgot.

N: No, he didn't. You're always taking his side. You're always protecting him.

M: Oh, I'm so tired of this argument. It's the same thing every time. Sid?!

SID: What, Mum?

M: Did you forget to give Nancy a message this morning?

S: I don't remember. I'm not her secretary.

N: Huh, what?

S: Well, I'm sick of answering the phone for you.

N: Huh, you're just jealous because nobody ever phones you.

M: Now come on you two.

S: It's not me. She's always trying to cause trouble.

N: Well, he never gives me my messages. I'm fed up with it.

S: Oh, you're so pathetic!

N: Look who's talking! You . . .

M: Be quiet both of you!!

Recording 59

1 HUSBAND: No, I half expected it to happen, I think.

FRIEND 1: Really?

H: Oh, yes. I found it in her handbag about a month ago.

F1: Oh, no. Who was it from?

H: Someone she works with. Stan Something.

F1: Good heavens. And what did he say?

H: Well, he said that he wanted to get some . . .

2 SONNY: Oh, no! Oh, no!

COLLEAGUE: What? What's up?

S: I've deleted it! I don't believe it!

C: Have you checked in deleted texts?

S: I've checked everywhere – it's gone!

C: Was it important? What did it say?

S: It was about last year's budget. He was asking if there were a few . . .

3 FRIEND 2: Well?! Did you see it last night?

FRIEND 3: No. What happened? Anything exciting?

F2: Are you joking? Marlene finally told Charlene about Janie and Bobby!

F3: Oh, no! I can't believe it! Well, what did she say? How did she explain it?

4 FRIEND 4: Has Serena been away? I haven't seen her for ages.

TANYA: Well, I talked to her about a week ago. She sounded a bit strange.

F4: Yeah?

T: Yeah. She said she was really bored with her life, with everything. She said she wanted a complete change!

F4: Serena?! Change? I don't believe it. I mean, she's so, I don't know, conservative.

T: Yeah, I know. I'm a bit worried. I wonder if she's all right. I've tried to ring her a few times since then but there's never any answer. I might go round to her place.

F4: So what else did she say?

T: Well, she said that she'd met this guy at a party . . .

Recording 60

NEWSREADER: . . . and John Tidings is in central London now, talking to one of the organisers. John?

JOHN: Yes, Helen. I'm here with Ted Cross from Planet of Love who organised the march. Now Ted, there were two thousand people on the march and . . .

TED: That's the police estimate. We think it was closer to ten or eleven thousand.

J: Yes, but now look around – is this what you wanted to happen?

T: Of course not. We started a peaceful march at twelve o'clock and it was a bit noisy. I was with my girlfriend, chanting, you know, but a small group of maybe twenty people started throwing things and a police officer in riot uniform got hit by a bottle or something and then *BAM!* Suddenly I saw hundreds of police on horses charging towards us and the riot police running at us from the other side – we got trapped in the middle and we couldn't run anywhere. Then Cheryl . . .

J: Your girlfriend.

T: Er, yeah, er Cheryl got knocked down by a police horse, but the rider didn't stop or anything, so I picked her up and we just ran into the park. I mean the police were waiting for just one little thing to happen. It changed from quite peaceful to a complete riot in about thirty seconds – horrible! Now it's all out of control and shops are getting wrecked and a lot of people are getting hurt for no reason.

J: And the people who started the trouble didn't get arrested?

T: The police don't usually arrest other police officers.

J: Er, this is John Tidings, for the four thirty news, central London. Agh! What the . . . ?!

Recording 61

INTERVIEWER: Well, Mr Chalmers, this is quite a change from your prison cell, isn't it?

MR CHALMERS: Ah, well, yes. Still, they couldn't keep an innocent man in prison.

I: But you're out because you've finished your sentence, not because you're innocent. The jury found you guilty.

MR C: Ah, yes. But the jury was given false information. They weren't told the whole story. One day the truth will come out! I'm innocent!

I: So are you saying that you really intended to start this company?

MR C: Absolutely. I got people to invest their money in good faith, but unfortunately I was never informed about how the money was spent.

I: But weren't you the financial director?

MR C: Um, yes. It was my responsibility to get the money. But the actual business side was the responsibility of the business director, old Seymour . . .

Recording 62

INTERVIEWER: But weren't you the financial director?

MR CHALMERS: Um, yes. It was my responsibility to get the money. But the actual business side was the responsibility of the business director, old Seymour . . .

I: Ah, yes. I'm glad you mentioned him. Didn't you know, Mr Chalmers, right from the beginning, that Seymour Cripes-Tottingly was a known criminal?

MR C: Um, well. He's an old friend and we all do crazy things when we're young!

I: But he was arrested for fraud when he was thirty-six.

MR C: Ah, well . . .

I: And couldn't you see that he was simply putting the money into foreign bank accounts – that he was lying to people who trusted you!

MR C: Yes, exactly. I'm very sorry that he did those terrible things.

I: But the accounts were in your name, Mr Chalmers.

MR C: Yes, well he's a clever man, that Seymour. Clever, but criminal. That's why unfortunately I have cut off all business connections with him. Very sad.

I: But haven't you and your wife just returned from a holiday with Mr Cripes-Tottingly and his wife?

MR C: Um, well – holidays aren't business as such, really . . .

Recording 63

1 MAN 1: Well, I'm fairly sure it's against the law. I mean you're not allowed to sound your horn unless there's immediate danger or something – just to say "Look out! Get out of the way!" – otherwise it's illegal to use it, I think . . . I mean you can't just use it when you're angry but that doesn't stop people doing it. I hear them all the time in the street outside my flat – I mean it's not just selfish, it's stupid. I mean a fourteen-car traffic jam and suddenly car eleven starts going "Beeep beep beep, beeep beep beep . . ."

2 WOMAN 1: Well, it's not illegal, of course, you can chat quietly, I suppose, but it's rude to talk as if you're at home watching TV. It's just really annoying for the rest of the audience and it's not good manners. The cinema doesn't belong to you. I mean it's fine to react – you don't have to stay completely silent – but you're supposed to keep a bit quiet while other people are trying to watch the film. I told one guy to be quiet once and he just said: "Why should I? It's not against the law, is it?"

And I thought: "Well, no", but I mean how can people be so selfish?

3 WOMAN 2: You're not supposed to talk in a library. It's as simple as that. It's against the rules and it's extremely irritating for the people who're trying to get some work done. You can't talk loudly, you can't eat or drink, but it's not about rules – it's just about being polite – you know, trying not to be anti-social. You shouldn't talk in a library – is that so complicated to understand?

Recording 64

1 MAN: Yeah, jaywalking's a really strange thing. Um, I . . . I . . . you know, I . . . here in this country I jaywalk all the time. You know, when the light's red or when there's no sort of crossing . . . passage, but in America, where I'm from, it's actually a major crime. Um, in California you get really huge tickets . . . something like . . . you know . . . like fifty to a hundred dollars for jaywalking. So I wouldn't jaywalk in California. But here, why not?

2 WOMAN: This reminded me of a story an Italian friend told me. When he was on a train, um, in Italy, in Rome. He hadn't had time to buy a ticket. And the inspector came along and asked him for his ticket. And he apologised and said he hadn't had time to buy it. And to his surprise the inspector took his hat off and sat down next to him and looked really miserable and he said: "What am I supposed to do? I'm meant to check people's tickets on this train and not one single passenger on this train has had a ticket. What is the point of all this?"

Recording 65

1 WOMAN: I suppose my favourite kind of films are things . . . romantic comedies. I like to be entertained so I like something funny. And I'm a bit of a softy. Um, things I really can't stand are these sort of action films where there's just guns and noise and . . . all the time. And luckily my boyfriend can't stand them either, so we'll . . . we'll give those a miss.

2 MAN: Well, you know, I like the usual stuff. I like crime and I like thrillers. Um, sometimes I . . . if I'm in the mood I . . . I'll go and see a horror film, um, although I don't do that very much any more. My wife really likes musicals and comedies, you know, American-type comedies. Um, I don't really enjoy them but I'll go and see one or two with her, um, but it's not something that I would go out and see on my own.

Recording 66

1 FRIEND 1: I knew it would be rubbish! I hate films like that – huge expensive Hollywood blockbusters!

FRIEND 2: So why did you come, then?

F1: Well, I read a review in the paper that said it was really good – and you said it would be great!

F2: Well, I thought it was great! I mean the special effects were amazing! Really realistic!

F1: Yeah, I suppose . . .

F2: And the music was excellent! I'm going to buy the soundtrack!

F1: Who was it by? Who wrote it – do you know?

F2: No, I don't know. I wanted to read the credits at the end of the film, but you wanted to leave.

F1: Oh, sorry . . .

2 DIRECTOR: OK, honey, it's like a modern version of a classic story. Got it?

ACTRESS: Yeah, sure.

D: It's based on a novel by Charles Dickens.

A: Who?

D: It doesn't matter. And it's set in London. Modern day London.

A: Where?

D: Lon. . . er, don't worry about it. Anyway, it's about a girl of twenty and her father, who work on a boat . . .

A: I play the girl, huh?

D: No! You play the boat! Yeah, you play the girl! Now, in the first scene, you and a man are in a boat . . .

A: Ah, like *Titanic*?

D: I wish it were like *Titanic*. Er . . . now, one more time . . . you and a man are in a boat . . .

3 FRIEND 3: Where are you going?

FRIEND 4: I can't see the screen from back here! I'm going to sit in the front row.

F3: What?! What do you mean you can't see the screen? It's enormous!

F4: I know, but I've forgotten my glasses and I can't read the subtitles!

F3: Oh, really!

F4: And I don't speak Danish.

F3: Oh, I don't believe it! What?! Hey! Don't take the popcorn. I haven't eaten any yet.

F4: Excuse me! I paid for it! I'll see you at the end.

Recording 67

JAKE: . . . Um, you know. I think the answer's no. Huh, I mean, I think I've stayed to the end of every film I've ever been to. I never leave. I just can't, um, I mean, it just seems silly to spend all that money and then walk out. Really, I always sit through the whole film, even if I hate it, you know. But in fact I . . . I suppose I never really hate films. I mean, all films have some good points, I think, don't they? You know, I just like cinema . . . I suppose . . . good and bad.

Recording 69

BETSY: You said you knew the way! We should be in Los Angeles by now!

BUD: I know! I know! Darn it! But the storm's getting worse and we'll have to stay here in this big dark old house tonight. Oh gee, there's nobody . . . Hey, the door's opening.

BETSY: Now Bud, don't . . .

BUD: Great! Hey, come on in, honey. Come out of the rain.

Recording 71

BETSY: I'm trying to remember. It's all so confused . . . I . . . OK. We arrived around midnight, I guess, the door opened – I mean it just opened and Bud went in. He asked me to come out of the rain – you know it was really raining – but, well I refused to take one more step. It was dark! Real scary. But Bud was standing there and I was getting real wet and so finally I agreed to go in . . . and as soon as I was inside *BANG!* the door closed and gee . . . I got scared! I told Bud and he was so sorry for everything. He apologised for bringing me to the house, he apologised for getting lost – I mean it wasn't his fault really. Um, so anyway, then he wanted me to hold the candle while he tried to fix the electricity – you know down in the cellar, when suddenly this huge monster, I mean, a man, just appeared and put his hand on the door. We just looked at him . . . and he looked at us . . . and then he spoke – real deep and, and slow – and he warned us not to go into the cellar. He said it was um "strange" . . . yeah "strange". So Bud was calm and he promised not to go down there. And this man seemed satisfied. He said he was the servant, er . . . Glutz? Yeah, Glutz, he said. Then, as if nothing's wrong, he offered to get our bags from the car and then he . . . he offered us a glass of milk! A glass of milk! Then he told us to go upstairs . . . well . . . so we did. But then I thought I heard someone laughing, and Glutz, he told us not to come back down . . . and we just . . . but then I heard the laughing again later that night and . . . and Bud went to look and that's the last time I saw him! There's something in that cellar! You've got to come with me! You've got to help me!

Recording 72

1 GIRL: Excuse me.

MAN 1: Yes?

G: Sorry to bother you but would you mind taking our picture?

M1: No, not at all.

G: Oh, thanks a lot!

M1: Now, how do you work it?

G: Oh, you just push that button, um, at the front . . . the blue one.

M1: Ah, yeah. OK. Right . . . say "Cheese!".

GIRLS: Cheese!

2 SIMON: Mr Clark?

MR CLARK: Yes? Oh, hi, Simon.

S: Um, hi. I was wondering . . . er . . . Do you mind if I leave a bit early on Friday? You see, my sister's coming . . . just for the weekend.

MR C: No, of course not. That's fine.

3 WOMAN 1: So do you want to go to the concert?

MAN 2: Yeah, it sounds good.

W1: OK, I'll ring and book. Um, is it OK if I use your phone? I'll do it now.

M2: Sure – go ahead.

4 MAN 3: That CD looks really good. Um I know you've just bought it, but um, could I borrow it?

MAN 4: Yeah, sure.

MAN 3: Just for the weekend? To tape it.

MAN 4: Yeah . . . no problem.

5 MOTHER: Brian! Can you get that?

BRIAN: Mmm. Sure.

M: Brian! Can you please answer the phone?

B: Yeah. Yeah. OK . . . Hello . . . Hello?

M: Who is it?

B: Dunno. They've hung up.

Recording 74

MAN: Excuse me.

WOMAN: Hello?

M: Hello. I'm terribly sorry to bother you but would you mind turning your music down a bit? You see, I'm afraid I have to get up very early for work and it's three a.m. I'm afraid I'm getting awfully tired.

W: Oh dear. I'm afraid we can't. You see, we're having a party. It would be very difficult for us to turn it down right now. Could you possibly wait . . . a few hours?

M: Oh dear. That might be difficult. Um, do you mind if I phone the police?

W: No, not at all. Go ahead. Um, would you mind leaving us alone now?

M: No, not at all. No problem. Thanks so much.

W: That's OK. Bye now.

M: Bye.

Recording 75

FREDDY: I say, that soup looks awfully good. Do you mind if I take just the teeniest bit?

WOMAN: I, well I, er . . .

F: Mmm! Delicious. Oh, and that wine smells divine. Is it a rioja? Could I possibly take just a sip . . .

W: Well, actually, . . . I was just about to drink it.

F: Mmm! Heaven! Now, let's see . . . um . . . would you mind ordering some meat, perhaps a steak?

W: I'm afraid I don't eat meat. I've ordered the vegetarian moussaka.

F: Oh, excellent choice. They do a wonderful moussaka here. That'll be fine, fine. Now pass me one of those cigars, would you? You know, just while I'm waiting . . .

W: Sorry, they're my husband's.

F: Really? Jolly good quality, too, yes . . . Oh, I just love the Riviera this time of year, don't you? People are so friendly . .

Recording 77

1 MAN: I think the worst thing that parents do, when they take their children on holiday, is that they of . . . they always take them to really boring places, and they . . . the children never enjoy these . . . these . . . places they think they'll probably enjoy, um, like museums and galleries and . . . and . . . and . . . cultural things that maybe the parents think the children should . . . should learn about, um, and the other thing I think that parents always do is, especially when you're younger, er . . . is they always intr . . . want to introduce you to everybody: "This is my son, this is my daughter" and they always try and make you play with other kids and you don't want to and always making you do things you don't want to do . . .

2 WOMAN: I think when . . . when children go on holiday they're . . . they're very much thinking of it from their point of view . . . what . . . what they want to do, um, and perhaps they want to do the same thing every day, for example, if you go to the seaside, the children want to go to the beach, every day . . . and then when they get to the beach it's: "I want an ice cream, I want this I want that" and the . . . for the parents I think this could be, potentially, a little bit stressful when a . . . a holiday is supposed to be a relaxing thing . . .

Recording 78

RECEPTIONIST: Good evening, madam. Can I help you?

SARAH: Yes, er could I have the key to, er, room four oh nine, please?

R: Just a moment. Oh, I'm afraid room four oh nine is occupied, madam.

S: Er, no. I'm sorry. The room can't be occupied! That's my room. The long-haul business suite?

R: Yes, it's the business suite. Um, but I'm afraid it is booked. You may be in another room. What's the name?

S: Carmichael. Sarah Carmichael. C–A–R–M–I . . .

R: No. I'm sorry. You aren't on the list at all!

S: B–But I must be on the list! My company made this booking months ago! Can you check the computer again? You must be looking at the wrong day or something!

R: No, no, it's the right day, madam. Are you sure you booked into the King's Hotel? You might be thinking of the Queen's Hotel? Or the Royal?

S: No. It's the King's Hotel. It's tonight. I'm very tired . . .

R: Well, the booking could be under your husband's name, he is . . .?

S: No! No husband. No different room. No different hotel. Can I just have my key, please . . .

Recording 80

RECEPTIONIST: There's nothing I can do . . .

SARAH: You must have made a mistake. It's as simple as that. Can you check yesterday's reservations, please? You might have written the reservation on a different day.

RECEPTIONIST: I'm sorry, madam, but I can't have made a mistake about the reservation. You see, your name isn't anywhere in our records. Nowhere.

S: Well, I can't have dreamt it all! I'm not mad!

R: Please calm down, madam. Your travel agent might have booked you into another hotel. Or you might have cancelled your reservation and then forgotten about it. I really don't know. I only know you can't stay here. We're full.

S: I didn't use a travel agent. I told you. It's business . . . my company booked . . . Oh, wait! Of course! Is there a message for me?

R: I'll have a look – what was the name again?

S: Carmichael! My company must have changed the hotel at the last minute. They're always doing that!

R: Yes, here you are.

S: Oh! I knew it! Oh, I don't believe this! Can you phone me a taxi, please?

Recording 82

GUY: Oh, you're going to Cuba?

KATE: Yes, we got a really good deal. Come on. You're the expert. You've got to tell me all about it. What about the crocodile farm? I've heard it's really amazing.

G: No, no, I wouldn't bother. It isn't worth it. It was the only guided tour I went on. It takes five hours to get there and the crocodiles just lie there. It was really boring. Everyone just stood around for an hour and then got back on the bus and left . . .

K: Oh, but I'm really looking forward to the Havana Café. I mean . . .

G: Oh, I went there. It's a waste of time – and money! It's just this huge tacky place, really plastic, ten dollars a drink if you want to sit next to the stage . . . and there's this ten-piece salsa orchestra. I mean, they just come on stage, sing a couple of tourist pleasers and walk off! But you've got to stay in the Hotel Nacional!

K: Yeah, but isn't that really expensive?

G: Yeah, but it's worth every penny.

K: I don't know . . .

G: Well, if you don't stay there, just go and have a look. I mean, it's definitely worth seeing. Really amazing!

Recording 83

GUY: So, anyway, as I said . . . the Havana Café is a complete rip-off. It's awful.

DEREK: The real Havana Café? In Cuba? Oh, it isn't that bad.

G: Oh, have you been to Cuba?

D: Yeah, I was there last year. I really enjoyed it. I think it's the most fantastic place I've ever been.

G: Oh, come on! It isn't that good.

D: I loved it.

G: Oh, I give up.

D: It's got an amazing atmosphere. And all the women are so beautiful.

G: Oh, they aren't that good-looking.

D: Anyway, Kate, I really think you'll love it!

K: Oh, sorry? I wasn't listening . . .

Irregular verb list and Guide to pronunciation

Verb	Past Simple	Past participle
be	was / were	been
beat	beat	beat
become	became	become
begin	began	begun
bend	bent	bent
bite	bit	bitten
blow	blew	blown
break	broke	broken
bring	brought	brought
build	built	built
burn	burned / burnt	burned / burnt
buy	bought	bought
catch	caught	caught
choose	chose	chosen
come	came	came
cost	cost	cost
cut	cut	cut
deal (with)	dealt (with)	dealt (with)
dig	dug	dug
do	did	done
draw	drew	drawn
dream	dreamed / dreamt	dreamed / dreamt
drink	drank	drunk
drive	drove	driven
eat	ate	eaten
fall	fell	fallen
feel	felt	felt
fight	fought	fought
find	found	found
fly	flew	flown
forget	forgot	forgotten
forgive	forgave	forgiven
freeze	froze	frozen
get	got	got
give	gave	given
go	went	gone
grow	grew	grown
hang	hung	hung
have	had	had
hear	heard	heard
hide	hid	hidden
hit	hit	hit
hold	held	held
hurt	hurt	hurt
keep	kept	kept
know	knew	known
learn	learned / learnt	learned / learnt
leave	left	left
lend	lent	lent
let	let	let
lie	lay	lain
light	lit	lit
lose	lost	lost
make	made	made
mean	meant	meant
meet	met	met
pay	paid	paid
put	put	put
read	read	read
ride	rode	ridden
ring	rang	rung
rise	rose	risen
run	ran	run
say	said	said
see	saw	seen
sell	sold	sold
send	sent	sent
set	set	set
shake	shook	shaken
shine	shone	shone

Verb	Past Simple	Past participle
shoot	shot	shot
show	showed	shown
shut	shut	shut
sing	sang	sung
sink	sank	sunk
sit	sat	sat
sleep	slept	slept
smell	smelt	smelt
speak	spoke	spoken
spell	spelt	spelt
spend	spent	spent
split	split	split
stand	stood	stood
steal	stole	stolen
stick	stuck	stuck
swear	swore	sworn
swim	swam	swum
take	took	taken
teach	taught	taught
tear	tore	torn
tell	told	told
think	thought	thought
throw	threw	thrown
understand	understood	understood
wake (up)	woke (up)	woken (up)
wear	wore	worn
win	won	won
write	wrote	written

Guide to pronunciation

Vowels

/ə/	again, doctor, finally, seven
/æ/	cat, glad
/ʌ/	mum, run
/ɑː/	half, arm
/e/	red, any
/ɪ/	miss, ill
/iː/	seat, see
/ɒ/	boss, on
/ɔː/	forty, awful
/ɜː/	bird, early
/ʊ/	put, good
/uː/	food, true
/ɪə/	beer, year
/ʊə/	cure, tourist
/eə/	hair, care
/eɪ/	plane, play
/ɔɪ/	join, boy
/aɪ/	wife, eye
/əʊ/	go, boat
/aʊ/	out, town

Consonants

/p/	pop, shop
/b/	bike, job
/f/	five, cough
/v/	video, wave
/t/	time, sit
/d/	dad, read
/θ/	thing, healthy
/ð/	then, weather
/tʃ/	church, question
/dʒ/	jar, agent
/s/	soft, rice
/z/	magazine, noise
/ʃ/	shut, ambition
/ʒ/	television, pleasure
/k/	coast, black
/g/	girl, bag
/m/	make, home
/n/	name, fun
/ŋ/	sing, long
/h/	hot, who
/l/	live, level
/r/	rock, married
/w/	wet, away
/j/	yellow, use

Acknowledgements

The authors and publishers would like to thank the following teachers for piloting and / or reporting on the manuscript:

In **Brazil**, Anna Szabó (Cultura Inglesa, São Carlos), Ana Beatriz Medeiros de Sousa (Cultura Inglesa, Rio de Janeiro), Giselle Maria Paula e Silva Soffiatti (Sociedade Brasileira de Cultura Inglesa, Curitiba); in **Italy**, Sophie Salaman (University of Florence Language Centre), Monica Martino (UPTER Università popolare di Roma), Wendy Armstrong (International House, Milan), Claire Wroe (MCD, Milan), Gian Piero Bonacossa (Liceo Sc. St. "Taramelli", Pavia); in **Poland**, Hanna Kaczmarczyk (Warsaw University Studium), Anna Nowakowska (SJO Proficiency, Sopot); in **Spain**, Alejandro Zarzalejos (Escuela Oficial de Idiomas, Las Rozas, Madrid), Ana Fraile del Pozo (Escuela Oficial de Idiomas de Alcalá de Henares), Mike Carter (CLIC International House, Seville), Birgit Ferran Eichmann (Escola Oficial d'Idiomes de L'Hospitalet de Llobregat), Fernando Alba Navarro (Escuela Oficial de Idiomas de Valdemoro) Matthew Cruickshank, Claire Balch, Jura Zymantos, Jackie Neff, Michael Tregebov (ESADE Idiomes, Barcelona); in **the UK**, Sue Wharton and the MA students on the MSc TESOL course at Aston University Language Studies Unit (Vicdan Erkir, Sarah Gasparinatou, Effie Migga-Vlachou, Esra Sagol, Jenny Bartlett, Katherine Jaehnig, Tessa Osborne, Marion West, Debbie Jagaraki, Marilena Nikolaou-Koutsoupaki, Anastasia Kinali, Fotini Vareltzis, Julia Rodriguez, Wolfgang Luhrer, David Coulson, Katherine de Vries, Keith Delves, Flora Tate), Patrick Dare (Wimbledon School of English), Gerald Kelly (Francis King School, Victoria), Steve Perry and Jo Thorpe (Bell Language School, London), Martin, Kaz Janowski (BBC English), David Game and Patrick Barden (David Game College, London), Russell Stannard, Katy Mann (Crawley College), Martin Williams, Carolyn Jones, Anne Cox, Lynne Rushton.

The Wavelength publishing team:

Jenny Colley (Publisher), Rose Wells (Editorial Assistant), Paul Katumba (Production Controller), Hilary Morgan (Picture Editor).

The publishers would particularly like to thank Brigit Viney, Shona Rodger, Ruth Atkinson and Rob Briggs for their work on this Coursebook.

We are grateful to the following for permission to reproduce copyright photographs:

The Art Archive for 46 bottom left and 46 bottom right; Bridgeman Art Library for 32 right, 46 top left and 46 top right; Camera Press for 48 bottom right and 50 top right; The Comedy Store, London for 34 top; Corbis Images for 48 top, 64 and 75 bottom; Corbis Stock Market for 74 top; El Deseo, S.A. for 17; Mary Evans Picture Library for 52; Eye Ubiquitous for 100 middle left; Getty One Stone for 77 right; Ronald Grant Archive for 15 left, 94 top right, 95 top, 95 bottom; Sally and Richard Greenhill for 74 bottom; Robert Harding Picture Library for 22 top; Hulton Getty for 49 bottom right; Image Bank for 106; Images Colour Library for 100 middle right; Kobal Collection for 14 left, 14 top right, 15 right, 49 top, 50 bottom, 66 top, 92/93, 94 bottom, 96 top, 96 bottom right and 97 bottom; Kobal Collection, Barcelona for 14, bottom right, 96 left and 97 top; Moviestore Collection for 66 bottom, 67 top left, 67 top right, 67 bottom, and 94 top left; PA Photos for 22 bottom and 50 top left; Paragon Ltd for 43 bottom, left, middle right and right; Pearson Education/Trevor Clifford for 24 and 73 and /Peter Lake for 8, 20, 28, 34 bottom, 72 and 103; The Photographers Library for 38; Picador for 78 bottom; Pictor International for 75 top and 100 top left; Popperfoto for 32 left, 32 middle, 32 middle left, and 32 middle right; Redferns for 49 bottom left; Retna for 91 top and 91 bottom; Rex Features for 44, 50 middle left and 50 middle right; Ben Rowden for 48 bottom left; Spectrum Colour Library for 100 bottom left; Frank Spooner Pictures for 22 middle and 84/85; Sporting Pictures (UK) Ltd for 31 (background); Superstock for 43 top and 43 middle; Telegraph Colour Library for 75 middle, 78/79 (background) and 100 top right; Topham Picturepoint for 40 and 53 and Victoria and Albert Museum Picture Library for 43 bottom middle right.

Freelance Picture Research by Louise Edgeworth and commissioned photography by Ann Thomson and Hilary Fletcher.

We are grateful to the following for their help with the location photography:

The Bull & Crown, Chingford; Cheshunt Marriot Hotel; KLM UK Ltd; The Slaters Arms, Romford.

The back cover photographs of the authors by Charles Yacoub.

We are grateful to the following for permission to reproduce copyright material:

Applause Theatre Book Publishers for an adapted extract from *The Collected Works Of Paddy Chayefsky 1995* © 1954 by Paddy Chayefsky; The Basement from *The Very Best of Herman* by Jim Unger for page 36 top right; Barry Cadish for adapted extracts from the website www.regretsonly.com; Barry Cadish is also the author of *Damn! Reflections on Life's Biggest Regrets* © 2001 Barry Cadish; John Callahan from *Digesting the Child Within* published by Statics for page 36 middle left; Carlton Books for a story rewritten from *Just like on TV* by Yorik Braun and Mike Flynn from *The Best Book of Urban Myths ever*; Chronical Publishing Company, San Francisco, USA from *Too Bizarro* by Piraro, 1987, 1988 for page 36 top left; Chronical Publishing Company, San Francisco, USA from *Too Bizarro* by Piraro, 1992 for page 36; Private Eye Publications for page 36 bottom; Express Newspapers for an adapted extract from the article "Houdini the dead hamster" by Margaret Hussey from *The Daily Express* 22.10.99; Guardian News Service for adapted extracts from the articles "A little help from our friends" from *The Guardian* 13.5.00 and "Top 100 Movies" from *Observer* Magazine 6.2.00; HarperCollins Publishers for the cover and an adapted extract from *Men Are From Mars, Women Are From Venus* by John Gray; HarperCollins/authors' agent Christopher Little for the cover and an adapted extract from *How To Make Anyone Fall In Love With You* by Leil Lowndes; Las Vegas Weddings for an adapted extract from "Make your wedding a legend" from www.lasvegasweddings.com/elvis; Little Brown for the cover and an adapted extract from *Don't Say 'Yes' When You Want To Say 'No'* by Fensterheim & Baer published by Futura/Warner Books/Little Brown; Macmillan/the author's agent – Abner Stein Ltd for an extract adapted from *American Beauty* by Alan Ball, © Dreamworks 1999 published by Film Four Books; Macmillan for the cover and an extract from *Bridget Jones's diary* by Helen Fielding; Michael O'Mara Books Ltd for an extract from *The One Hundred Stupidest Things Ever Done* by Ross & Kathryn Petras; Mystery Café for source material from www.mysterycafe.net; News International Syndication for an adapted extract from the article "The Immortals" by Maureen Freely in the Brainpower Series in *The Sunday Times*; The New York Times for an extract from the article "The Op-Ed" by Gail Collins in *The New York Times* 1.4.00; the author John G. Nilsen for adapted extracts from www.artoftravel.com; Nitro Grill for source material from www.nitrogrill.com; Orion Publishing Group for an adapted extract from *Black And Blue* by Ian Rankin; Penguin Books Ltd for an adapted extract from *How The Mind Works* by Steven Pinker published by Allen Lane The Penguin Press 1997. Copyright © Steven Pinker, 1997; Picador for an adapted extract from *Arabia* by Jonathan Raban; Private Eye publications for page 36 middle right; © Quino/Quipos for page 58; The Random House Archive and Library for the cover and an adapted extract from *One-Minute Stress Management* by David Lewis – published by Vermilion/Ebury Press; Rainforest Cafe for source material from www.rainforestcafe.com/RFC; Serpent's Tail Ltd for a slightly adapted extract from *The Glass Citadel* by Alison Love and Valentine's Weddings for an adapted extract from www.esbnyc.com.

We regret that we have been unable to trace the copyright holder of a story about an e-mail heard on the BBC Radio 4 programme *The News Quiz* and would appreciate any information which would enable us to do so.